NEW TEEN TITANS

TERRA INCOGNITO

NEW TEEN TITANS

TERRA INCOGNITO

MARV WOLFMAN Writer

GEORGE PÉREZ Penciller

ROMEO TANGHAL   PABLO MARCOS Inkers

ADRIENNE ROY Colorist

JOHN COSTANZA   BEN ODA   TODD KLEIN Letterers

GEORGE PÉREZ Original Series Covers

NEW TEEN TITANS CREATED BY MARV WOLFMAN & GEORGE PÉREZ

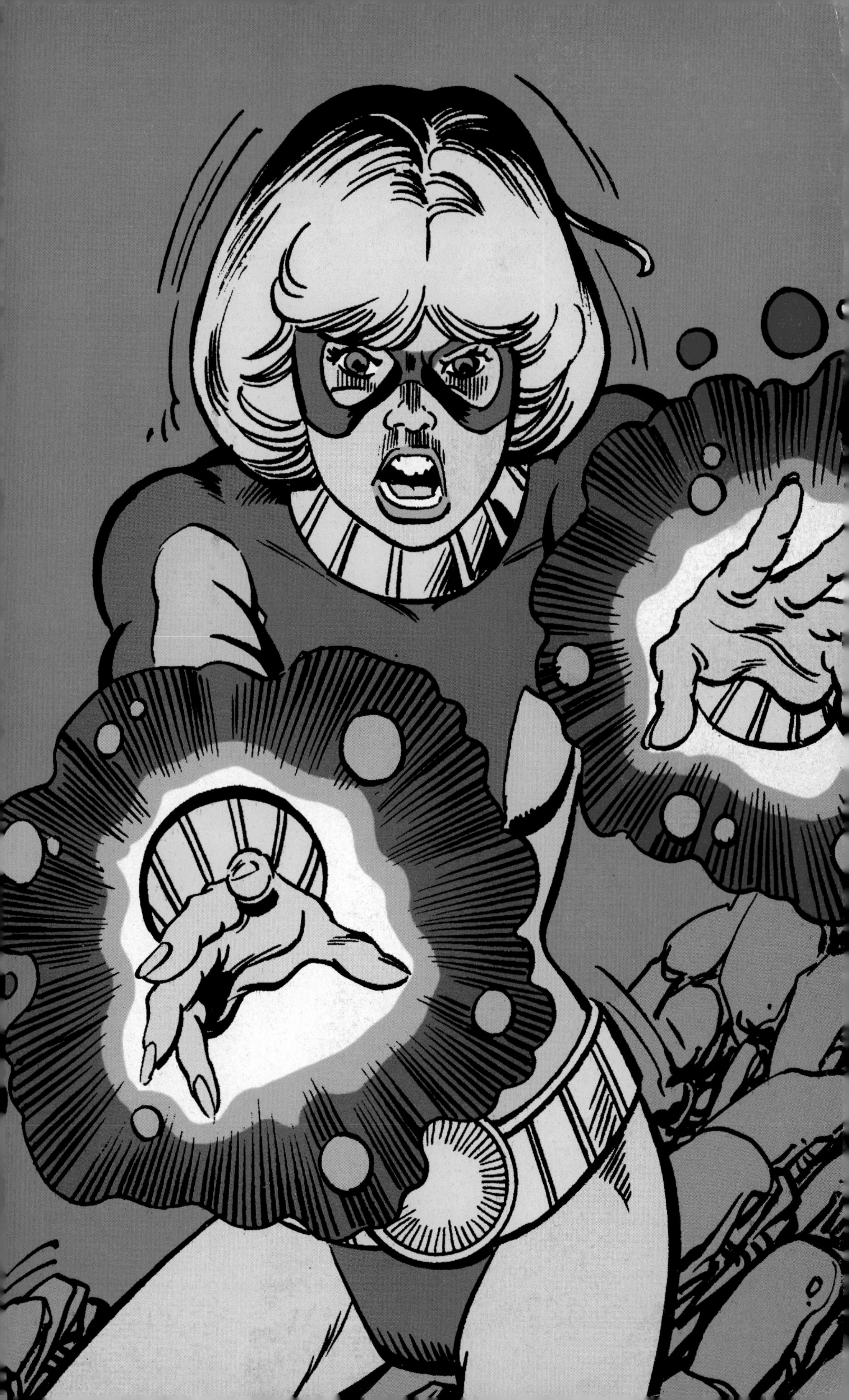

Dan DiDio
Senior VP-Executive Editor

Len Wein
Editor-original series

Bob Joy
Editor-collected edition

Robbin Brosterman
Senior Art Director

Louis Prandi
Art Director

Paul Levitz
President & Publisher

Georg Brewer
VP-Design & DC Direct Creative

Richard Bruning
Senior VP-Creative Director

Patrick Caldon
Executive VP-Finance & Operations

Chris Caramalis
VP-Finance

John Cunningham
VP-Marketing

Terri Cunningham
VP-Managing Editor

Stephanie Fierman
Senior VP-Sales & Marketing

Alison Gill
VP-Manufacturing

Hank Kanalz
VP-General Manager, WildStorm

Jim Lee
Editorial Director-WildStorm

Paula Lowitt
Senior VP-Business & Legal Affairs

MaryEllen McLaughlin
VP-Advertising & Custom Publishing

John Nee
VP-Business Development

Gregory Noveck
Senior VP-Creative Affairs

Cheryl Rubin
Senior VP-Brand Management

Jeff Trojan
VP-Business Development, DC Direct

Bob Wayne
VP-Sales

NEW TEEN TITANS: TERRA INCOGNITO

Published by DC Comics. Cover and compilation copyright
© 2006 DC Comics. All Rights Reserved.
Originally published in single magazine form in NEW TEEN
TITANS 26, 28-34; NEW TEEN TITANS ANNUAL 2. Copyright ©
1982, 1983 DC Comics. All Rights Reserved. All characters, their
distinctive likenesses and related elements featured in this
publication are trademarks of DC Comics. The stories,
characters and incidents featured in this publication are
entirely fictional. DC Comics does not read or accept
unsolicited submissions of ideas, stories or artwork.
DC Comics, 1700 Broadway, New York, NY 10019
A Warner Bros. Entertainment Company
Printed in Canada. First Printing.
ISBN: 1-4012-0972-6
ISBN 13: 978-1-4012-0972-8
Cover art by George Pérez
Cover color by Richard & Tanya Horie

NEW TEEN TITANS
TERRA INCOGNITO

Writer: Marv Wolfman
Color restoration by Pacific Rim Graphics

PROLOGUE
From New Teen Titans #26
George Pērez – Artist
Romeo Tanghal – Inker
Ben Oda – Letterer

TERRA IN THE NIGHT
From New Teen Titans #28
George Pērez – Artist
Romeo Tanghal – Inker
John Costanza – Letterer

FIRST BLOOD
From New Teen Titans #29
George Pērez – Artist
Romeo Tanghal – Inker
John Costanza – Letterer

NIGHTMARE!
From New Teen Titans #30
George Pērez – Artist
Romeo Tanghal – Inker
Ben Oda – Letterer

INFERNO!
From New Teen Titans #31
George Pērez – Layouts
Romeo Tanghal – Embellisher
Ben Oda – Letterer

THUNDER AND LIGHTNING!
From New Teen Titans #32
George Pērez – Layouts
Romeo Tanghal – Embellisher
Ben Oda – Letterer

WHO KILLED TRIDENT?
From New Teen Titans #33
George Pērez – Layouts
Romeo Tanghal – Embellisher
Ben Oda – Letterer

ENDINGS... AND BEGINNINGS!
From New Teen Titans #34
George Pērez – Layouts
Romeo Tanghal – Embellisher
Todd Klein – Letterer

THE MURDER MACHINE
From New Teen Titans Annual #2
George Pērez – Layouts
Pablo Marcos – Embellisher
John Costanza – Letterer

PRELUDE...

LOST AGAIN! STUPID GAME! SOMETIMES I THINK *ATARI* HATES ME PERSONALLY.

SKRRREEE

NUTS! IT FIGURES... THE *EMERGENCY SIGNAL!*

UH-OH, SOMETHING'S UP AT THE *STATUE OF LIBERTY.* WELL, GUESS I SHOULD *CALL* IN THE OTHERS.

THEN AGAIN, I COULD LET THE *COPS* HANDLE IT AND TRY ANOTHER ROUND OF *SWORDQUEST.*

NAH! WHO AM I *KIDDING?* I'M A SUPER-HERO. WE'RE SUPPOSED TO PUT OUR *LIVES* ON THE LINE TO HELP OTHERS.

GOD, WE'RE STUPID.

KEEP AN *EYE* ON HER... DON'T LET HER *ESCAPE.*

HOW ARE WE SUPPOSED TO DO THAT?

YOU SEE HER *POWERS?*

MEANWHILE...

WELL, WELL, *LOOK* WHAT WE HAVE HERE.

HALF OF NEW YORK CITY'S *FINEST* HAVE GATHERED TO STOP--*HER?*

HI, HONEY-- WHAT'S THE *PROBLEM?* LOSE YOUR *BOYFRIEND?*

COME TO UNCLE CHANGELING-- I CAN *HELP* YOU IF SOMETHING'S WRONG.

CHANGELING? STAY AWAY FROM ME.

DON'T GET *CLOSE* OR I'LL HAVE TO *KILL* YOU.

I HAVE MY ASSIGNMENT. I HAVE TO *DESTROY* THIS STATUE.

YEAH, YEAH, I KNOW. IT'S A *DIRTY* JOB. BUT HONEY, *YOU* DON'T HAVE TO DO IT.

YOU LOOK LIKE YOU'RE IN *TROUBLE,* LET ME *HELP.*

NO-- STAY AWAY.

YOU DON'T *UNDERSTAND.*

BUT YOU'RE STILL GOING TO TRY TO *STOP* ME, AREN'T YOU?

7

OKAY, THE *STATUE* STAYS IN ONE PIECE... I *CAN'T* LET MYSELF BE CAUGHT.

FOR NOW, *CHANGELING,* YOU *WIN!*

BUT THE *NEXT* TIME WE MEET, I WILL HAVE TO *KILL YOU!*

WHAT THE HECK IS SHE DOING?

JUMPING?

IN AN INSTANT, THE TITANS, RESIDENT *METAMORPH* ALTERS HIS HUMAN SHAPE...

...AND...

DON'T TRY TO *CHASE* ME, CHANGELING. IT CAN'T BE *DONE!*

I'VE GOT *POWERS* YOU HAVEN'T EVEN *DREAMED* OF!

I'M CALLED *TERRA*-- THAT'S AS IN *EARTH POWERS!*

CRUNCH!

I CAN DO MOST *ANYTHING* -- INCLUDING ERUPTING A SOLID COLUMN OF *EARTH* SKYWARD TO SLOW MY FALL--

--AND SMASH *YOU* INTO OBLIVION!

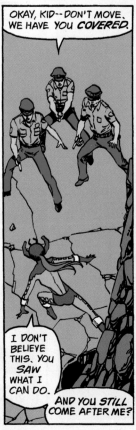

OKAY, KID-- DON'T MOVE, WE HAVE YOU *COVERED.*

I DON'T BELIEVE THIS. YOU *SAW* WHAT I CAN DO.

AND YOU *STILL* COME AFTER ME?

SHE'S GOING TO *DO* SOMETHING -- *FIRE!*

ARE YOU PEOPLE *INSANE?* ALL I HAVE TO DO IS RAISE AN EARTHEN SHIELD AND YOUR BULLETS ARE *STOPPED* IN THEIR TRACKS!

AND IF THE SHIELD ISN'T ENOUGH, I CAN *CHANGE* THAT COLUMN--

--INTO AN UNSTOPPABLE *MONSTER!*

SO PLEASE LET ME GO BEFORE YOU MAKE ME KILL YOU.

I DON'T WANT TO DO ANY OF THIS IN THE *FIRST* PLACE!

DON'T MAKE IT *HARDER* ON ME, PLEASE!!

SORRY, SHORT-STUFF, BUT YOU'RE *NOT* STOPPING ME.

LOOK, LET'S GET THIS STRAIGHT. I'M THE *GOOD GUY* AND YOU'RE THE *BAD GUY.*

IF I LET YOU GO, I'D HAVE TO TURN IN MY SUPER-HERO *UNION* CARD!

AND YOU KNOW HOW *LONG* IT TOOK FOR ME TO *GET* THE BLASTED THING!

SKRUNCH!

OH-NO -- I DON'T *LIKE* THIS.

THEY'RE COMING FROM ALL SIDES. I'M NOT *READY* FOR A BIG BATTLE.

GOT TO GET OUT OF HERE.

BLAST! I THOUGHT I WAS SO MUCH *BETTER,* THOUGHT I HAD IT ALL WORKED OUT.

THEY'LL *KILL* ME FOR FOULING UP. THEY'LL JUST *KILL* ME.

AS IF PRO-PELLED FROM THE HEART OF A *VOLCANO,* THE GIRL NAMED TERRA SOARS OFF...

...*VANISHING* INTO THE FAR DISTANT MISTS...

SHE'S ESCAP-ING... AND I'M --I'M OUT OF *POWER!*

WHO *IS* SHE?

9

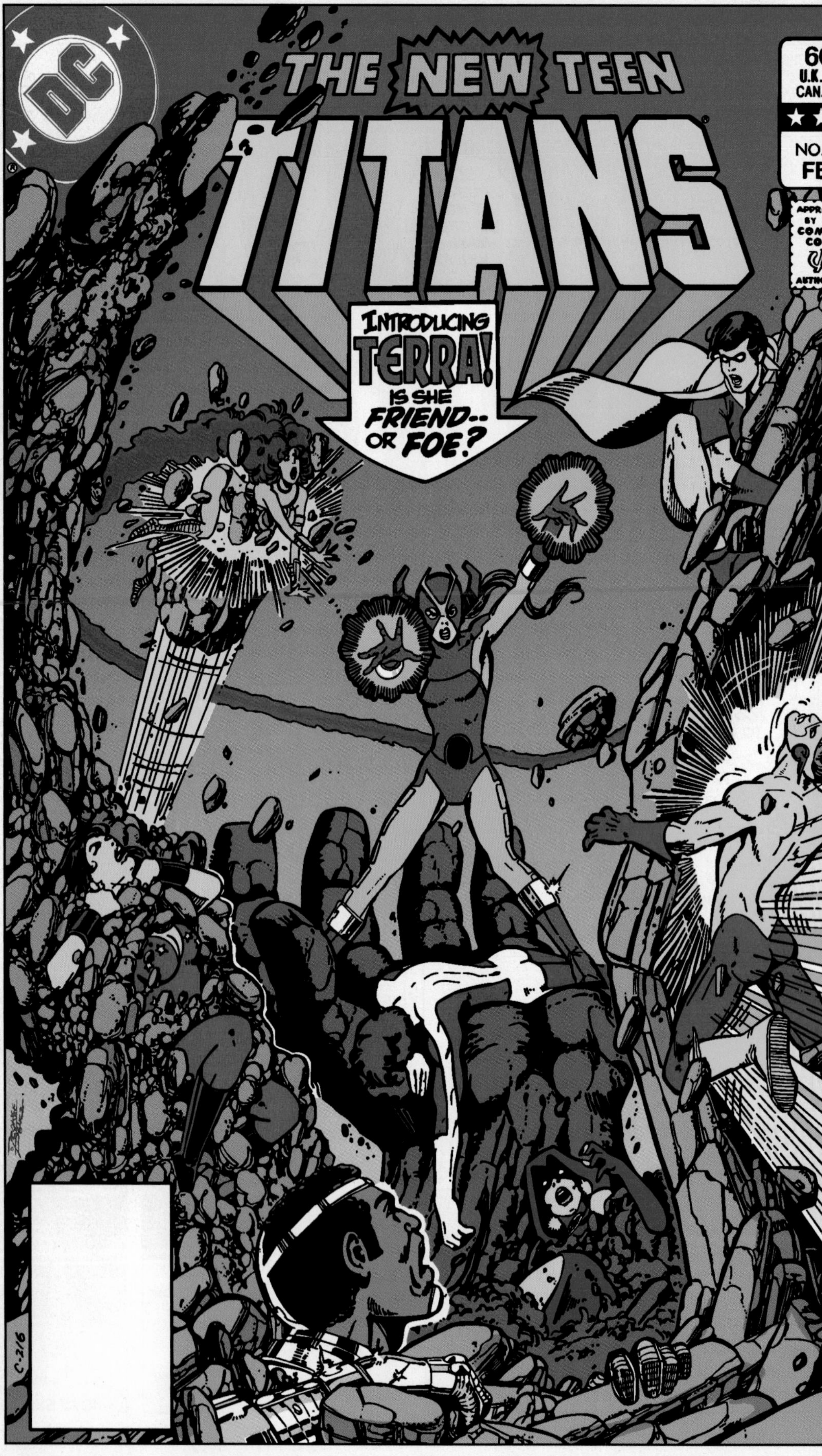

DC
THE NEW TEEN
TITANS
60¢
U.K. 25p
CAN. 75¢
NO. 28
FEB.
APPROVED BY THE COMICS CODE AUTHORITY
INTRODUCING
TERRA!
IS SHE
FRIEND..
OR FOE?
C-216

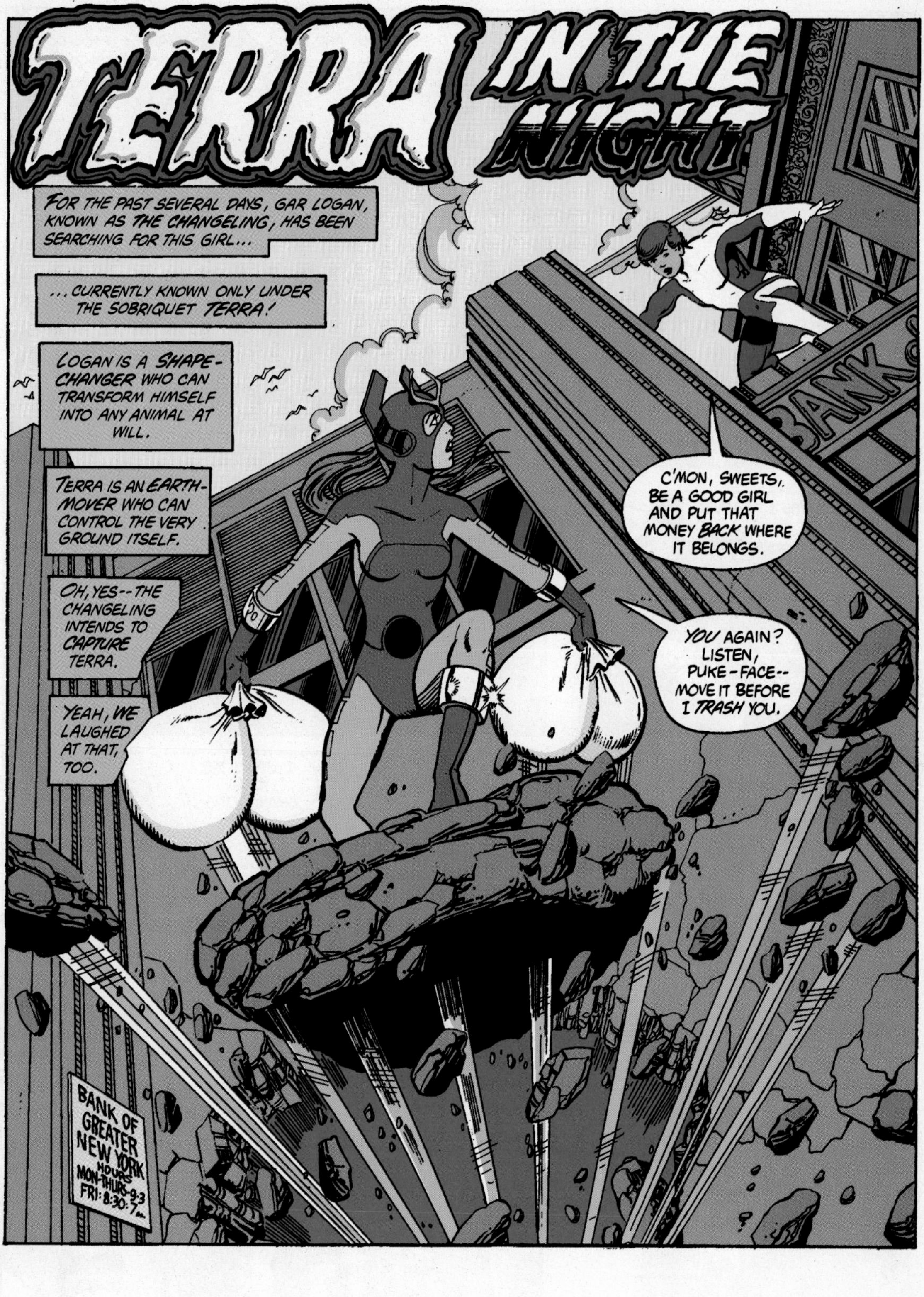
TERRA IN THE NIGHT
FOR THE PAST SEVERAL DAYS, GAR LOGAN, KNOWN AS THE CHANGELING, HAS BEEN SEARCHING FOR THIS GIRL...
...CURRENTLY KNOWN ONLY UNDER THE SOBRIQUET TERRA!
LOGAN IS A SHAPE-CHANGER WHO CAN TRANSFORM HIMSELF INTO ANY ANIMAL AT WILL.
TERRA IS AN EARTH-MOVER WHO CAN CONTROL THE VERY GROUND ITSELF.
OH, YES--THE CHANGELING INTENDS TO CAPTURE TERRA.
YEAH, WE LAUGHED AT THAT, TOO.
C'MON, SWEETS, BE A GOOD GIRL AND PUT THAT MONEY BACK WHERE IT BELONGS.
YOU AGAIN? LISTEN, PUKE-FACE--MOVE IT BEFORE I TRASH YOU.
BANK OF GREATER NEW YORK
HOURS
MON-THURS 9-3
FRI: 8:30-7

"PUKE-FACE"? NOW YOU'VE DONE IT, GORGEOUS. YOU'VE WOUNDED MY FRAGILE EGO. YOU'VE CUT ME SEVERELY TO MY EVER-CUTE QUICK.

IF I WEREN'T SANFORIZED, I'D SHRIVEL UP AND DIE.

YOU STILL MAY, CREEP--IF YOU DON'T LEAVE ME ALONE.

HONEY, WITH A FACE LIKE YOURS, I'D FOLLOW YOU ANYWHERE...

AT LEAST UNTIL I RECOVER THAT MONEY YOU STOLE.

TELL YA WHAT. FORGET THIS CRIME JUNK. LET'S CATCH A MOVIE, EAT SOME POPCORN, MAYBE NECK A LITTLE...

BOY, YOU DON'T QUIT, DO YOU?

I TOLD YOU BEFORE, I HAVE TO DO THIS. THERE'S TOO MUCH AT STAKE FOR ME TO STOP.

DON'T YOU THINK I CAN'T TELL THAT, TERRA? HEY, HARD AS IT IS TO BELIEVE, I'M MORE THAN JUST A GREAT-LOOKING HUNK.

I CAN HELP! WHAT'S WRONG?

I CAN'T TELL YOU, CHANGELING.

AND I'M REALLY SORRY I HAVE TO DO THIS--

--BUT MY *PARENTS' LIVES* ARE AT STAKE!

SKROOM

THEY'LL *DIE* UNLESS I FINISH THIS MISSION.

YOUR *PARENTS?* TERRA. *LISTEN* TO ME... I'M BEING *SERIOUS* NOW.

THE TITANS CAN *HELP.*

NO ONE CAN *HELP* ME, CHANGELING.

I'VE RELIED ON OTHERS FOR *TWO YEARS* AND I'VE ALWAYS FAILED. I'VE *GOT* TO DO THIS MYSELF.

YOU'RE NOT GOING TO GIVE ME THE CHANCE TO PLAY *HERO?*

TERRA, TERRA, *TERRA*-- THIS IS WHAT I *LOVE* DOING SECOND MOST IN THE WORLD.

C'MON, WE'LL TEAM UP AND *SAVE* YOUR PARENTS.

I SAID-- *NO!* GO AWAY!

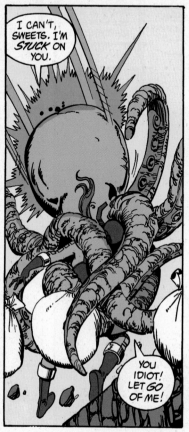

I CAN'T, SWEETS. I'M *STUCK* ON YOU.

YOU *IDIOT!* LET *GO* OF ME!

I'LL *CRUSH* YOU IF I HAVE TO!

HEY, WAIT! STICKS AND STONES MAY BREAK MY--

AGHHHH!

TERRA? ARE YOU ALL RIGHT?

ONE OF HER OWN STONES *HIT* HER. SHE LOOKS DAZED, *HURT.*

C'MON, BEAUTIFUL-- YOU GOTTA *TALK.*

BLAST, SHE ISN'T *MOVING.* DON'T TELL ME THAT KI--

JERK!

SKODM!

YOU FELL FOR THE *OLDEST* TRICK IN THE WORLD!

SEEYA AROUND, NERD!

TERRA?

TERRA?

I DON'T *LIKE* THIS. SHE'S OBVIOUSLY IN TROUBLE. SHE *NEEDS* MY HELP. SHE NEEDS *ME.*

AND AGAIN I *FAILED.*

I'VE BEEN *USELESS* FOR MONTHS NOW --ALMOST *AFRAID* TO USE MY POWERS TO THEIR FULLEST...

...EVER SINCE WHAT HAPPENED TO *MADAME ROUGE*...EVER SINCE I ACCIDENTALLY KIL--

GAR LOGAN'S THOUGHT FADES AS WE SHIFT EASTWARD...

ZANDIA: A SMALL BALTIC ISLAND. ITS CHIEF EXPORT IS VIOLENCE, FOR ZANDIA IS AN ISLE RUN BY TERRORISTS.

EVEN AS ITS CHURCH IS OPERATED BY THE CULT OF *BROTHER BLOOD,* A MAN WHOM, IT IS SAID, HAS LIVED MORE THAN SEVEN HUNDRED YEARS.

ALL IS SERENE IN HIS CATHEDRAL OF DEATH.

ALL PERIMETERS CLEAR...NOW CHECKING SOUTHERN BORDERS...

4

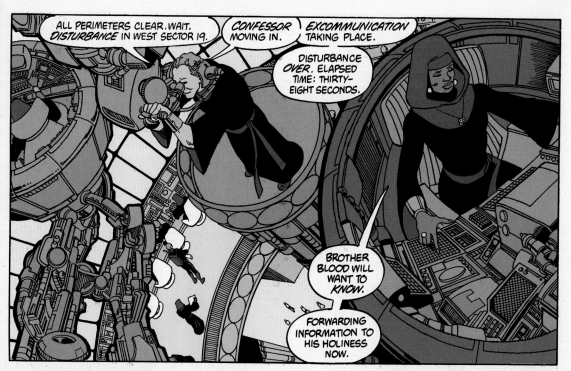

ALL PERIMETERS CLEAR. WAIT. *DISTURBANCE* IN WEST SECTOR 19.

CONFESSOR MOVING IN.

EXCOMMUNICATION TAKING PLACE.

DISTURBANCE *OVER.* ELAPSED TIME: THIRTY-EIGHT SECONDS.

BROTHER BLOOD WILL WANT TO *KNOW.*

FORWARDING INFORMATION TO HIS HOLINESS NOW.

DELICATE FINGERS DANCE ACROSS THE KEYBOARD.

THEN...

WH-WHAT? HELP!

HER NAME IS *SISTER SADE.* SHE HAS BEEN A LOYAL BELIEVER IN--AND LOVER OF--BROTHER BLOOD FOR THREE YEARS.

IT IS TOO LATE. AT THE AGE OF FOUR, SISTER SADE, THEN HELEN GEARY, DEVELOPED A TERRIBLE FEAR OF *SNAKES.*

NOW THAT FEAR PROVES HER UNDOING.

SISTER SADE? WHAT *IS* IT? WHAT'S *WRONG?*

WHAT'S SHE *DOING?*

DON'T YOU SEE THEM? THEY'RE ALL OVER ME. *HELP* ME.

I DON'T SEE *ANYTHING.*

SOMETHING'S *WRONG.* SET ALARMS IMMEDIATELY.

PLEASE-- TAKE THEM *OFF* ME.

15

NOW SISTER SOUL TURNS TOWARD THE CONSOLE, READY TO ALERT BROTHER BLOOD'S MERCENARY MISSIONARIES...

I DON'T UNDERSTAND THIS. SHE'S *DEAD*.. HER HEART *STOPPED*.

THERE'S NO REPORT OF ANY *BREAK-INS.* NOTHING ON MY *SCANNERS.* I--

SUDDENLY THE GROUND BENEATH HER OPENS, AND SISTER SOUL BEGINS A MILE-LONG *FALL*

LORD! OH, NO-- NO!

HELP ME! *HELP* ME!

TH-THEY'RE ALL OVER...

STOP HIM! HE'S GOING *CRAZY!*

I'VE GOT TO *STOP THEM!* I'VE GOT TO *KILL THEM!*

BAM BAM

SINCE SHE CAN REMEMBER, SISTER SOUL HAS SUFFERED FROM EXTREME *VERTIGO.*

HE'S *KILLING* OUR OWN *TROOPS!*

CAN'T HOLD ONTO HIM. HE'S LIKE AN *ANIMAL!*

BAM BAM BAM BAM

NOW HER WORST FEAR HAS COME TO LIFE.

WE HAVE NO *CHOICE.*

CAN'T LET HIM KILL ANYONE *ELSE!*

BAM

BLAM

6

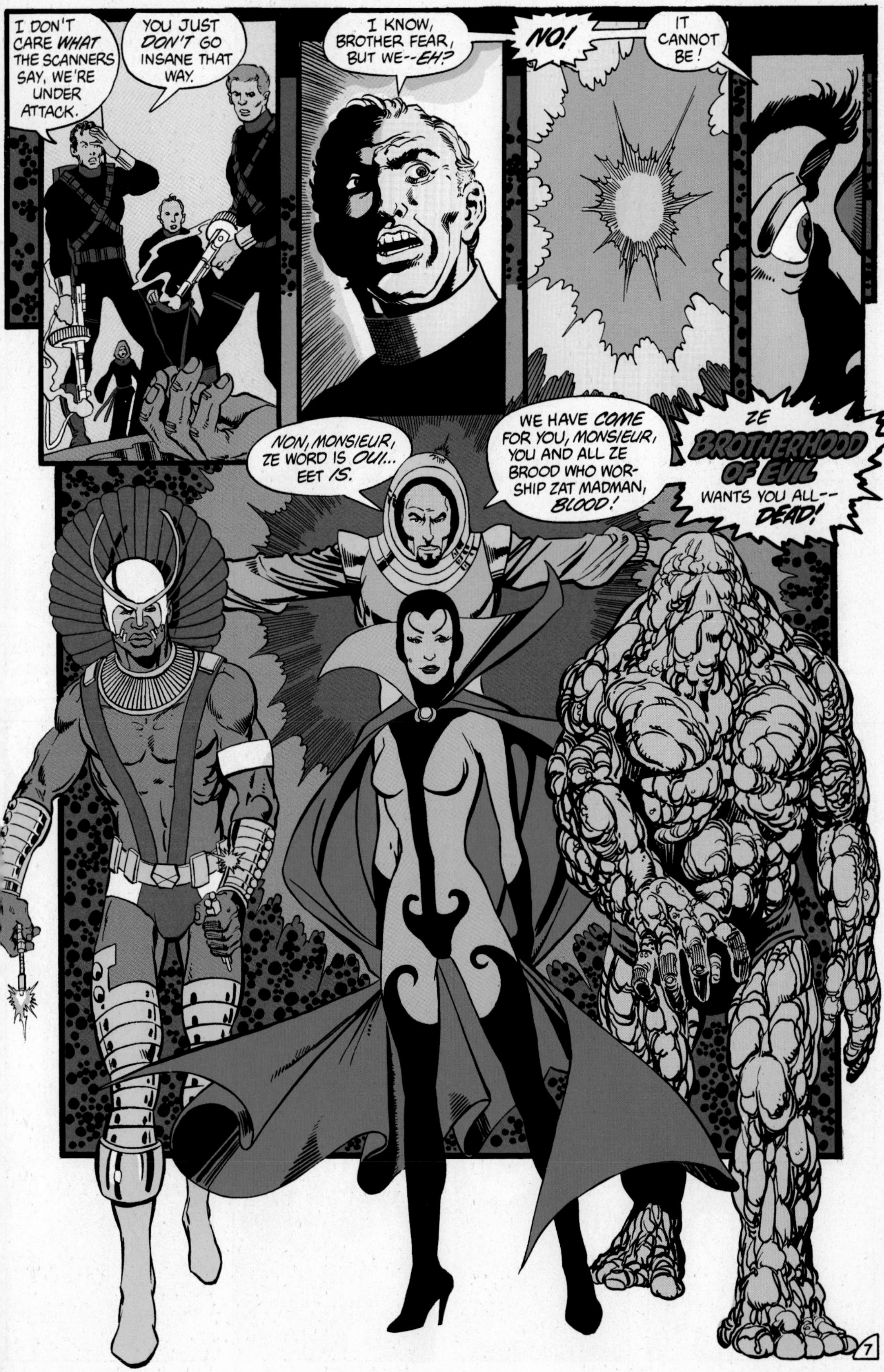
I DON'T CARE *WHAT* THE SCANNERS SAY, WE'RE UNDER ATTACK.
YOU JUST *DON'T* GO INSANE THAT WAY.
I KNOW, BROTHER FEAR, BUT WE--*EH?*
NO!
IT CANNOT BE!
NON, MONSIEUR, ZE WORD IS *OUI*... EET *IS.*
WE HAVE *COME* FOR YOU, *MONSIEUR,* YOU AND ALL ZE BROOD WHO WOR-SHIP ZAT MADMAN, *BLOOD!*
ZE BROTHERHOOD OF EVIL WANTS YOU ALL-- *DEAD!*
7

W-WE'VE JUST GOT ORDERS FROM *BROTHER BLOOD.*

IS HE GOING TO *HELP* US?

N-NO... HE SAYS HE'S PREPARING OUR *LAST RITES!*

BUT I DON'T WANT TO *DIE.*

A *SHAME* ZEN, EH, *MONSIEUR*? FOR YOU *WILL.*

ZE BROTHERHOOD HAS POWERS *MAGNIFIQUE.* I, *WARP,* CAN *TWIST SPACE* ITSELF...

...AND SEND YOU MILES AWAY TO YOUR *DOOM*...AT ZE BOTTOM OF ZE *BALTIC SEA.*

DERE DEATHS ARE *EASY,* HERR *WARP.* BUT ZESE FOOLS SHALL FEEL *MY* TERRIBLE POWER.

THE VERY TOUCH OF *PLASMUS* MEANS A BURNING, AGONIZING END.

I HAF BEEN REDUCED TO DIS *PLASMIC MASS.* MY POWERS ARE DARK AND EVIL.

ACH! I *HATE* VHAT I HAF BECOME, BUT I *USE* VHAT I NOW AM FOR DER GOOD OF DER BROTHERHOOD!

DERE! YOU ARE REDUCED TO A *PROTOPLASMIC BLOB* EVEN AS I AM--ONLY *YOU* ARE DEVOID OF LIFE.

NEW YORK CITY: FAR FROM ZANDIA'S TROUBLED SHORES, BUT SOON TO HAVE ENOUGH TROUBLES OF ITS OWN.

FOR NOW, HOWEVER, THERE IS *PEACE* HERE IN THE PENTHOUSE APARTMENT OF DONNA TROY AND KORY ANDERS...

EVERYTHING SEEMS *PERFECT* BETWEEN YOU AND DICK. I'M SO *GLAD* FOR YOU, KORY.

PERFECT? I DON'T KNOW ABOUT *THAT*, DONNA.

HE'S BEEN ACTING SO *STRANGE* LATELY. SO *TIRED* AND SO...I GUESS *GRUMPY* IS THE WORD.

I WONDER IF HE REALLY *CARES* ABOUT ME? HAVE I DONE SOMETHING *WRONG*?

DON'T PUT YOURSELF DOWN, HONEY. THIS IS *DICK'S* PROBLEM.

I'VE SEEN HIM GO THROUGH THESE TIMES *BEFORE*.

DICK'S *PUSHING* HIMSELF. HE WORKS WITH US, ON HIS OWN, HE GOES TO SCHOOL, AND THEN HE WORKS ALONGSIDE THE BATMAN.

AND YOU KNOW HOW HE *FEELS* ABOUT THE BATMAN. HE WANTS TO BE AS *GOOD*...

...EVEN THOUGH HE NEVER *CAN* BE.

HE'S JUST NOT *DRIVEN* THE WAY THE BATMAN IS. HE HASN'T GOT THAT SAME *FANATICAL* OBSESSION.

SO DICK'S ALL *TENSE* TRYING TO DO TOO MANY THINGS AT ONCE. THE BEST *YOU* CAN DO IS GET HIM TO *RELAX*.

I KNOW HE'S *SHORT-TEMPERED* NOW, BUT WHEN HE'S NOT TRYING TO LIVE UP TO SOME IMPOSSIBLE IMAGE--

--HE'S ONE OF THE MOST *WONDERFUL* PEOPLE I KNOW.

WERE *YOU* EVER IN LOVE WITH HIM?

ROMANTICALLY? NO. BUT I LOVE HIM AS ONE OF MY DEAREST *FRIENDS*.

9

C'MON, KORY-- ANSWER THE *DOOR*.

ANSWER IT!

BLZZZZ

DICK. YOU'RE RIGHT ON TIME.

AREN'T I *ALWAYS*? READY TO GO?

YOU LOOK *TIRED*.

YEAH, WELL, I'VE BEEN DOING SOME WORK AT THE CIRCUS. AND... HEY, THAT'S NOT WHY I CAME HERE. LET'S *GO*.

NO. LET'S *STAY* HERE FOR A CHANGE. WE'RE ALWAYS GOING OUT.

CAN WE *UHH-- RELAX...*? JUST FOR ONE EVENING? I'D MUCH RATHER STAY HOME TONIGHT.

BESIDES, I'M *LEAVING--* SO THE PLACE IS ALL YOURS. TERRY AND I HAVE PLANNED A *NIGHT* OF IT.

HE'LL *NEED* IT. HE'S SPENDING THE DAY WITH HIS EX-WIFE AND KID.

YOU'RE LOOKING *GREAT*, DONNA.

I HOPE A CERTAIN *MR. LONG* THINKS THE SAME.

KORY, DON'T *WAIT UP* FOR ME.

YOU TWO HAVE FUN. OH, DICK, I'LL SEE YOU LATE TOMORROW TO GO OVER THOSE *PLANS*.

TA TA, CREW.

NOW DON'T DO ANYTHING *I* WOULDN'T DO.

OKAY, WE'RE STAYING HOME. *NOW* WHAT DO WE DO?

OH, SOMEHOW WE'LL THINK OF *SOMETHING*.

10

MEANWHILE, LESS THAN FIFTEEN BLOCKS AWAY, AT THE CENTRAL PARK ZOO...

GET *AWAY* FROM ME. I DON'T WANT ANY OF YOU *FOLLOWING* ME.

DON'T YOU PEOPLE UNDERSTAND? *STAY AWAY!*

SHE'S *SCARED.* STARTING TO LASH OUT AT EVERY- ONE.

TROUBLE IS, HER BEING *SCARED* COULD MEAN SOMEONE *DIES.*

WELL, HERE GOES GAR LOGAN SCREWING UP HIS COURAGE, AND-- OH, *NO!*

CAGES BLASTED OPEN...THE ANIMALS ARE *ESCAPING!*

BETTER CHANGE *FORM...* EVEN THOUGH I'M GETTING *TIRED...* TOO MANY TRANSFORMATIONS IN TOO SHORT A TIME.

NO *CHOICE* THOUGH. THIS IS PRETTY MUCH GONNA *WIPE ME OUT* FOR THE BETTER PART OF A DAY--

--BUT I'VE GOT TO LEND A HELPING *TRUNK* TO STOP THIS ZOO-CREW FROM GETTING OUTTA HAND.

PARDON ME.

EXCUSE ME.

EXCUSE ME.

SORRY.

11

NUTS!

FIGURES, DOESN'T IT.

SHE'S USING THIS CONFUSION TO PONY-TAIL IT *OUTTA* HERE.

GAR LOGAN IS *WORRIED* ABOUT THIS GIRL NAMED TERRA. SHE SEEMS SO FRIGHTENED, SO *VULNERABLE*...

SHE NEEDS *HELP*, GAR *THINKS*.

BUT TO HELP...

HONEY?

WHAT?!?

LIGHTS OUT!

BLAMM!

...HE CANNOT BE GENTLE.

MEANWHILE, BELOW...

I SEE IT, BUT I DON'T *BELIEVE* IT. *HOW?*

WELL, SIR, THERE WAS THIS *GREEN ELEPHANT* WHO TURNED INTO A GREEN *BIRD* AND FLEW OFF AFTER THIS GIRL ON A FLYING ROCK, AND...

SAY, FELLAS, DO ME A FAVOR AND *RETURN* THIS MONEY.

AND MAKE CERTAIN YOU DON'T *APPRO-PRIATE* ANYTHING ON THE WAY.

I'D HATE TO HAVE TO HUNT YOU GUYS DOWN.

I *KNOW* HIM, HE'S FROM THE TITANS, HE'S THAT *BEAST BOY* KID.

SIGH! I SPEND ONE MILLION OF MY DAD'S MONEY, HIRE THE BEST *CONSULTANTS* TO COME UP WITH A GLITZY NEW *NAME* FOR ME...

...AND THOSE JERKS DOWN THERE *STILL* CALL ME BEAST BOY.

I TELL YOU, TERRA, THERE'S NO *JUSTICE* IN THIS WORLD!

LATER...

WHAT'S *WRONG*, DICK?

OH, NOTHING. SOMETIMES I JUST LIKE BEING *ALONE.*

YOU'D RATHER I WASN'T *HERE?*

OH, NO -- *NO.*

DICK, I --

LOOK, I'M SORRY. I HAVE A LOT ON MY *MIND* RIGHT NOW.

DICK, I *LOVE* YOU. I REALLY DO. I --

KORY, PLEASE. I'D RATHER NOT TALK ABOUT *US* RIGHT NOW.

YOU *CARE* FOR ME, DON'T YOU?

OF COURSE. LOOK, I'M *SORRY.* IT'S THAT I HAVEN'T HAD MORE THAN THREE HOURS' *SLEEP* IN THE LAST THREE DAYS --

-- AND WHILE YOU WERE IN THE *SHOWER,* I READ THIS NEW COLUMN BY BETHANY SNOW.

SHE'S BLAMING THE *TITANS* FOR EVERYTHING THAT'S *BAD,* WITH THE POSSIBLE EXCEPTION OF THE NEW *TV* SEASON.

I DON'T LIKE *SAYING* THIS, KORY, BUT I'D LOVE TO PLANT MY FIST UP THAT SNOOTY *NOSE* OF HERS.

SNOW STORM by Bethany Snow

IT'S NOT *YOU,* REALLY. I'M JUST ALL *NERVES* RIGHT NOW.

WOULD YOU LIKE A *BACK RUB?* IT WILL MAKE YOU FEEL BETTER.

KORY -- *PLEASE!* DON'T YOU EVER WANT TO ENJOY A *BAD* MOMENT? I JUST WANT TO *THINK.*

AND MAYBE SEE IF *ADRIAN CHASE* HAS CHECKED OUT BETHANY SNOW'S CONNECTIONS WITH *BROTHER BLOOD.*

LET ME *COME* WITH YOU, DICK.

OKAY?

PLEASE?

13

TITANS TOWER, LOCATED IN NEW YORK'S MUDDY EAST RIVER...

INSIDE SITS A YOUNG *EMPATH*, DEEP IN MEDITATION.

HER NAME IS *RAVEN*. SHE HAS THE POWER TO TAKE YOUR PAINS AND MAKE THEM HER OWN.

BUT RECENTLY SHE HAS NOT BEEN ABLE TO *DISPEL* THOSE PAINS. THEY *LINGER* WITHIN HER. THEY *HURT* HER. THEY MAY VERY WELL *KILL* HER.

MEDITATION WIPES AWAY THE FIRST LEVEL OF BEING. SHE REACHES *INSIDE* HERSELF.

THERE IS A *WALL*. DARK, MENACING...SO VERY COLD. SHE REACHES FOR THE WALL. REACHES...TOUCHES...

NOK! NOK!

HER TRANCE ENDS, ALL TOO ABRUPTLY.

HI, RAVEN, DID I *BOTHER* YOU?

N-NO. I... HAVE NOT *SEEN* YOU FOR AWHILE, WALLACE.

AND I SENSE SOMETHING *DISTURBING* YOU.

WHAT IS *WRONG*?

WHAT ELSE? *SCHOOL*. I'M HAVING TROUBLE STUDYING. YOU HAVE TROUBLES AT *YOUR* SCHOOL?

IN AZARATH I LEARNED *HOW* TO STUDY. YOUR SCHOOLS ARE NOT *DIFFICULT* FOR ME.

MAN, I WISH *I* COULD SAY THAT. I'M FAILING *FRENCH TWO*.

AND I CAN'T *GIVE UP* SCHOOL. I SIMPLY *CAN'T*.

AND I'M NOT LIKE *DICK*. I CAN'T *JUGGLE* HALF A DOZEN PROBLEMS AT ONCE AND STILL DO EVERYTHING SO PERFECTLY.

I CAN'T FOCUS. HALF THE TIME I'M *KID FLASH*. HALF THE TIME I'M A *STUDENT*. IT'S NOT WORKING.

SOMETIMES I *ENVY* HIM THAT TALENT.

14

I NEVER REALLY WANTED TO *BE* KID FLASH, AND I--

HEY! SOMEONE HERE! HELP!

HUH?

GARFIELD. HE'S CALLING FOR *HELP*.

WELL, NO PROBLEM *THERE*. I PRESS MY RING AND MY COSTUME SHOOTS OUT--

--EXPANDING ON CONTACT WITH THE *AIR*.

SOMETHING *WRONG*, RAVEN? WHY DIDN'T YOU *TELEPORT* TO HELP GAR?

I DO NOT TELE-PORT. I MOVE BETWEEN DIM-ENSIONS.

AND GARFIELD'S NEEDS ARE NOT QUITE SO *DESPERATE* AS HE MAKES THEM OUT TO BE.

BUT, MOMENTS LATER...

WELL, WELL, GAR, YOU CAN'T GO CALLING FOR THE TITANS JUST BECAUSE YOU MADE SOME GIRL SWOON.

WHO'S YOUR *FRIEND*?

IS THAT *HER*? THE ONE YOU *TOLD* US ABOUT?

WELL, SHE SURE AIN'T *VALERIE BERTINELLI*.

HIYA, FLEET-FEET. LONG TIME, NO SEE.

I ASKED YOU... WHO'S THE *GIRL*?

THAT'S NO *GIRL*, THAT'S MY *STRIFE*!

HER NAME'S *TERRA*, LIKE IN EARTH AND GROUND. ONLY IT SHOULD BE TERROR-- AS IN-- *HOLY COW, WATCH OUT, FELLAS!*

SHE'S *HURT*, BUT I CAN *HELP* HER...

HELP? N-NO... DON'T *TOUCH* ME. I KNOW ALL ABOUT YOU.

HEY, CALM DOWN, RAVEN WAS JUST TRYING TO *HELP*!

15

25

I TOLD YOU BEFORE, JERK-- I DON'T *WANT* HELP.

GET OUTTA MY WAY. LET ME *OUTTA* HERE.

SHE'S *ESCAPING.*

I WILL--

A LITTLE *SUPER-SPEED VIBRATION* AND I SIPHON OFF THE *AIR* AROUND HER.

NAH, LET *ME* HANDLE HER, RAVEN.

SHE GOES DOWN FROM MOMENTARY *LOSS OF OXYGEN.*

YOU CREEPS REALLY WANNA *FIGHT,* DON'T YOU?

OKAY, I'LL TAKE YOU *ALL* ON IF I HAV--

OH, NUTS.

I HEARD *SHOUTING.*

WHAT'S *WRONG?*

16

DON'T TELL ME. *YOU'RE* THE REASON MY BEAUTY REST WAS INTERRUPTED.

PUT ME *DOWN*, YOU WALKING GARBAGE CAN!

WHOSE IS SHE, ANYWAY?

GAR FOUND HER. HER NAME'S *TERRA*.

LOGAN? *FIGGERS!*

DON'T TAKE HER TOO *LIGHTLY*, RUST-HEAD. SHE'S *MEANER* THAN SHE LOOKS.

SHE'D *HAVE* TO BE.

OKAY, JERK--YOU *ASKED* FOR IT.

WHAT IN--?

SKRUNCHH!

I *WARNED* YOU, DIDN'T I? BUT WOULD YOU LISTEN--? *NOOOOO!*

SHE'S GOT POWER OVER THE EARTH. AND THAT MEANS MORE 'N JUST MAKING *MUD-PIES!*

POWER ALONE ISN'T ENOUGH TO *STOP* HER.

WE'VE GOT TO *CONVINCE* HER WE CAN HELP.

THERE... CYBORG, *CATCH* HER.

UHHH, THAT *HURTS!*

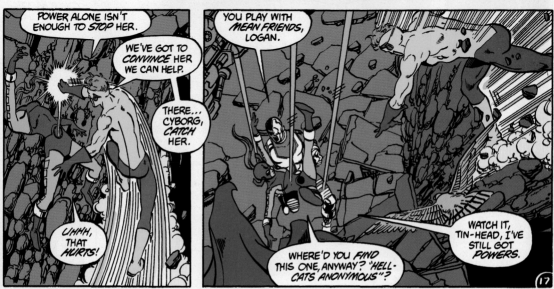

YOU PLAY WITH *MEAN FRIENDS*, LOGAN.

WHERE'D YOU *FIND* THIS ONE, ANYWAY? "HELL-CATS ANONYMOUS"?

WATCH IT, TIN-HEAD, I'VE STILL GOT *POWERS.*

(17)

27

TERRA, IT'S REAL DUMB TO KEEP FIGHTING. SO HOW ABOUT GIVING US A CHANCE?

OKAY, OKAY, I *BELIEVE*. JUST KEEP TWINKLE-TOES AWAY FROM ME.

GOD, I'VE GOT A *HEADACHE*. WHAT DID YOU *DO*?

JUST A SUPER-SPEED *NERVE PINCH*. SORRY.

LISTEN, YOU GOTTA REALIZE, IT'S BEEN A WHILE SINCE I COULD *TRUST* SOMEBODY.

YOU'RE LOOKING AT ME LIKE I JUST STEPPED OUT OF A *PADDED CELL*. OKAY, I'LL EXPLAIN.

MY PARENTS... WELL, THEY'RE IN CHARGE OF ANOTHER *COUNTRY*... AT LEAST MY *DAD* IS.

I'M SORTA THE NATIONAL *EMBARASSMENT*. MY *REAL* MOM DIED IN CHILDBIRTH, AND I WAS RAISED HERE IN *AMERICA* SO DAD'S *WIFE* WOULDN'T HAVE A CORONARY.

'BOUT TWO YEARS AGO I RETURNED TO MY HOMELAND ONLY TO FIND DAD AND GUESS-WHO *KIDNAPPED!* MY BROTHER, THAT'S BRION, HE AND I *SEARCHED* FOR THEM...

...ONLY WE GOT SEPARATED 'BOUT THE TIME I RAN ACROSS THESE TERRORISTS WHO SAID THEY WERE *HOLDING* MY DAD AND THE QUEEN.

THE TERRORISTS THREATENED TO *KILL* 'EM BOTH IF I DIDN'T USE MY POWERS IN THEIR CAUSE.

I DIDN'T KNOW WHAT *ELSE* TO DO. BRION WAS OFF SOMEWHERE IN SOUTH AMERICA. I WAS *SCARED*.

EVERYTHING WILL BE *ALL RIGHT*, TERRA.

PLEASE, CALL ME *TARA*, THAT'S MY *REAL* NAME. THE TERRORISTS THOUGHT IT WAS CUTE TO CALL ME *TERRA* INSTEAD, 'CAUSE A MY *POWERS*.

IT IS NOTHING... *NOTHING*.

THOUGH I DO NOT LIKE THESE *FEELINGS* I SENSE.

OBVIOUSLY YOU WEREN'T *BORN* WITH YOUR POWERS ...OR *WERE* YOU?

WHAT DO YOU THINK I *AM* ANYWAY? SOME KINDA FREAKY *MUTANT*?

SORRY, TERRA. SAY, HOW *OLD* ARE YOU ANYWAY?

ALMOST *SIXTEEN*. HEY, I DON'T LIKE THAT *LOOK* IN YOUR EYES. I DON'T WANT *PITY*.

I'VE DON'T PRETTY WELL, CONSIDERING.

LOOK, YOU DON'T WANNA *HELP*, JUST TELL ME AND I'LL TAKE OFF.

ACROSS TOWN...

DONNA TROY STEPS FROM THE CAB BEFORE TERRY LONG'S APARTMENT. SHE IS VERY HAPPY. DURING THESE PAST MONTHS THEY HAVE BECOME CLOSER THAN SHE EVER FELT SHE COULD BE TO ANYONE.

RAVEN, YOU LOOK LIKE YOU SWALLOWED A PIGEON. SOMETHING *WRONG*?

BUT DON'T *STARE* AT ME LIKE I'M POSTER GIRL FOR *"MISS SPAT-UPON OF THE NINETEEN EIGHTIES."*

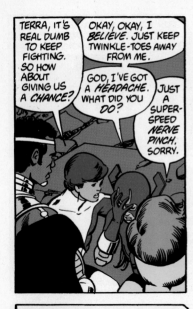

18

THOUGH BORN MORTAL, SHE WAS RAISED ON PARADISE ISLAND, LEGENDARY HOME OF THE AMAZONS. SHE WAS RAISED AWAY FROM MEN, RAISED TO SOMETIMES *DISTRUST* MEN AND THEIR PROCLIVITIES TOWARD VIOLENCE.

AND FOR MANY YEARS SHE SHARED THAT DISTRUST, UNTIL SHE MET DICK GRAYSON, THEN ROY HARPER, WALLY WEST AND ALL THE OTHERS.

AND, SLOWLY SHE LEARNED TO *LOVE*.

SLOWLY SHE LEARNED TO JUDGE FOR HERSELF.

TERRY, DON'T WORRY, IT'S *ME*.

I LET MYSELF--

OHH, I'M SO *SORRY*.

DONNA? DON'T TELL ME IT'S ALREADY TIME. C'MON *IN*.

YOU TWO HAVEN'T MET, BUT THIS IS *MARCIA*.

WE WERE JUST GOING OVER SOME PAPERS.

TERRY, IF I'M INTERRUPTING SOMETHING *IMPORTANT*...

NO, NO, YOU'RE *SUPPOSED* TO BE HERE, HONEY. I'M SO SORRY. TIME SLIPPED BY.

SO THIS IS *DONNA*. TERRY, YOU DIDN'T TELL ME SHE WAS SO... *YOUNG*.

YOUNG ENOUGH *NOT* TO HAVE DEVELOPED A *SARCASTIC* STREAK.

WE STILL HAVE JENNY'S *SCHOOL* TO DISCUSS, TERRY.

YOU *DO* FEEL THAT'S IMPORTANT, DON'T YOU?

I MEAN, YOU HARDLY SPEND ANY *TIME* WITH HER IN THE FIRST PLACE.

PLEASE, MARCIA, DO WE HAVE TO DISCUSS THIS *NOW*?

TERRY, IT'S OBVIOUS I'M *INTERRUPTING*...

NO, DONNA. STAY, PLEASE.

I'D RATHER *NOT*, HONEY.

I'M SORRY ABOUT THIS, DONNA. SHE JUST WOULDN'T LEAVE.

I UNDERSTAND. BELIEVE ME.

LOOK, NO HARD FEELINGS. WE CAN MAKE IT ANOTHER DAY.

DADDY, DADDY, YOU GOTTA SEE WHAT I DID.

IT'S JUST GREAT. YOU'LL LOVE IT.

IT'S YOU, DADDY, AND I--

WHO'S THAT, DADDY?

SHE'S DONNA. SHE'S MY, UHH...

SHE'S DADDY'S FRIEND, JENNIFER.

NOW, TERRY, DO I HAVE YOUR ATTENTION?

GO RIGHT AHEAD, MRS. LONG. I'M LEAVING.

I'LL CALL YOU TOMORROW.

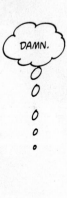
DAMN.

LONG ISLAND CITY: WHERE THE CITY'S TRAINS GO TO SLEEP. HERE, IN THIS SEEMINGLY ENDLESS SUBWAY GRAVEYARD, A FUTILE ATTEMPT IS MADE TO REPAIR A TRANSPORTATION SYSTEM THAT WAS BUILT AT THE DAWN OF THE TWENTIETH CENTURY.

BUT, WITH BUDGET CUTBACKS, MAINTENANCE CREWS HAVE LONG SINCE VANISHED.

NOW THE ONLY ONES HERE ARE THE VERMIN. THE FOUR LEGGED...

...AND THE TWO-LEGGED KIND AS WELL.

20

TERRA WAS CORRECT. SHE WAS *EXPECTED* BACK HERE.

I *KNOW* YOU. YOU'RE FROM THE TITANS.

TELL US WHERE YOU HOLD HER *PARENTS*.

TELL US *NOW!*

GET *BACK*, LADY. I'M NOT *TALKING*.

YOU DON'T *HAVE* TO TALK.

NOT WHEN I CAN *REACH* INTO YOUR VERY SOUL AND *TAKE* WHAT I NEED.

SOMETHING IS *WRONG*. THIS MAN KNOWS *NOTHING* OF TERRA'S PARENTS.

ONE OF YOU WILL BE *GLAD* TO TALK.

NO WAY, SPEED-BOY. WE HAVE OUR JOB AND WE'RE *DOING* IT.

ONE MOVE AND I SWEAR HER PARENTS WILL *DIE*.

HE'S PROBABLY JUST *HIRED HELP*, RAVEN. DON'T WORRY. SOMEHOW WE'LL FIND OUT WHAT WE WANT.

RIGHT, BOYS?

NOW DON'T YOU REALLY FEEL LIKE A *JERK*?

HEY, GUYS-- I THINK I'VE GOT THE *LEADER* HERE.

HE'S THE ONE WHOSE *I.Q.* TOPS *75*.

BONK!

HE RUNS NOW, SEEMINGLY FRIGHTENED. RUNS PAST RAILROAD CARS, HOPING AGAINST HOPE THE TITANS WON'T FOLLOW.

NATURALLY, HE'S WRONG.

LAST *STOP*, MUSCLE-HEAD.

THIS IS AS FAR AS YOU *GO*.

CLUNK

OVER HERE. I *GOT* HIM.

21

MAKE HIM TELL WHERE MY *PARENTS* ARE.

IF *YOU* DON'T, I *WILL*.

BE *CALM*, TERRA, WE WILL LEARN THE TRUTH.

YEAH. *LISSEN* TO THE WITCH, SHRIMP. MUSH-FOR-BRAINS HERE'S GONNA TALK.

RIGHT?

I WANT MY *PARENTS*. WHERE *ARE* THEY? *TELL* ME!

TH-THEY'RE *DEAD*...THEY'VE *BEEN* DEAD ALL ALONG.

THEY DIED BEFORE THEY WERE EVEN TAKEN OUT OF THEIR COUNTRY.

WE'VE JUST BEEN *USING* YOU.

NOW... GASP... LET GO...*LET GO!*

NO! YOU'RE LYING. THEY *CAN'T* BE DEAD!

I'VE BEEN *SEARCHING* FOR THEM. I KNOW THEY'RE *ALIVE*.

YOU'RE LYING!

AND YOU'LL PAY FOR IT!

SHE'S CREATING AN *EARTHQUAKE*.

DIDN'T KNOW SHE WAS *THIS* POWERFUL.

IT'S OKAY. I'LL *STOP* HER. I CAN DO IT.

22

DON'T *DO* IT, TERRA. PLEASE...EVERYTHING'LL BE *OKAY.* I PROMISE YOU.

MY PARENTS DIED, TOO. I PULLED THROUGH.

ONLY YOU WON'T BE *ALONE* LIKE I WAS. PLEASE, TERRA, LET US *HELP.*

NO! I WANT TO *KILL* THIS FILTH. MY PARENTS *CAN'T* BE DEAD.

THEY'RE THE ONLY REASONS I'VE KEPT *GOING.*

THEY'RE THE ONLY ONES WHO EVER *MATTERED* TO ME.

TRUST US, TERRA. DON'T KILL THEM. PLEASE... *DON'T.*

OH, GOD, GAR--I DON'T KNOW WHAT TO *DO* ANY MORE.

I...FEEL SO ALONE.

YOU DON'T *HAVE* TO BE, TERRA. *I'M* HERE.

WE WILL *HELP* YOU IF THAT IS WHAT YOU TRULY WANT.

MAYBE YOU'RE *RIGHT.* MAYBE I NEED TIME TO THINK.

WHAT DO *YOU* THINK, VIC?

DUNNO. JUST DON'T KNOW.

SOMETHING...*BOTHERS* ME, BUT I DON'T KNOW WHAT IT IS.

THE GIRL MUST BE FRIGHTENED. SHE SAYS SHE FEELS *ALONE.*

YET WHY DO I SENSE SOMETHING...

...*ELSE?*

WHY?

23

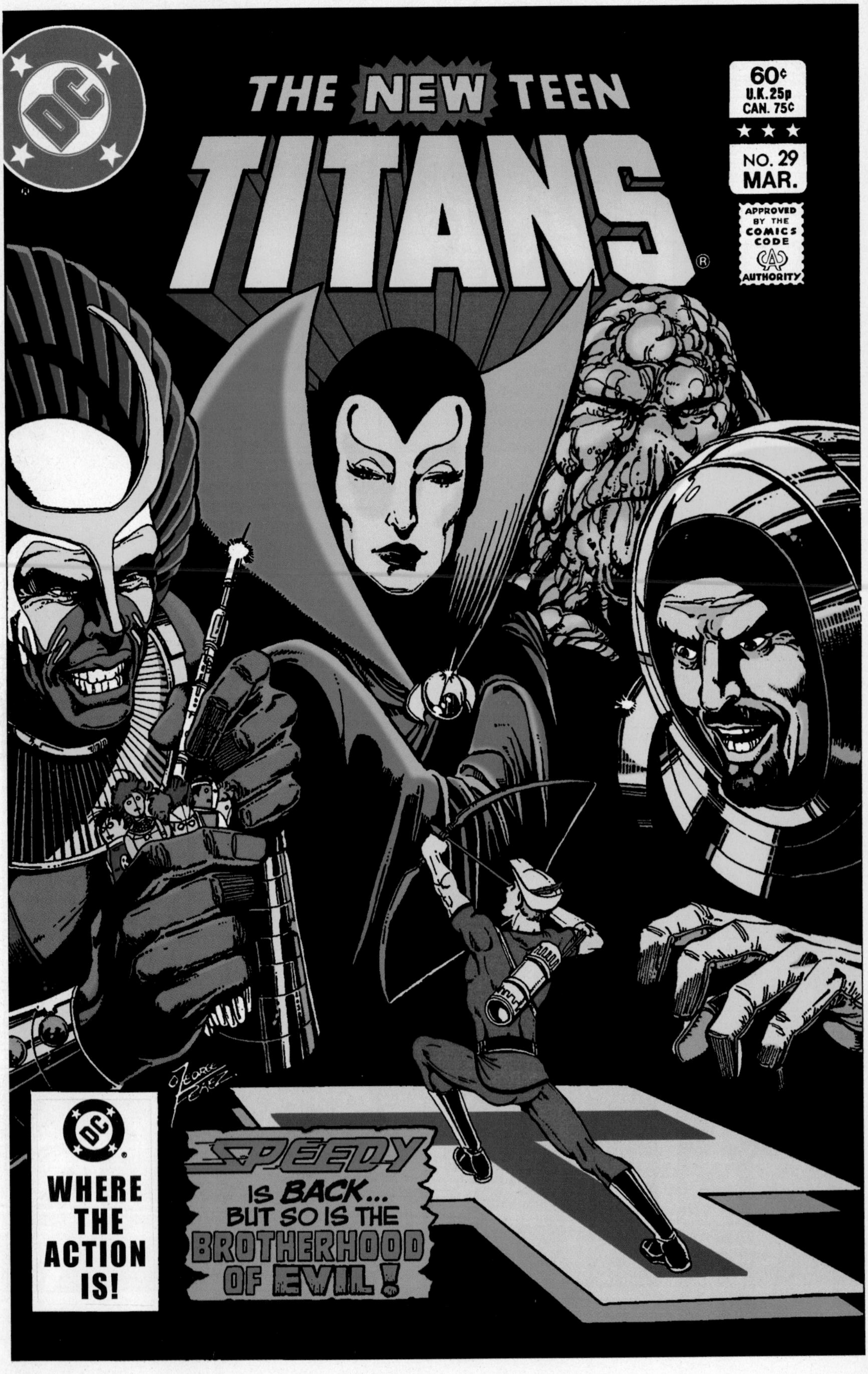
DC
THE NEW TEEN
TITANS
60¢
U.K. 25p
CAN. 75¢
NO. 29
MAR.
APPROVED BY THE COMICS CODE AUTHORITY
DC
WHERE THE ACTION IS!
SPEEDY
IS BACK...
BUT SO IS THE
BROTHERHOOD
OF EVIL!

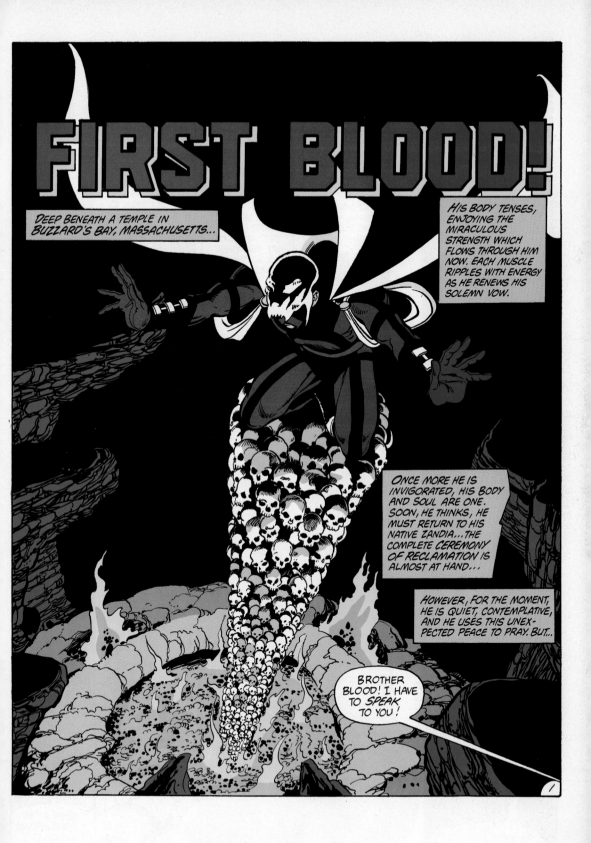

FIRST BLOOD!

DEEP BENEATH A TEMPLE IN BUZZARD'S BAY, MASSACHUSETTS...

HIS BODY TENSES, ENJOYING THE MIRACULOUS STRENGTH WHICH FLOWS THROUGH HIM NOW. EACH MUSCLE RIPPLES WITH ENERGY AS HE RENEWS HIS SOLEMN VOW.

ONCE MORE HE IS INVIGORATED, HIS BODY AND SOUL ARE ONE. SOON, HE THINKS, HE MUST RETURN TO HIS NATIVE ZANDIA...THE COMPLETE CEREMONY OF RECLAMATION IS ALMOST AT HAND...

HOWEVER, FOR THE MOMENT, HE IS QUIET, CONTEMPLATIVE, AND HE USES THIS UNEXPECTED PEACE TO PRAY. BUT...

BROTHER BLOOD! I HAVE TO SPEAK TO YOU!

MOTHER MAYHEM, YOU KNOW MY RULE AGAINST INTERRUPTING MY *MEDITATION.*

I *DO*-- AND I WOULD NEVER DISTURB YOU WITHOUT GOOD *REASON.*

THE *BROTHERHOOD OF EVIL* HAS LEFT ZANDIA. THEY'RE COMING HERE TO AMERICA-- OBVIOUSLY FOR *YOU.*

I AM *AWARE* OF THEIR DEPARTURE, AND I AM AWARE OF THEIR TRUE *DESTINATION.*

NOTHING OCCURS IN MY HOMELAND WITHOUT MY KNOWLEDGE.

BUT I HAVE ALREADY TAKEN *PRECAUTIONS,* THANK YOU. NOW PLEASE *LEAVE* ME.

BUT THERE'S MORE THAT YOU MAY NOT BE FULLY AWARE OF, SIRE. OUR *TEMPLES* WERE DEFILED.

OUR ACOLYTES TORTURED AND THEN *SLAIN.*

THE BRAIN AND HIS BROTHERHOOD ARE *TREACHEROUS.* THEY *FRIGHTEN* ME.

THEN I WILL COMFORT YOU LATER IN MY CHAMBERS, AND ONCE AGAIN YOU WILL LEARN WHY *BROTHER BLOOD* FEARS NO MAN, BEAST OR THING.

BUT FIRST, SPREAD THE WORD TO ALL MY BELIEVERS. INSTRUCT THEM TO ATTEND MY *SERMON* TONIGHT.

I SENSE A TIME OF GREAT *URGENCY* BEFALLING US. I WANT ALL WHO WORSHIP ME *PREPARED.*

2

"TELL THEM, TOO, THAT THEIR BROTHERS AND SISTERS WHO *DIED* DEFENDING MY CHURCH SHALL BE *AVENGED.*

"THE TEMPLE OF BROTHER BLOOD MAY *NEVER* BE DEFILED."

"AND NONE SHALL EVER *PUNISH* MY BELIEVERS, SAVE BROTHER BLOOD HIMSELF.

"GO NOW, SPREAD MY WORD QUICKLY AND THEN RETURN THAT I MAY SOOTHE YOUR DEEPEST FEARS AS ONLY *I* CAN."

ZANDIA: BROTHER BLOOD'S CHURCH FADES BENEATH THE SPEEDING JET AS IT LIFTS FROM THE WAR-TORN AIRPORT, RISING HIGH INTO THE DARK, ACRID SKIES.

THE STENCH OF DEATH FILLS ITS HULL, NOT WITH REMORSE, BUT WITH JOY...

YOU HAVE DONE *WELL,* MY BROTHERHOOD. ZE BRAIN IS *PLEASED.*

THEN YOU WILL BE *ECSTATIC* WHEN WE RETURN FROM AMERICA, OUR MISSION *COMPLETE.*

INDEED, PHOBIA. ZHAT I SHALL.

ACH! DEN VE VILL KILL DEM *ALL*, BRAIN.

BUT REMEMBER, ZE ONE WE SEEK WILL BE *WELL-GUARDED*. THEY WILL FIGHT TO ZE DEATH TO PREVENT HER *ABDUCTION*.

OUI, MONSIEUR PLASMUS, ZE LOVELY ZEY CALL *RAVEN* WILL BE *OURS!*

BUT I *WORRY*, WARP. REMEMBER, WE MET THESE TITANS ONCE BEFORE. THEY ARE *POWERFUL*.

ZE BROTHERHOOD SHALL STILL *SLAY* THEM. DO NOT WORRY SO, MONSIEUR HOUNGAN.

NON, MONSIEUR WARP, HOUNGAN IS *CORRECT*. DO NOT BELITTLE OUR ENEMY. ZEY *ARE* STRONG.

FOR ALMOST AN HOUR THE JET THUNDERS ACROSS THE ATLANTIC ON A STEADY COURSE. THEN, SUDDENLY...

MEIN GOTT! DER PLANE-- VAT IS *HAPPENING*?

BUT THEY WILL *NOT* STOP US! GO AND BRING ZIS RAVEN TO ME.

WE'RE PLUNGING TOWARD THE *OCEAN*-- GOING TO *CRASH!*

DER PILOT, *HE* DOES THIS. DERE IS NO *MALFUNCTION* WIT DIS JET.

BEFORE I BECAME DIS CREATURE, I VAS A *PILOT*. I KNOW DESE JETS--

-- HE IS *DELIBERATELY* DESTROYING US!

DID YOU TINK DIS FLIMSY STEEL DOOR VOULD KEEP ME *AVAY* FROM YOU?

SCHWEIN! DID YOU TINK VE VOULD NOT *STOP* YOU?

VELL, YOU ARE *WRONG*, SCHWEIN! YOU VILL *PAY* FOR THIS!

4

PLASMUS' BURNING HAND GRABS THE PILOT, PULLING HIM BACK...

YET, THE PILOT SAYS NOTHING AS HIS CLOTHING BEGINS TO BURN.

THERE IS NO CRY OR PLEA AS HIS FLESH BEGINS TO SIZZLE...

...AND-- MELT?

LIEBER GOTT! HE'S A-- ROBOT!

BROTHER BLOOD IS BEHIND THIS.

I VANT HIM--MORE DAN EVER.

THEN HURRY, YOU FOOLS! LOOK!

VE MUST NOT DIE!

DO SOMETHING. PILOT THIS JET!

I--I CANNOT. DE CONTROLS ARE STUCK! DEY VILL NOT WORK!

DAMN BROTHER BLOOD! DIS TIME HE HAS--

SKA-BLAMM!

YOU'RE DETERMINED TO *HURT* YOURSELF, AREN'T YOU?

I'M DOING JUST *FINE*, DONNA. NO *PROBLEMS*.

PHYSICALLY YOU'RE RIGHT. MENTALLY, YOU'RE *TORTURING* YOURSELF TO ACHIEVE SOME *IDEAL* THAT'S IMPOSSIBLE TO REACH.

YOU'LL NEVER BE *THE BATMAN*. DICK, WANT TO TALK?

NOTHING TO TALK *ABOUT*.

I'M *FINE*. LET ME BE.

DICK, THERE'S ABSOLUTELY NO ONE I'M *CLOSER* TO IN THE TITANS THAN YOU. I CAN'T LET THIS GO.

I CARE TOO *MUCH*. YOU'RE DRIVING YOURSELF *INSANE*.

YOU'RE TRYING TO DO IT ALL, BUT YOU *CAN'T*. I HATE TO LET YOU IN ON THIS, PAL--

--BUT YOU'RE ONLY *HUMAN*. YOU'VE GOT TO *STOP*. WORKING WITH *US*. WORKING *ALONE*. WITH *THE BATMAN*. GOING TO SCHOOL...

YOU'VE SET YOUR-SELF AN *IMPOSSIBLE* CHALLENGE.

DONNA, I APPRECIATE YOUR CONCERN, BUT YOU'RE *WRONG*. I CAN DO THIS.

I *HAVE* TO.

OKAY, I WON'T PUSH... NOT *TODAY*. JUST TAKE CARE OF YOURSELF. AND TALK WHEN YOU CAN.

SURE, TAKE CARE. I'LL *SEE* YOU.

7

JUST WISH I KNEW *WHY* DICK IS PUSHING HIMSELF. IT'S DRIVING *KORY* UP THE WALL.

POOR KID KEEPS THINKING IT'S SOMETHING *SHE* DID.

GREAT! I'M WORRYING ABOUT EVERYONE ELSE WHEN I'VE GOT MY *OWN* PROBLEMS.

I WAS AN ABSOLUTE *IDIOT* LAST NIGHT WITH TERRY.

BUT I FELT SO *UNCOMFORTABLE* SEEING HIM AND HIS WIFE... NO, IT'S NOT HIS *EX.* SHE DOESN'T BOTHER ME.
IT WAS HIS *DAUGHTER.* SHE'S THE ONE. I SAW A *FAMILY* IN HER...

NO MATTER WHAT'S *HAPPENED* BETWEEN HER PARENTS, SHE WILL ALWAYS *KNOW* WHO THEY ARE.

WHICH IS MORE THAN I DO ABOUT *MINE.*

THE ROOM IS SMALL, BUT LARGE ENOUGH FOR RAVEN'S NEEDS. THE AIR IS SCENTED WITH JASMINE, FAR TOO SWEET FOR WALLY WEST, BUT HE SAYS NOTHING.

WALLACE, I CANNOT DO YOUR SCHOOL WORK *FOR* YOU...

FORGET SCHOOL. I NEED TO GET *US* FIGURED OUT.

THERE CAN BE NO "US." I LIKE YOU... DEEPLY. BUT WHAT I AM *PRECLUDES* MY LOVING YOU.

I DARE NOT ALLOW MYSELF THAT EMOTION.

JUST OUTSIDE THE CLOSED DOOR...

SOMETIMES I FEEL I'M DENYING MY OWN EMOTIONS, RAVEN. NOT KNOWING WHO I AM *DOES* THAT TO ME.

SOMETIMES I DON'T FEEL LIKE I BELONG. I SHOULDN'T. BUT I *DO.*

I KNOW THAT, RAVEN, BUT I *LOVE* YOU.

BUT *I* CANNOT LOVE *YOU.* IF I FAIL TO REIGN IN MY EMOTIONS, THAT PART OF ME WHICH IS MY FATHER *TRIGON* CAN BURST FREE.

I'VE GOT TO DO SOMETHING ...SOON. I CAN'T KEEP *DENYING* MY HERITAGE.

I'VE GOT TO *KNOW* WHAT I TRULY AM.

YOU CANNOT UNDERSTAND THE *PAIN* I LIVE WITH, TRYING TO *CONTROL* MY DARKER SIDE.

YOU ASK FOR ADVICE? *LEAVE* THE TITANS! RETURN TO SCHOOL. *FORGET* ME.

IF YOU STAY, I SWEAR I SHALL BE THE *DEATH* OF YOU! /8

A SMALL ISLAND IN THE MID-ATLANTIC...

GULF-STREAM WATERS WARM THIS VEST-POCKET ISLE, MAKING IT A VERITABLE *PARADISE*...

WHICH IS EXACTLY THE THOUGHT OF THESE FOUR HAGGARD TRAVELERS...

WH-WHERE ARE WE?

VHERE HAF YOU *TELEPORTED* US, WARP?

I AM NOT SURE, MON AMI... I HAD TO WARP US OFF THAT PLUNGING JET TOO QUICKLY TO *CHOOSE* MY DESTINATION.

ARE YOU STRONG ENOUGH TO TELEPORT US TO *AMERICA?*

NON... GIVE ME A MOMENT. TO CARRY ALL *FOUR* OF US IS A TERRIBLE *STRAIN.*

I CANNOT *WAIT,* HERR WARP. MY ANGER TOWARD BROTHER BLOOD GROWS WITH EVERY SECOND.

ALRIGHT, PLASMUS-- BUT WE MUST MAKE ZIS VOYAGE IN *STAGES...*

I DO NOT HAVE ZE *ENERGY* TO TAKE US SO *FAR.*

AND, AS SIMPLY AS THAT, THEY ARE *GONE.*

9

AND, IN AMERICA...

WHAT A *GROUP* WE HAVE. SOMETIMES I FEEL WE SHOULD SELL OUR LIFE STORIES TO *GENERAL HOSPITAL.*

STILL, I GUESS I HAVE THE *LEAST* TO COMPLAIN ABOUT.

MY *PAST* MAY BE A SHAMBLES, BUT MY *FUTURE* LOOKS CERTAIN. I'M GENERALLY HAPPY. I CERTAINLY LOVE *TERRY,* AND--

KORY? WHAT ARE *YOU* DOING UP HERE?

OH, HI, DONNA. JUST *THINKING.*

DON'T TELL ME. *DICK?*

IT'S *UNHEALTHY,* KORY. YOU'RE BEGINNING TO LIVE JUST FOR *HIM.*

BUT I *LOVE* HIM.

ARE YOU CERTAIN YOU'RE NOT JUST IN LOVE WITH *BEING* IN LOVE?

I DON'T KNOW WHAT YOU *MEAN.*

NEVER MIND, HONEY. DICK'S GOING THROUGH SOME EMOTIONAL PROBLEMS. IF YOU REALLY LOVE HIM, LEAVE HIM *ALONE.*

LOOK, GO OUT AND HAVE SOME *FUN.* ENJOY YOURSELF.

WHERE ARE *YOU* GOING?

TO SEE *TERRY.* I LEFT HIS PLACE A TAD *ANGRY* LAST NIGHT.

AND I DON'T LIKE *DOING* THAT.

AND DON'T WORRY ABOUT *DICK.* HE'LL COME AROUND.

TAKE *CARE OF YOURSELF,* HON.

10

FROM NOTHINGNESS THERE COMES LIGHT.

AND FROM THE LIGHT APPEARS THE BROTHERHOOD OF EVIL...

NOW VHERE ARE WE, HERR WARP?

NOT FAR FROM OUR GOAL, MON AMI. BUT PLEASE, LET ME REST.

TO USE MY POWERS SO BROADLY WEAKENS ME.

THEN VE VAIT. BUT DO NOT DELAY. DER FORCES WHICH CHURN WITHIN ME... DEMAND I SLAY OUR ENEMY.

YOU WILL GET YOUR CHANCE, MON AMI-- AFTER WE ABDUCT THIS RAVEN,...NOT BEFORE.

MINUTES PASS, THEN...

WHAT?

LASERS!?!

PHOBIA SNAPS TO ATTENTION, HER HEAD CRANING UPWARD, GAZING AT THE JET-AND-CRIMSON FIGURES WHO SLIDE IN ON MINI-FLYERS.

THESE ARE BROTHER BLOOD'S MISSIONARIES, SET TO CARRY OUT THE ORDERS OF EXCOMMUNICATION.

BUT...

MY POOR, DELUDED FRIENDS, WE ARE NOT YOUR ENEMY. GAZE INTO THE EYES OF PHOBIA--

--AND YOU WILL LEARN WHO YOU MUST TRULY FEAR.

11

NEW YORK CITY. WINTRY DAYS TAKE HOLD AS THE LONG INDIAN SUMMER FINALLY FADES...

AND THIS GIRL *SHIVERS* WHILE GAZING LONGINGLY AT THE FAMILIAR SITE HALFWAY ACROSS THE EAST RIVER.

THESE PAST MONTHS SHE HAS BEEN SO *FRIGHTENED*, BUT NOW SHE KNOWS WHAT MUST BE DONE.

AND, MARVELLING AT THE *CONTROL* SHE HAS GAINED IN SO SHORT A TIME, SHE RISES SEVERAL *FEET* INTO THE AIR...

...GLIDING QUICKLY TOWARD HER DESTINATION.

WHILE WITHIN...

HIYA, BEAUTIFUL. HOW'S IT GOING?

EVERYTHING IS JUST *FINE*, ROY. ARE YOU ENJOYING YOUR VISIT HERE?

WITH GIRLS LIKE *YOU* AROUND, WHO WOULDN'T? WANNA TAKE IN A FLICK?

SOMETHING WRONG, STARFIRE? IS IT *DICK*?

I'M *SORRY*. I DIDN'T KNOW I WAS SO OBVIOUS.

ROY, YOU'VE *KNOWN* HIM A LONG TIME. WHY HAS HE BECOME SO MOODY?

IS HE *ANGRY* WITH ME?

YOU KNOW, SOMETIMES I BECOME SO *CONFUSED*. I STILL DON'T UNDERSTAND YOU EARTHLINGS.

MY GORGEOUS, BEAUTIFUL FRIEND, I *AM* AN EARTHLING, AS YOU SO SWEETLY PUT IT--

--AND EVEN *I* DON'T UNDERSTAND OUR POOR RICHARD GRAYSON.

WHY DON'T YOU *FORGET* ABOUT HIM? *I* COULD CERTAINLY CHEER UP THAT DOUR FACE.

12

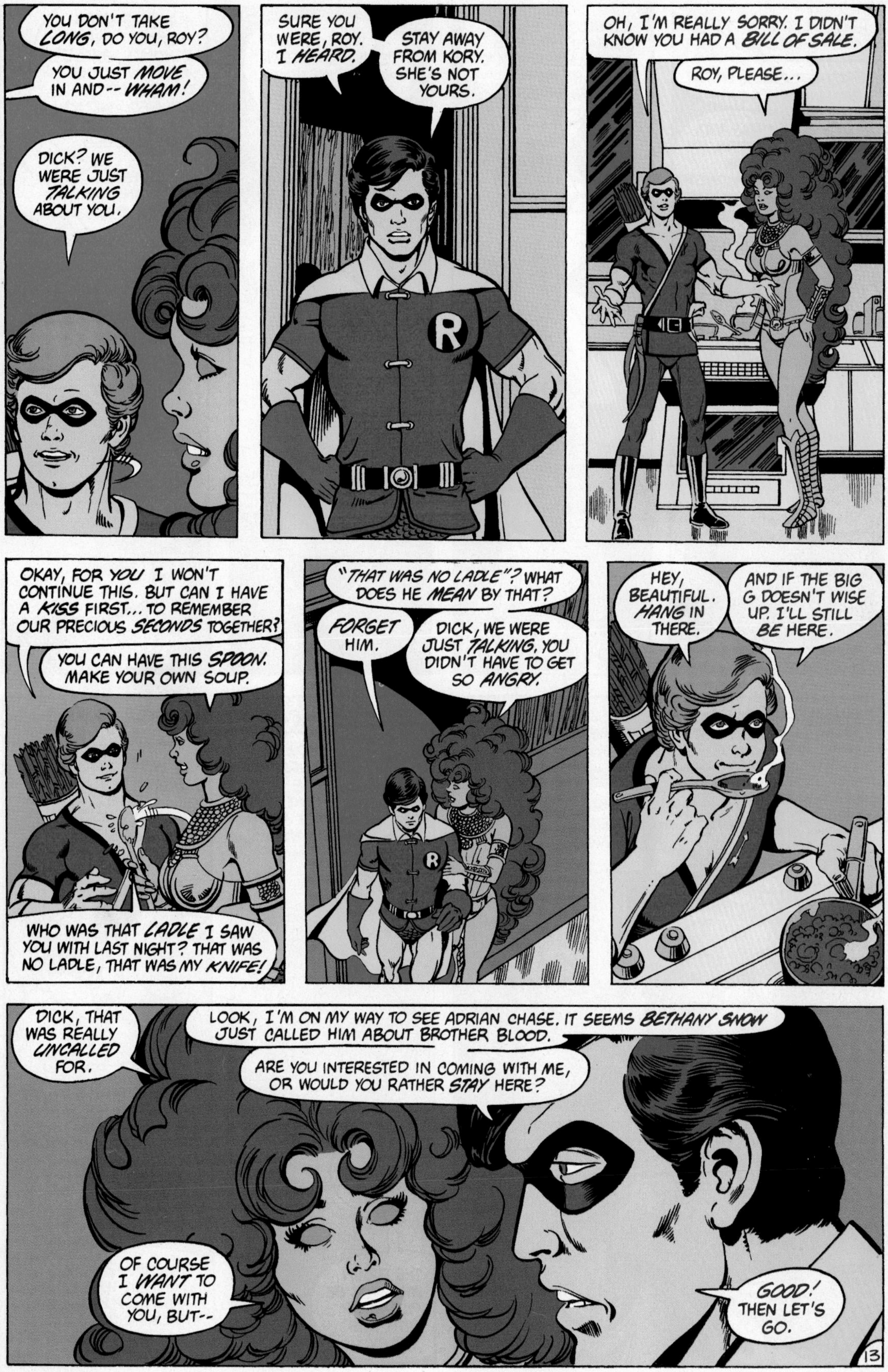
YOU DON'T TAKE LONG, DO YOU, ROY?
YOU JUST MOVE IN AND-- WHAM!
DICK? WE WERE JUST TALKING ABOUT YOU.
SURE YOU WERE, ROY. I HEARD.
STAY AWAY FROM KORY. SHE'S NOT YOURS.
OH, I'M REALLY SORRY. I DIDN'T KNOW YOU HAD A BILL OF SALE.
ROY, PLEASE...
OKAY, FOR YOU I WON'T CONTINUE THIS. BUT CAN I HAVE A KISS FIRST... TO REMEMBER OUR PRECIOUS SECONDS TOGETHER?
YOU CAN HAVE THIS SPOON. MAKE YOUR OWN SOUP.
WHO WAS THAT LADLE I SAW YOU WITH LAST NIGHT? THAT WAS NO LADLE, THAT WAS MY KNIFE!
"THAT WAS NO LADLE"? WHAT DOES HE MEAN BY THAT?
FORGET HIM.
DICK, WE WERE JUST TALKING. YOU DIDN'T HAVE TO GET SO ANGRY.
HEY, BEAUTIFUL. HANG IN THERE.
AND IF THE BIG G DOESN'T WISE UP, I'LL STILL BE HERE.
DICK, THAT WAS REALLY UNCALLED FOR.
LOOK, I'M ON MY WAY TO SEE ADRIAN CHASE. IT SEEMS BETHANY SNOW JUST CALLED HIM ABOUT BROTHER BLOOD.
ARE YOU INTERESTED IN COMING WITH ME, OR WOULD YOU RATHER STAY HERE?
OF COURSE I WANT TO COME WITH YOU, BUT--
GOOD! THEN LET'S GO.
13

BUZZARD'S BAY, MASSACHUSETTS...

BROTHER BLOOD, SISTER BETHANY IS HERE.

CHASE AND THE TITANS HAVE AN APPOINTMENT WITH ME, FOR LATER.

EXCELLENT, SISTER BETHANY. DO THIS TASK WELL AND YOU WILL BE AMPLY REWARDED.

I WILL, M'LORD. I'VE MEMORIZED ALL THE INFORMATION. THEY WILL BELIEVE ME.

MAKE CERTAIN THEY DO. I NEED ZANDIA'S AGREEMENT WITH THE UNITED STATES RATIFIED. AND YOU ARE THE KEY TO THAT SUCCESS.

SISTER BETHANY, DO NOT FAIL ME.

SOMEWHERE IN THE ATLANTIC LIE THE REMAINS OF BROTHER BLOOD'S MISSIONARIES. THEIR DEATHS WERE SWIFT, AND FOR SOME--PAINLESS.

WHILE, ACROSS THE OCEAN, THEIR MASTER SMILES; ALL GOES WELL.

ABOVE THIS ISLE DE MORTE...

HOW KIND OF BLOOD TO SUPPLY US WITH THESE FLIERS. IT MAKES MY WORK THAT MUCH EASIER, NON?

EASIER, WARP--BUT NOT FASTER.

THE BRAIN WILL NOT BE PLEASED WITH THIS DELAY.

C'EST LA GUERRE, EH?

I WORK WITH ZE BRAIN, NOT FOR HIM.

AH, MONSIEUR HOUNGAN-- AND YOU?

I WORK FOR HIM, MONSIEUR WARP. I OWE HIM BOTH MY LIFE AND MY POWER TO CONTROL THESE COMPUTERIZED FETISHES.

14

TITANS TOWER...

...I'M NOT SAYING I DON'T TRUST YOU, TERRA-- BUT WHY DIDN'T YOU USE YOUR EARTH-SHIFTING POWERS TO STOMP THOSE TERRORISTS?

CAN THE QUESTIONS, BOZO. MIND YOUR OWN BUSINESS.

YOU SHUT UP TOO, ARCHER.

HI, GUYS. HOW'S IT GOING?

YEAH, I GUESS IT WILL BE A NICE DAY IF IT DOESN'T RAIN.

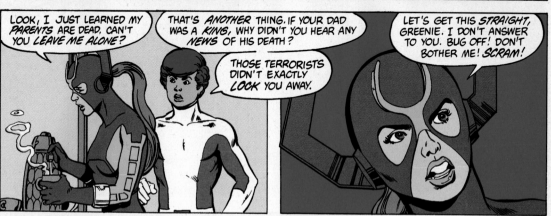

LOOK, I JUST LEARNED MY PARENTS ARE DEAD, CAN'T YOU LEAVE ME ALONE?

THAT'S ANOTHER THING. IF YOUR DAD WAS A KING, WHY DIDN'T YOU HEAR ANY NEWS OF HIS DEATH?

THOSE TERRORISTS DIDN'T EXACTLY LOCK YOU AWAY.

LET'S GET THIS STRAIGHT, GREENIE. I DON'T ANSWER TO YOU. BUG OFF! DON'T BOTHER ME! SCRAM!

CALM DOWN, TERRA. WE TITANS DON'T ARGUE AMONG OURSELVES LIKE THIS. WE WORK TOGETHER.

NOW ISN'T THAT JUST SWEETNESS AND LIGHT?

FIRST OFF, I'M NOT A TITAN.

SECOND, I'M NOT BECOMING ONE.

AND THIRD-- BUTT OUT!

OOOF!

SKTK

TERRA? WAIT A SECOND. COME BACK HERE!

LOGAN?

NOT NOW, VIC. I'M IN A RUSH.

TERRA!?!

15

49

VICTOR, MY FRIEND, I THINK *REFORMING* TERRA'S BECOME LOGAN'S PERSONAL CRUSADE.

IF THAT'S THE CASE, HARPER, THEN I THINK HE'S *BITTEN OFF* EVEN MORE THAN HIS OVER-SIZED MOUTH *CAN* CHEW.

I GOT SOME WORK TO DO UP IN THE MACHINE SHOP. WANNA *HELP?*

NAH! STILL HAVEN'T HAD *LUNCH*.

SUIT YOURSELF.

WHILE, IN ANOTHER ROOM...

NO USE. THIS STUFF PUTS ME *TO SLEEP*. I THOUGHT *CONRAD* WAS SUPPOSED TO BE BRILLIANT.

THE GUY USES FOUR THOUSAND WORDS WHEN *TWO* WOULD DO.

NEVER BEEN MUCH OF A READER ANY-WAY-- EH? PICKING UP *VIBRATIONS*... EMERGENCY ALARM'S ABOUT TO RING.

WHAT'S THAT?

SOUNDS LIKE ME TRYING TO *SING*.

TROUBLE! SOMEONE *UNAUTHORIZED* LANDED ON THE ISLAND.

NO, VICTOR...IT IS *NOT* TROUBLE.

"I SENSE...A FRIEND."

HI, WALLY.

FRANCES KANE? I DON'T BELIEVE IT.

Y-YOU'RE *FLOATING?* BUT I THOUGHT YOU *LOST* YOUR POWERS.

I'M SO *HAPPY* TO SEE YOU, WALLY. FOR A WHILE I DIDN'T THINK I'D HAVE THE *NERVE* TO COME BACK HERE--AFTER WHAT HAPPENED.

I THOUGHT EVERY-THING WAS GOING TO *CHANGE*. BUT THEN THE *MAG-NETIC POWERS* CAME BACK... AND I GOT SO SCARED AGAIN...

I *HAD* TO SEE YOU.

16

AND, MERE MOMENTS LATER...

WELL, WELL, I *KNEW* THERE WAS A REASON I HUNG AROUND.

MY NAME'S *SPEEDY*, BUT THAT'S NOT INDICATIVE OF *EVERYTHING* I DO.

LONG TIME, FRAN. HOW'S THINGS?

WHAT IS *WRONG*, FRANCES? I SENSE *CONCERN*.

I AM, RAVEN. SOMETHING'S *WRONG.*

LISTEN, IT'S *COLD* OUT HERE. LET'S GO INSIDE. I'LL MAKE SOME *HOT CHOCOLATE.*

I DON'T GET IT. SO FAR I'VE *STRUCK OUT* WITH EVERYONE BUT TERRA--

--AND I *NEVER* MAKE A PLAY FOR GIRLS WHOSE *AGE* IS SMALLER THAN MY STRING SIZE!

DON'T *WORRY* ABOUT IT, ARCHER. FRANCES AN' WALLY GO WAY BACK.

SO? THAT'S *NEVER* STOPPED ME BEFORE.

I MUST BE *LOSING* THE OL' ROY HARPER CHARM.

LEMME KNOW HOW THINGS WORK OUT. SEEYA LATER, MAN.

HYDRAULIC LEGS PROPEL CYBORG TOWARD MANHATTAN, AT THE MOMENT VICTOR STONE IS HAPPY.

TRUST US WHEN WE SAY, THAT SOON WILL CHANGE.

MEANWHILE, IN MANHATTAN...

ADRIAN SAID HE'D BE RIGHT OUT. YOU CAN-- UH--*WAIT* FOR HIM.

THANK YOU, MRS. CHASE.

PLEASE, CALL ME DORIS.

YOUR CHILDREN ARE *BEAUTIFUL*, DORIS. I LOVE CHILDREN. DON'T YOU, ROBIN?

THEY'RE SO *INNOCENT*, SO FULL OF LIFE.

STARFIRE, WE'RE HERE ON *BUSINESS.*

I KNOW, BUT WE CAN STILL *ENJOY* SOME PLEASURES.

17

GEE, WHAT'S *SUPERMAN* AN' *BATMAN* REALLY LIKE? THEY'RE MY ABSOLUTE *FAVORITES*, RIGHT AFTER *E.T.*

YEAH, *MINE* TOO. MRS. CHASE, WILL ADRIAN BE *LONG?*

HOW DO YOU SEE WITHOUT *EYES?*

OH, I SEE PERFECTLY, HONEY... AND I *DO* HAVE EYES.

RELAX, ROBIN-- WE HAVE PLENTY OF *TIME* TO GET TO BETHANY SNOW'S STUDIO.

I DON'T THINK *MEN* CAN RELAX. AT LEAST MY ADRIAN CAN'T. SOMETIMES I WISH HIS *WORK* WOULD JUST GO AWAY.

THAT, MY DEAR, WILL NEVER HAPPEN UNTIL MEN DECIDE *GREED* DOESN'T PAY.

AND *FORTUNATELY* FOR *MY* INCOME, THAT'S NOT ABOUT TO HAPPEN. READY, ROBIN?

FRANCES KANE'S EYES CLOSE, HER BROW FURROWS AS SHE BEGINS HER CONCENTRATION...

JUST WATCH. I FEEL THE *ENERGY* BUILDING.

MY *MAGNETIC POWERS* MAKE IT CHILD'S PLAY TO LIFT THAT SIXTY-POUND MOTOR.

OF COURSE, IT GETS *HARDER* AS THE WEIGHT INCREASES.

VERY LARGE OBJECTS I CAN'T LIFT MAGNETICALLY... I CAN ONLY *SHOVE* THEM.

UP UNTIL A FEW *HUNDRED* POUNDS. AFTER THAT I'M USELESS.

FRAN, DO YOU *REALIZE* SOMETHING? YOU KNOW YOU CAN'T RETURN HOME...

BUT WITH THOSE POWERS YOU CAN *STAY HERE*-- BECOME *ONE* OF US.

NO...NO. THAT'S *NOT* WHY I CAME, WALLY. I'M *SCARED* OF THESE POWERS.

I DON'T THINK I *WANT* THEM. PLEASE, *HELP* ME, WALLY. I NEED YOUR HELP.

OKAY, FRAN-- LET'S TALK.

WE'RE *BOTH* IN THE SAME BOAT.

18

52

IT IS TIME TO MOVE ON, ROY HARPER THINKS, POURING HIMSELF THE LAST OF THE TOMATO-RICE SOUP. THE TRIP WAS SUCCESSFUL, BUT...

HE HEARS THE QUIET POP OF RUSHING AIR BEHIND HIM JUST MOMENTS BEFORE THE LIGHT EXPLODES.

THEN...

I TOLD YOU I WAS STRONG ENOUGH TO WARP THE LAST MILES HERE.

WHILE...

WALLACE, I SENSE--THE BROTHERHOOD? THEY ARE IN THE KITCHEN.

WHO?

HE'S STILL COMING AT ME. I HAVE NO CHOICE--I HAVE TO SHOOT.

NOT THAT I THINK IT WILL STOP HIM.

C'MON, YOU DON'T REALLY WANNA FIGHT ME, DO YOU?

NO, SCHWEIN--I VANT TO KILL YOU.

I VANT TO REDUCE YOUR MISERABLE FLESH TO ITS BASIC PROTOPLASMIC SLIME!

DIS IS TITANS' TOWER? VHERE ARE THE TITANS? TELL ME!

HOO BOY, SOMETHING TELLS ME YOU'RE NOT FRIENDS DROPPING IN.

OH, GOD-- JUST WHAT WE DIDN'T NEED. HALF THE TEAM'S OUT.

FRAN, YOU STAY HERE. C'MON, RAVEN-- LET'S GO.

STAND BACK, JELLO-FACE. AND THAT GOES FOR THE REST OF YOU.

WELL, UGLY, YOU CAN'T GET EVERYTHING YOU WANT.

WATCH THESE GUYS. THEY'RE DANGEROUS.

THAT YOU DIDN'T HAVE TO TELL ME.

19

KID FLASH? *GOOD!* I CAME PREPARED. MY *FETISH* IS ALREADY PROGRAMMED TO YOUR CELL TYPE.

A SINGLE TOUCH WITH MY *COMPUTERIZED NEEDLE* AND SCIENCE AND SORCERY WORK AS ONE.

MY LEG!!

WITHOUT TOUCHING HIM, THE NEEDLE *CUTS* THROUGH FLESH AND MUSCLE, RIPPING THROUGH TENDON AND BONE.

KID FLASH *STUMBLES* IN PAIN. HE FALLS AND *STAYS DOWN.*

THERE IS RAVEN...I WILL SEND HER TO OUR *WAITING STATION.* SHE WILL *NOT* BE ABLE TO ESCAPE.

NO!

THE SOMBER EMPATH *SENSES* THE TRAP EVEN BEFORE IT IS SPRUNG.

AND EVEN AS HER BODY FALLS THROUGH THE SPATIAL WARP, HER SOUL SELF SLIPS FREE.

WHY HAVE YOU *DONE* THIS TO ME?

AND WHERE HAVE YOU SENT MY *CORPOREAL BODY?* SPEAK TO ME? TELL ME!

RAVEN!

WARP IS NOT YOUR FOE. *LOOK* AROUND YOU. SEE YOUR *WORST* FEAR COME ALIVE.

HE IS HERE. NOW!

HE WILL *DESTROY* YOU. DESTROY EVERYTHING YOU HOLD DEAR.

N-NO!

THERE? BUT THAT IS WAL--

TRIGON?

AZAR GUIDE ME! MY FATHER HAS SLAIN WALLACE!

NO, RAVEN-- IT'S ME. MY GOD-- STOP, RAVEN!

20

WHATEVER YOU'VE DONE TO HER-- *STOP IT!*

FOR GOD'S SAKE, RAVEN-- CAN YOU *HEAR ME?* STOP!

BUT RAVEN HEARS NOTHING SAVE THE POUNDING OF HER FEARFUL HEART.

HER *SOUL-SELF* IS THE PART OF HER WHICH IS TRIGON. NOW THAT *SOUL-SELF* IS *OUT OF CONTROL.*

I COULDN'T STAY BACK, WALLY. I--

OH, NO-- WHAT'S GOING ON HERE?

WALLY?

IT *HURTS*...PLEASE... STOP, RAVEN-- YOU'RE *KILLING ME.*

SO COLD...IT'S *HORRIBLE*... I--I CAN'T TAKE IT.

FRANCES KANE *REACTS* WITHOUT THINKING. ONCE, MANY YEARS AGO, SHE HAD LOVED WALLY WEST...

SHE MAY *STILL* LOVE HIM.

BUT WHATEVER HER FEELINGS, SHE WILL *NOT* SIT BACK AND WATCH HIM DIE.

STOP HER! SHE MUST NOT PREVENT US FROM CON- TROLLING RAVEN.

DO NOT VORRY, PHOBIA. SHE VILL NOT USE DOSE *POWERS* ON THE ONE VE VANT.

DER BRAIN SENT US FOR RAVEN. *NOTHING* VILL STOP US FROM ABDUCTING HER.

AND, IF I MUST *KILL* TO ASSURE OUR GOAL, DEN SO BE IT.

DAT VHICH I AM CRIES OUT FOR BLOOD.

REALLY, PAL, THEN TRY *MINE*-- IF YOU'RE MAN ENOUGH.

YOU *ARE* A MAN BENEATH ALL THAT MUCK, AREN'T YOU?

21

YOU SCHWEIN, I VILL--

SPLAHMM!

MY BODY-- SO COLD. VHAT HAF YOU...YOU... UNHHHH.

WELL, WHADDAYA KNOW, IT *WORKED*.

WHEREVER YOU ARE, OLLIE, I *OWE* YOU ONE.

PLASMUS ON A STICK. NOT BAD, EH? STILL, I THINK I'LL STICK TO *CHIPWICH*.

WHAT HAVE YOU *DONE* TO HIM?

OH, JUST ATTACHED THE FRIDGE'S *COOL-ING* UNITS TO A COMMON *EXPLOSIVE ARROW*. THAT'S IT.

NOW, SINCE I GATHER *YOU'RE* THE ONE WHO DROVE RAVEN CRACKERS--

SILENCE, CHILD. YOUR ARROWS ARE USELESS AGAINST ME AS I DELVE INTO YOUR SUBCON-SCIOUS...

AH, I SENSE YOUR DEEPEST *FEARS*, A MISTAKE YOU ONCE MADE--

RELIVE THOSE DARK DAYS, CHILD. RELIVE THE TORTURES OF A *DRUG-INDUCED MIND!*

RELIVE YOUR PAINS OF *WITHDRAWAL*, REMEMBER--

UNHHHH!

FRAN! THANK HEAVEN. THANKS.

HELP ME... WE'VE GOT TO SAVE WALLY, HELP ME.

HOLD IT, FRAN--GET BACK!

WE CAN'T GO NEAR HER--

I'VE GOT TO, SPEEDY. I CAN'T LET HIM DIE.

HELP ME! THE PAIN! THE PAIN!

22

BUT...

NO!

WHAT HAVE I DONE?

THE SOUL-SELF VANISHES. THEN...

HEY, PAL, HOW ARE--

SH-SHE WAS SO COLD...LIKE DEATH...LIKE THE DYING...

SHE--SHE WANTS TO KILL ME. THE HATE...I SAW HER HATE. I COULD TOUCH IT.

I SAW HER...GOD, FOR THE FIRST TIME-- I SAW HER...

SAW HER...SAW TRIGON...MY GOD...HER SOUL...TRIGON...THEY--THEY'RE LIKE ONE...

I--I NEVER KNEW ...SHE-SHE COULD HAVE DESTROYED ME.

I RETRIEVED MY BODY--WITHOUT THE BROTHERHOOD PRESENT, THEIR TRAP COULDN'T HOLD ME.

WALLACE! THANK AZAR. I THOUGHT I HAD SLAIN YOU.

GET AWAY FROM ME, RAVEN. STAY AWAY!

YOU WOULD HAVE KILLED ME.

WALLACE, PLEASE UNDERSTAND. MY SOUL-SELF WAS OUT OF CONTROL. I COULD NOT CONTAIN MY DARK SIDE.

IT WAS NOT ME.

STAY AWAY FROM ME, RAVEN.

JUST STAY AWAY!

I--I CANNOT TAKE YOUR HATE...I MUST LEAVE....MUST GO...MUST THINK!

WELL, ROY, HOW DID YOU SPEND YOUR WINTER VACATION?

SHE'S GONE, BUT I DON'T THINK SHE KNEW WHAT SHE WAS DOING.

SHE KNEW, FRAN--BELIEVE ME. SHE KNEW!

AND MORE-- SHE ENJOYED IT!

23

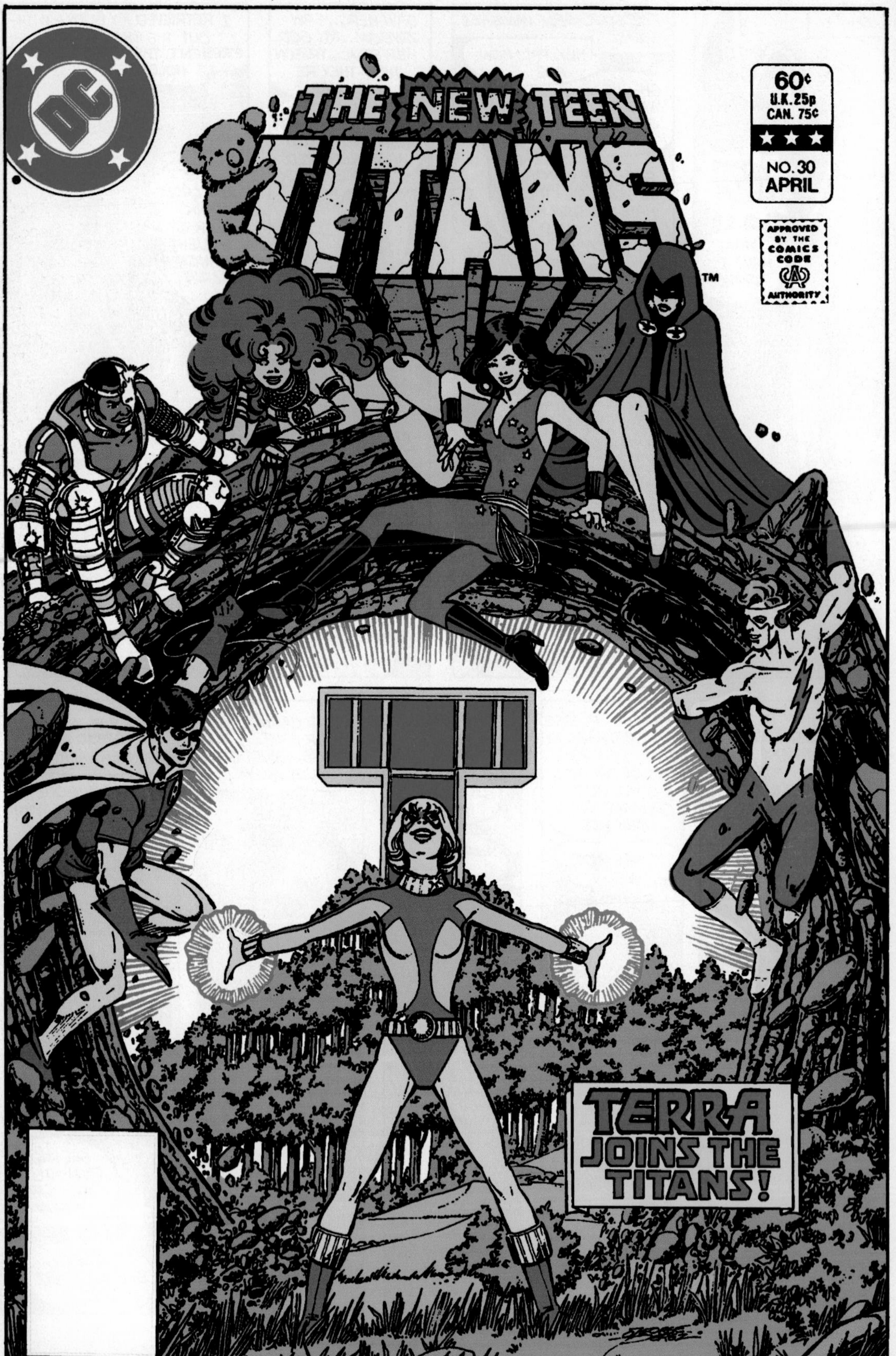
THE NEW TEEN
TITANS
TM
60¢
U.K. 25p
CAN. 75¢
NO. 30
APRIL
APPROVED BY THE COMICS CODE AUTHORITY
TERRA
JOINS THE
TITANS!

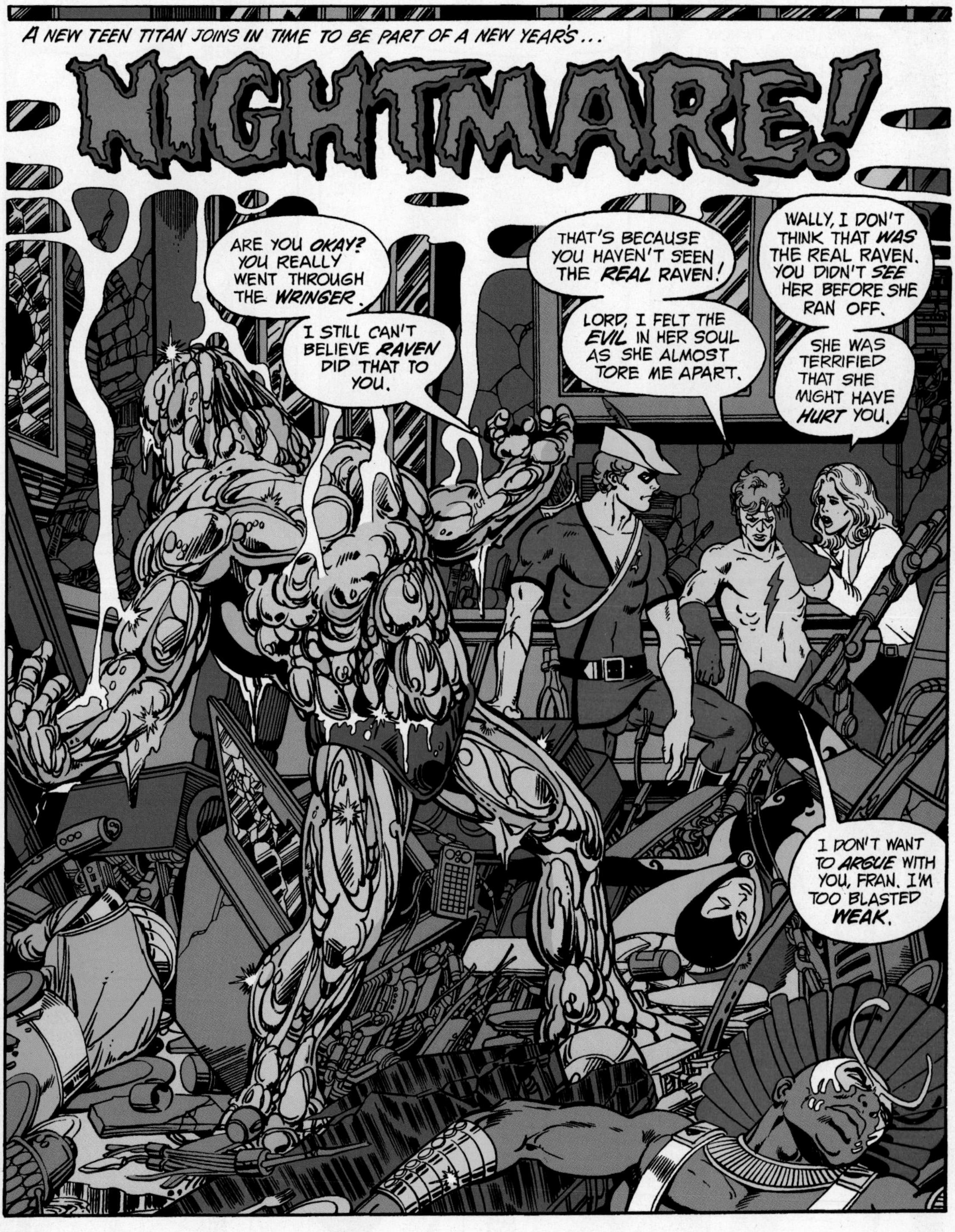

A NEW TEEN TITAN JOINS IN TIME TO BE PART OF A NEW YEAR'S...
NIGHTMARE!
ARE YOU OKAY? YOU REALLY WENT THROUGH THE WRINGER.
I STILL CAN'T BELIEVE RAVEN DID THAT TO YOU.
THAT'S BECAUSE YOU HAVEN'T SEEN THE REAL RAVEN!
LORD, I FELT THE EVIL IN HER SOUL AS SHE ALMOST TORE ME APART.
WALLY, I DON'T THINK THAT WAS THE REAL RAVEN. YOU DIDN'T SEE HER BEFORE SHE RAN OFF.
SHE WAS TERRIFIED THAT SHE MIGHT HAVE HURT YOU.
I DON'T WANT TO ARGUE WITH YOU, FRAN. I'M TOO BLASTED WEAK.

HOLD ON, WALLY. I'M BRINGING A A CHAIR FOR YOU *MAGNETICALLY.*

MAYBE I DON'T KNOW RAVEN LIKE *YOU* DO, BUT I STILL DON'T THINK SHE'S *EVIL.*

FRAN'S RIGHT, PAL. YOU TOLD US YOURSELF THAT HER FATHER TRIGON, WAS *PART* OF HER SOUL-SELF.

THE PART SHE FIGHTS TO *SUPPRESS.*

BUT WHEN *PHOBIA* DUG INTO RAVEN'S SUBCONSCIOUS, SHE LEARNED THAT HER GREATEST FEAR WAS *UNLEASHING* HER EVIL SIDE.

RAVEN COULDN'T *HELP* WHAT HAPPENED TO HER.

I-I DON'T CARE. SHE'S *EVIL...* I KNOW THE TRUTH NOW.

H-HOW COULD I HAVE TRIED TO *LOVE* HER?

WALLY, I CAME HERE POSSESSING SUPER-POWERS I DIDN'T *WANT.*

SOMETHING TELLS ME *YOU* WOULD RATHER FORGET *YOUR* SUPER-HEROICS AS WELL.

WHY DON'T WE BOTH GO BACK TO *BLUE VALLEY*--PLEASE, WALLY?

LEAVE THE *TITANS?* FRAN, RIGHT NOW THAT SOUNDS SO *TEMPTING...*

LORD, I DON'T KNOW... I NEVER SEEM TO KNOW *WHAT* TO DO.

I HATE TO *SAY* THIS, PAL, BUT FRAN COULD BE *RIGHT.*

YOU'RE ALWAYS SAYING YOU CAN'T PLAY SUPER-HERO WHILE GOING TO *SCHOOL*--

--SO WHY DON'T YOU DO WHAT *I* DO--GO ON *RESERVE STATUS*... BE A *PART-TIME* TITAN.

PART- TIME? TH-THAT WOULD KEEP ME AWAY FROM RAVEN WHILE I THINK THINGS OVER.

I-I'VE GOT TO *THINK* ABOUT THIS, REALLY *THINK* ABOUT IT.

2

DERE IS NO *REASON* TO T'INK, NOT VEN YOU SHALL SOON *DIE!*

PLASMUS? HE'S *THAWED OUT!*

B-BUT, WHAT CAN *I* DO? I DON'T KNOW, *HELP ME!*

FRAN, I'M GOING TO NEED YOUR *POWERS.*

BEST DO *NOT'IN,* FRÄULEIN --

SWAK!

YOU ARE NOT *VUN* OF DESE TITANS...

...I DO NOT HAF TO *KILL* YOU.

SPRAAM!

PLASMUS, *FORGET* THEM. WE CAME HERE FOR THE GIRL CALLED *RAVEN*...

RAVEN? THEN SHE'S MIXED UP WITH *YOU?*

THAT DOES IT! I WANT *ANSWERS.*

EASILY, PHOBIA. MY COMPUTERIZED *VOODOO FETISH* HAS ALREADY BEEN PRO-GRAMMED WITH HIS *CELL STRUCTURE.*

IF I CONTINUED THE LETHAL SPRAY, HE WOULD *DIE!*

EXCELLENT, HOUGAN. NOW, FOR *YOU,* CHILD-- SHALL WE DISCUSS YOUR *LIFE*...

...AND WHAT MAKES YOU *SCREAM* FOR MERCY?

P-PLEASE ... I HAVEN'T *DONE* ANY-THING TO YOU. DON'T *HURT* ME.

HOUNGAN, *ELIMINATE* HIM.

IF I WANTED TO, THIS *GAS ATOMIZER* COULD *CRIPPLE* KID FLASH.

3

MY DEAR, PHOBIA HAS NO DESIRE TO *HARM* YOU.

I DO, HOW-EVER, WISH TO *WARN* YOU.

IF YOU DO NOT LIKE THIS SUDDEN FEELING OF *SPACE* CRUSHING IN ON YOU--

--STAY OUT OF OUR *WAY*. OR, WHEN *NEXT* WE MEET...

...I MAY NOT SO QUICKLY FREE YOU FROM THE CLUTCHES OF *CLAUSTROPHOBIA!*

JUST IN CASE, I HAD BETTER FIX A LOCK OF THIS ONE'S *HAIR* TO MY FETISH.

WE MAY ONE DAY *NEED* THIS, EH?

D-DON'T... PLEASE DON'T *DO* THAT AGAIN.

WELL, WARP, I HAVE GIVEN YOU RAVEN'S *DOLL*-- HAVE YOU HOMED IN ON HER *LOCATION?*

NOT *PRECISELY*, MONSIEUR, BUT I CAN BRING US *NEAR* HER.

NOW COME, LET US HURRY BEFORE SHE *VANISHES* AGAIN.

THE BROTHERHOOD IS PLEASED. THINGS HAVE GONE *WELL* THUS FAR, AND IF THEY *CONTINUE* THAT WAY, THEY WILL SOON HAVE RAVEN IN THEIR CLUTCHES...

...AND WITH HER, *THE SECRET OF BROTHER BLOOD!*

WALLY? SPEEDY? PLEASE ...SOMEONE... *HELP ME!*

PLEASE!!

WARP EXPLODES WITH LIGHT, TRANSPORTING HIMSELF AND HIS COMRADES ACROSS THE LENGTH OF MANHATTAN...

4

SEVERAL MILES SOUTH STANDS THE WORLD-FAMOUS *BROOKLYN BRIDGE*, SOLD TO ALL-TOO-MANY UNWARY TOURISTS LOOKING FOR A BIG APPLE *BARGAIN*.

YOU *LIVED* HERE, TARA? EVEN *COCKROACHES* WOULD PICKET A HOLE LIKE THIS.

THIS PLACE ISN'T EVEN FIT FOR *PIGEONS* TO DO YOU-KNOW-WHAT ON.

THIS DUMP'S NATIONAL BIRD IS *THE VULTURE!*

WILL YOU KNOCK OFF THE DUMB *JOKES*, LOGAN? I WAS BEING HELD *PRISONER* HERE, REMEMBER?

THERE AREN'T TOO MANY *TERRORISTS* WHO CAN AFFORD TO HOLE UP AT THE *PLAZA*.

YEAH, THAT'S SOMETHING I WAS *WONDERING* ABOUT. YOU HAD *SUPER-POWERS*. WHY DIDN'T YOU USE 'EM AND *FORCE* THOSE TERRORISTS TO TELL YOU ABOUT YOUR PARENTS?

I DON'T WANT TO *TALK* ABOUT THAT.

HEY, LOGAN, I HAVE NO PLACE TO *GO* NOW. YOU THINK I COULD STAY WITH *YOU* GUYS?

Y'KNOW, BECOME A *TEEN TITAN?* AH... *THERE* IT IS!

BECOME A *TITAN?* I *GUESS* SO. WE HAVEN'T GOT ANY *RULES* ABOUT THAT.

POLITICAL RISONERS

FREE

PLO

SO WHAT DID YOU *FIND* BACK THERE?

I ORIGINALLY MADE *TWO* COSTUMES TO WEAR AS *TERRA*-- BUT I SWORE I'D ONLY WEAR *THIS* ONE WHEN I WAS FINALLY *FREE*.

YEAH, IT STILL *FITS*.

SCREWBALL, TURN AROUND THIS WAY...

5

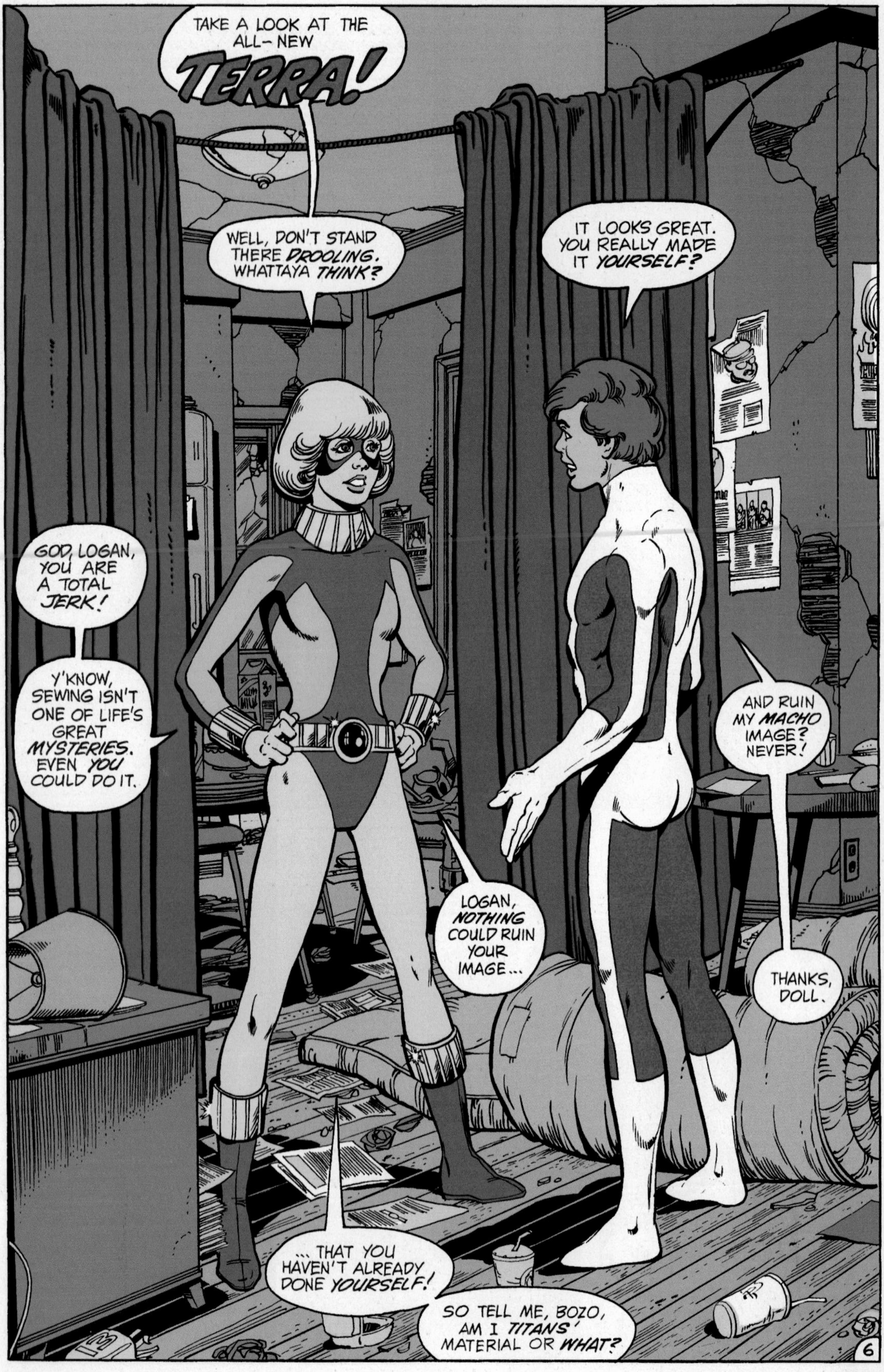
TAKE A LOOK AT THE ALL-NEW TERRA!
WELL, DON'T STAND THERE DROOLING. WHATTAYA THINK?
IT LOOKS GREAT. YOU REALLY MADE IT YOURSELF?
GOD, LOGAN, YOU ARE A TOTAL JERK!
Y'KNOW, SEWING ISN'T ONE OF LIFE'S GREAT MYSTERIES. EVEN YOU COULD DO IT.
AND RUIN MY MACHO IMAGE? NEVER!
LOGAN, NOTHING COULD RUIN YOUR IMAGE...
...THAT YOU HAVEN'T ALREADY DONE YOURSELF!
THANKS, DOLL.
SO TELL ME, BOZO, AM I TITANS' MATERIAL OR WHAT?
6

WELL, HOW ABOUT AN *ANSWER?*

WELL--AH-- ACTUALLY, IT'S NOT UP TO *ME.*

I GOTTA CHECK IT OUT WITH THE OTHERS. WE'RE SORTA *EXCLUSIVE.*

SURE, SURE. THEN LET'S PUT ON SOME *WING-SPEED,* WILLYA?

I WANT AN *ANSWER* ON THIS--*FAST!*

WHILE, BELOW...

CHASE, YOU HAVEN'T SAID A *WORD* THE WHOLE TRIP. WHAT'S *WRONG?*

WELL, KID, YOU REMEMBER THAT DRUG-PUSHER, ANTHONY SCARAPELLI? FROM THE *RUNAWAY* CASE?

HE JUST *BOUGHT* HIS WAY CLEAR.

SNOW STORM CABLE NEWS STARRING BETHANY SNOW

THIS IS WHAT *GETS* ME, ROBIN. I HAD SCARAPELLI DOWN *COLD*-- BUT NOW HE'S *FREE.*

LOOK, LET'S *FORGET* IT FOR NOW, OKAY? WE'RE AFTER *BROTHER BLOOD.*

YOU DO KNOW THIS IS PROBABLY A *SET-UP.* BETHANY SNOW *WORKS* FOR BLOOD.

TELL ME SOMETHING I *DON'T* KNOW.

YEAH, BLOOD'S *UP* TO SOMETHING... SOMETHING ABOUT THE UPCOMING *CONGRESSIONAL ELECTIONS.*

YOU REALLY THINK SHE'LL *HELP* US?

BEATS *ME,* STARFIRE-- BUT I CAN'T AFFORD TO OVERLOOK ANY OPPORTUNITIES.

BESIDES, I'M *PAID* TO WORK MY EIGHT HOURS.

THOUGH WHY YOU CLOWNS DO THIS FOR *FREE* I'LL NEVER KNOW.

THE DOOR'S *OPEN.*

ON THE AIR

STUDIO 11

THEN LET'S PLAY THE *FLIES* TO BETHANY SNOW'S *SPIDER.* C'MON!

7

WELL, MISS SNOW, WE'RE *HERE*.

WHY DID YOU *CALL* US?

OH, THANK GOD, I WAS GOING *CRAZY* WAITING FOR YOU.

LOOK, I KNOW YOU THINK I'M *LYING* ABOUT THIS, BUT I'M NOT.

I--I WANT BLOOD *STOPPED*.

OKAY, I *ADMIT* I WORKED FOR HIM. I HELPED HIM SET THE TITANS *UP* THAT'LL *PROVE* I'M BEING STRAIGHT.

ONLY IF YOU'RE WILLING TO GO ON THE *RECORD*.

I AM. *BELIEVE ME*.

WHY THE SUDDEN *CHANGE*, MISS SNOW?

BECAUSE I JUST LEARNED WHAT BROTHER BLOOD IS *REALLY* AFTER.

LOOK, I *BELIEVED* IN HIM. I REALLY *DID*. I THOUGHT HE WAS OUT TO CREATE A *BETTER* WORLD.

OH, I WASN'T *BLIND* TO HIS DARK SIDE, BUT I BELIEVED HIS ENDS *JUSTIFIED* HIS MEANS.

YOU STILL DON'T BELIEVE ME. THEN LOOK AT *THIS*.

WELL, WELL. BROTHER BLOOD WAS *THOROUGH* WITH HIS RECORDS. CAN WE *KEEP* THESE?

OF COURSE... SHOW THEM TO THE *PRESS*.

THESE PHOTOGRAPHS ARE *PROOF* OF BLOOD'S *REIGN OF TORTURE*.

8

X'HAL! WHY DIDN'T YOU *TELL* ME HE DID THIS TO YOU?

H-HE COULD HAVE *KILLED* YOU, ROBIN.

HE DIDN'T.

OKAY, SO WE *BUY* YOUR STORY -- FOR *NOW.* WHAT'S BLOOD UP TO?

IT'S THE *SPECIAL ELECTIONS* BEING HELD IN THREE STATES NEXT MONTH.

THESE PEOPLE -- THE FIRST TWO ARE CONGRESSMAN, THE OTHER ONE IS A *SENATOR.*

THEY *WORK* FOR BLOOD AND HE'S TRYING TO GET THEM *RE-ELECTED.*

BLOOD RUNS *ZANDIA* --AND *ZANDIA* NEEDS ARMS TO FIGHT A GROUP *CALLED THE BROTHERHOOD OF EVIL.*

THESE THREE ARE ON THE *ARMS COMMITTEE* -- AND THEY'RE SETTING UP A *TREATY* WITH ZANDIA TO SELL BLOOD THE *WEAPONS* HE NEEDS.

HOLD IT. DID YOU *HEAR* SOMETHING?

IF BLOOD *GETS* THOSE WEAPONS, THERE WILL BE *WAR.* THOUSANDS WILL DIE.

I--I CAN'T *ALLOW* THAT TO HAPPEN.

HEAR *WHAT,* ROBIN?

A *SCRAPING* SOUND-- HOLD IT.

LORD!

MOVE IT!

BA-WHAMMMM!

9

ROBIN, ARE YOU *OKAY?*

YEAH, YOU SEE WHO *DID* THIS?

HE'S RIGHT IN *FRONT* OF ME, TRYING TO *ESCAPE.*

HE WON'T GET *FAR.*

STARFIRE LUNGES FORWARD, EYES NARROWED IN ANGER, TEETH CLENCHED IN HATE.

BUT...

SKA-BLAMMM!

SHE SENSES THE *PAIN* IN ROBIN'S VOICE AND PROMISES HERSELF THAT THIS WOULD-BE KILLER WILL *PAY* FOR THIS DEED.

WHOEVER DID THIS *MINED* THE DOORWAY, PROBABLY WITH *ELECTRIC SENSORS.*

DON'T GO AFTER HIM *YOURSELF*, ROBIN. HE'S *DANGEROUS.*

DON'T WORRY ABOUT *ME*, I CAN HANDLE *MYSELF.*

NO GOOD. HE WAS *PREPARED.*

HE'S *GONE.*

MAYBE I CAN CHASE *AFTER* HIM. I'M ALL RIGHT NOW. I JUST HAD THE *WIND* KNOCKED OUT OF ME, THAT'S ALL.

DON'T BOTHER. WE KNOW *WHO* HE WAS WORKING FOR.

WELL, MISS SNOW, WHAT *NOW?*

LOOK, IF BLOOD *KNOWS* I'VE TURNED AGAINST HIM, HE'LL FIND SOME WAY TO *KILL* ME.

PLEASE, YOU'VE GOT TO *HELP* ME.

I'LL CONFESS TO *EVERYTHING!* JUST *SAVE* ME.

10

WHAT'S THIS BROTHERHOOD OF EVIL?

THE TITANS FOUGHT THEM SEVERAL MONTHS AGO. THEY'RE AN INTERNATIONAL TERRORIST GROUP--

-- AND THEY COME COMPLETE WITH SUPER-POWERS.

SOUNDS LIKE THEY'RE A MILLION LAUGHS. WHAT'RE THEY AFTER?

BROTHER BLOOD'S POWER, THEY MEAN TO GET IT THROUGH ONE OF THE TITANS... RAVEN!

ROBIN, I THINK YOU'D BETTER--

BUT EVEN BEFORE ADRIAN CHASE CAN COMPLETE HIS THOUGHT, ROBIN AND STARFIRE ARE GONE...

THEIR FRIEND IS IN TROUBLE.

UPTOWN: HIS NAME IS VICTOR STONE AND, SEVERAL YEARS AGO, HIS BODY WAS DESTROYED IN A LABORATORY ACCIDENT. HIS LIFE, HOWEVER, WAS SAVED BY HIS FATHER WHO TURNED HIM INTO A THING THAT IS HALF MAN / HALF MACHINE -- A CYBORG.

THOUGH HIS BODY WAS SAVED, HIS MIND SEETHED WITH ANGER TOWARD HIS FREAKISH APPEARANCE--

--UNTIL HE BECAME A MEMBER OF THE NEW TEEN TITANS.

--UNTIL HE MET A YOUNG WOMAN NAMED SARAH SIMMS, A TEACHER OF HANDICAPPED CHILDREN WHO SAW PAST HIS PROSTHETICALLY-ENHANCED BODY TO THE MAN INSIDE.

IN THE PAST MONTHS, THEY HAVE BECOME GOOD FRIENDS.

YES, WHO IS IT?

AND, VICTOR THINKS, PERHAPS EVEN MORE.

UH, MY NAME'S VIC STONE. THIS IS SARAH'S APARTMENT, ISN'T IT?

VICTOR? OH, I'M SORRY... I DIDN'T SEE THE METAL SIDE OF YOUR FACE.

PLEASE, COME IN. SARAH'S TOLD ME ALL ABOUT YOU. I'M MARK WRIGHT.

SPECIAL OLYMPICS

YOUR SHIRT... YOU WORK WITH SARAH.

USED TO. WE SET UP HER CENTER TOGETHER SEVERAL YEARS AGO.

SIT DOWN, VIC -- SARAH'S OUT SHOPPING FOR THE PARTY TONIGHT.

11

THIS IS REALLY A *PLEASURE*. SARAH'S SO *FOND* OF YOU.

YEAH, WE MAKE A GREAT *TEAM*. SAY, HOWCUM I HAVEN'T SEEN *YOU* AT THE CENTER? I'VE BEEN *WORKIN'* THERE SOMETIMES.

Y'KNOW, WE PARTED RIGHT AFTER WE GOT *ENGAGED*. BUT HER WORK KEPT HER UP HERE.

EN-ENGAGED?

OH, I WENT DOWN TO WASHINGTON ABOUT A YEAR AGO TO OPEN ANOTHER CENTER *THERE*.

I TELL YOU, BEING *APART* FROM SARAH'S BEEN *TERRIBLE*.

FOR A *YEAR* NOW. WE TALK ALL THE TIME BY *PHONE*.

ENGAG-- *HUH?*

UHH... JUST PICKED UP MY INTERNAL *ALARM*. SOMETHING'S WRONG AT *TITAN'S TOWER*.

SOMETHING *WRONG*, VICTOR?

LOOK, GIVE THIS TO *SARAH*. WISH HER *HAPPY NEW YEAR* FOR ME.

I'M SO SORRY YOU CAN'T *STAY*. SARAH WAS HOPING YOU'D *BE* HERE.

TELL HER I GOTTA GO SAVE *THE WORLD* OR SOMETHIN'!

7313

IT'S BEEN *GREAT*, VIC. WE'VE GOT TO TALK *MORE* SOME DAY.

YEAH, SURE.

HE LEAVES, NOT AT ALL HAPPY.

HADDA BE *CRAZY* THINKIN' WE MEANT THAT WAY TO EACH OTHER.

WHERE WAS YOUR *MIND*, STONE?

WHAT'VE YOU BEEN *THINKIN'* 'BOUT ALL THESE MONTHS?

SHE WAS A *FRIEND*, MADE ME FEEL GOOD INSIDE AN' I THOUGHT WE *LOVED* EACH OTHER MORE'N JUST FRIENDS DO.

NOT *ANGRY* AT HER. NOT EVEN *MAD* AT HER. AIN'T *HER* FAULT.

IT'S *MINE!* MINE!

12

KEEP *DELUDIN'* MYSELF, THINKIN' THERE'S GONNA BE A *REAL* LIFE OUT THERE FER ME.

FORGET THAT INSTEAD'A FLESH I GOT *PLASTIC.* INSTEAD'A BONE I GOT *MOLYBDENUM.*

MY FAULT, MAN... MY FAULT FOR THINKIN' I CAN JUMP HIGHER'N THE *RAINBOW.*

HANGIN' ROUND *FREAKS* SO MUCH, I FORGET *I'M* A FREAK, TOO.

WHY DO THEY ALLOW US FREAKS TO *HOPE?*

PLEASE *DO* THAT, MR. CHASE.

BROTHER BLOOD WILL *KILL* ME WHEN HE HEARS THAT I'VE TALKED.

VICTOR STONE'S HYDRAULIC LEGS CARRY HIM OVER THE CITY, WHILE *BELOW...*

I'LL CHECK INTO THE *FEDERAL WITNESS* PROGRAM FOR YOU, MISS SNOW.

WE'LL DO OUR BEST. DON'T *WORRY.*

BUT AS THE DOOR *CLOSES...*

WELL, WELL, SISTER SNOW. I *OVERHEARD* YOUR TALK WITH OUR DEAR *DISTRICT ATTORNEY.*

WHAT? WHO--?

YOU?

BROTHER BLOOD SENT ME HERE. HE *WANTED* ME TO OVERHEAR YOUR CONVERSATION WITH CHASE.

I'VE ALREADY REPORTED *BACK* TO HIM.

CONGRATULATIONS.

YOU *KNOW* IT, SISTER. THOSE FOOLS BOUGHT MY EVERY WORD.

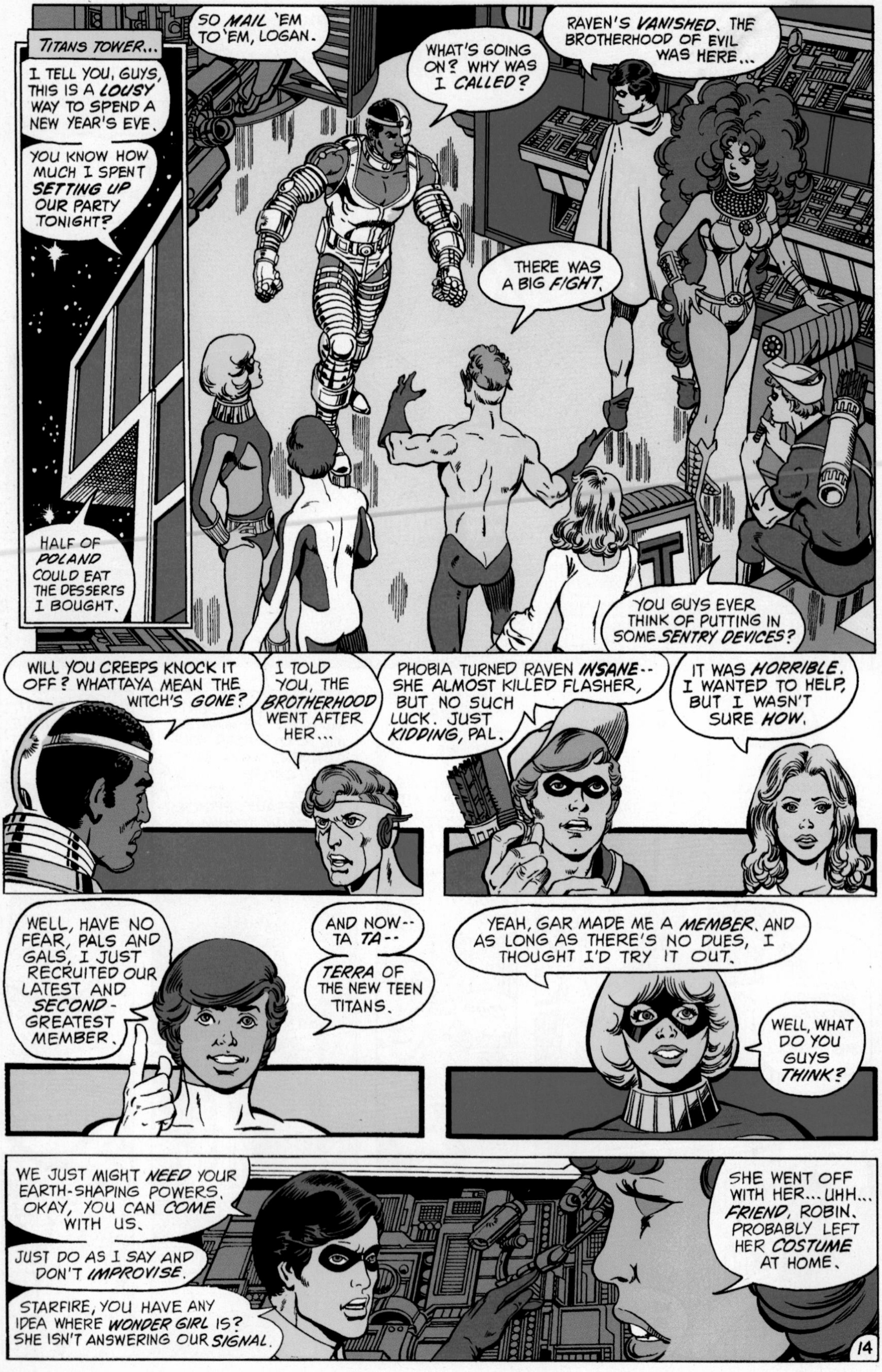

TITANS TOWER...
I TELL YOU, GUYS, THIS IS A LOUSY WAY TO SPEND A NEW YEAR'S EVE.
YOU KNOW HOW MUCH I SPENT SETTING UP OUR PARTY TONIGHT?
HALF OF POLAND COULD EAT THE DESSERTS I BOUGHT.
SO MAIL 'EM TO 'EM, LOGAN.
WHAT'S GOING ON? WHY WAS I CALLED?
RAVEN'S VANISHED. THE BROTHERHOOD OF EVIL WAS HERE...
THERE WAS A BIG FIGHT.
YOU GUYS EVER THINK OF PUTTING IN SOME SENTRY DEVICES?
WILL YOU CREEPS KNOCK IT OFF? WHATTAYA MEAN THE WITCH'S GONE?
I TOLD YOU, THE BROTHERHOOD WENT AFTER HER...
PHOBIA TURNED RAVEN INSANE-- SHE ALMOST KILLED FLASHER, BUT NO SUCH LUCK. JUST KIDDING, PAL.
IT WAS HORRIBLE. I WANTED TO HELP, BUT I WASN'T SURE HOW.
WELL, HAVE NO FEAR, PALS AND GALS. I JUST RECRUITED OUR LATEST AND SECOND-GREATEST MEMBER.
AND NOW-- TA TA--
TERRA OF THE NEW TEEN TITANS.
YEAH, GAR MADE ME A MEMBER. AND AS LONG AS THERE'S NO DUES, I THOUGHT I'D TRY IT OUT.
WELL, WHAT DO YOU GUYS THINK?
WE JUST MIGHT NEED YOUR EARTH-SHAPING POWERS. OKAY, YOU CAN COME WITH US.
JUST DO AS I SAY AND DON'T IMPROVISE.
STARFIRE, YOU HAVE ANY IDEA WHERE WONDER GIRL IS? SHE ISN'T ANSWERING OUR SIGNAL.
SHE WENT OFF WITH HER... UHH... FRIEND, ROBIN. PROBABLY LEFT HER COSTUME AT HOME.
14

WHERE IS *WONDER GIRL?* THE ANSWER LIES *HERE,* WITHIN THIS SKY-SCRAPING *RESTAURANT...*

THE RAINBOW

ROCKEFELLER PLAZA

MR. *LONG?* AHH, I SEE YOUR *RESERVATION.*

PLEASE FOLLOW ANDRE. HE WILL SEE YOU TO YOUR *TABLE.*

THANK YOU, ENRIQUE.

THIS IS *GORGEOUS,* TERRY. I'VE NEVER BEEN HERE BEFORE.

A CIRCULAR RESTAURANT SO YOU CAN SEE ALL ACROSS *MANHATTAN.*

TERRY, DON'T YOU THINK IT'S A TAD *EXPENSIVE?*

HONEY, THIS IS NEW YEAR'S EVE. I DIDN'T *CARE* ABOUT THE COST.

THIS, MY BEAUTIFUL *LOVE,* IS A VERY *SPECIAL* NIGHT FOR ME.

AND YOU WON'T TELL ME *WHY.* I CAN SEE THAT "I KNOW SOMETHING YOU DON'T KNOW" LOOK.

MY *DEAR,* YOU'LL FIND OUT SOON ENOUGH.

SAINT PETER'S CATHEDRAL:

THE PEWS ARE *EMPTY* NOW, THE DOOR HAS BEEN *LOCKED.*

BUT SEALED PORTALS ARE NO BARRIER TO THE DIMENSION-TRAVELING POWERS OF *RAVEN.*

RAVEN NEEDS TO BE *ALONE.* SHE NEEDS TO *THINK,* CONTEMPLATE WHO SHE IS...

AND, EVEN MORE... WHY SHE IS.

AND THIS CHURCH, ALTHOUGH ALIEN TO ONE WHO WAS RAISED IN THE DIMENSION-TOSSED LAND OF *AZARATH,* IS STILL A PLACE CONDUCIVE TO SUCH THOUGHT.

AND TO SUCH *PRAYER.*

15

WHY CAN I NOT *LOVE?*

WHY CAN I NOT *HATE?*

WHY CAN I NOT *FEEL?*

WHY AM I *DENIED* THE EMOTIONS ALL OTHERS POSSESS?

CAN I *HELP* YOU?

I--I AM SORRY. I AM NOT OF THIS FAITH. I DO NOT *BELONG* HERE.

OF COURSE YOU DO. IF SOMETHING IS WRONG, MAYBE I CAN *HELP.*

WILL YOU *LET* ME?

N-NO... IT IS IMPOSSIBLE. YOU CANNOT UNDER-STAND WHAT IS *WRONG* WITH ME.

FRANKLY YOU'D BE SURPRISED. PLEASE, RAVEN, GIVE ME A *CHANCE.*

YOU *KNOW* ME?

I READ THE PAPERS. I WATCH TV. IF YOU PROMISE NOT TO TELL, I EVEN ENJOY AN OCCASIONAL *VIDEO GAME.*

WE'RE NOT SEQUESTERED IN *DARK ABBEYS* ANY MORE.

PLEASE, STAY. EVERYONE IS *WELCOME* HERE.

EVEN *SATAN'S DAUGHTER?*

FATHER, SHE *CANNOT* BE HELPED.

COME TO US, RAVEN.

WHAT?!?

YOU KNOW EVENTUALLY WE'LL *GET* WHAT WE CAME FOR. WHY NOT JUST COME WITH US *PEACEFULLY?*

RAVEN FEELS THE *THUNDER* SCREAMING IN HER SOUL. SHE *SPEAKS* EVEN BEFORE SHE THINKS...

NEVER!

16

74

BECAUSE OF YOU, I ALMOST *KILLED* KID FLASH.

I WILL NEVER LET YOU *MANIPULATE* MY MIND AGAIN.

STOP!

THIS IS NOT THE PLACE TO *FIGHT!*

OH? SINCE WHEN HAVE *YOU* WORRIED ABOUT THE ARENA OF BATTLE?

DESPITE WHAT YOU *BELIEVE* ME TO BE, I WILL NOT DEFILE A *TEMPLE OF WORSHIP.*

LET US *DISCUSS* OUR DISAGREEMENT... OUTSIDE.

N-NO...I...I DO NOT FIGHT... I *CANNOT* FIGHT...

LEAVE ME ALONE! FOR AZAR'S SAKE-- *LEAVE ME ALONE!!*

SUDDENLY RAVEN IS VERY FRIGHTENED. SHE REALIZES *SHE* WAS THE ONE ANXIOUS FOR BATTLE.

SHE WAS READY TO RESORT TO *VIOLENCE.*

AFRAID, SHE VANISHES, EVEN AS THE *BROTHERHOOD OF EVIL* GIVES CHASE...

...LEAVING BEHIND A VERY TROUBLED FATHER PETER MALLORY.

HE SENSES SOMEHOW WHAT RAVEN *MEANT* WHEN SHE ASKED--"EVEN SATAN'S DAUGHTER?" ⑰

NEW YEAR'S EVE IN TIMES SQUARE HAS BECOME A NATIONAL TRADITION. MILLIONS AWAIT THE FALLING GLOBE, A HERALD OF HOPE FOR A BETTER TIME TO COME...

...I TELL YOU, EACH YEAR THE CROWD SEEMS TO GROW.

WHY, I CAN SEE PEOPLE PUSHED ALL THE WAY BACK TO 51ST STREET.

WELL, THE EXCITEMENT IS BUILDING DOWN THERE, JANE?

11:57:00

YOU'RE RIGHT, DICK. IN FACT, THE COUNTDOWN HAS ALREADY BEGUN. EVERYONE'S HAVING A BALL TONIGHT.

11:59:01

AND SPEAKING OF BALLS, WHEN OUR GOLDEN BALL DESCENDS, THAT SIGN WILL OFFICIALLY LIGHT UP THE NEW YEAR.

11:59:15

LET'S JOIN THE COUNTDOWN. 10, 9, 8, 7, 6, 5...

11:59:56

3, 2...

11:59:59

THE BALL STOPPED MOVING... AND THE SIGN--

12:00:00

SOMETHING'S WRONG. THE SIGN'S NOT LIGHTING!!

I'VE HAD LIVELIER NEW YEAR'S EVES HANGING AROUND CEMETERIES!

WHY AIN'T WE DOIN' SOMETHING? RAVEN'S LOST OUT THERE?

YOU TELL ME WHAT TO DO! WHERE DO WE GO?

RAVEN COULD'VE TELEPORTED ANYWHERE.

WHY DON'T WE JUST FORGET HER? WE SHOULD BE LOOKING FOR THE BROTHERHOOD OF EVIL.

AND THEY WANT RAVEN. FORGET THAT, FLEET-FEET.

C'MON, ARE WE JUST GONNA WATCH TV? LORD, YOU PEOPLE ARE DULL.

WE COULD ALWAYS HEAD UP TO MY ROOM AND NECK.

DON'T MAKE ME SICK.

HEY, HOW COME THE SIGN DIDN'T LIGHT? IT ALWAYS LIGHTS UP.

IF THIS IS HOW IT'S BEGINNING, I DON'T WANT TO KNOW FROM 1983.

18

CAN ANYONE *ELSE* SEE IT? THE SCREEN'S *SHIMMERING* NOW...

I DON'T BELIEVE IT!

1983

PINCH MY CHEEKS AND CALL ME GORGEOUS! IT'S *RAVEN!*

I *TOLD* YOU, RAVEN'S GONE *CRAZY.* MAYBE NOW YOU'LL BELIEVE ME.

MEANWHILE...

WHERE *IS* SHE?

MY COMPUTERIZED FETISH TRACED HER TO THIS AREA.... IT CAN'T *PIN-POINT* HER EXACT LOCATION.

WH-WHAT *ARE* THEY?

OH, GOD! LOOK!

LET ME *OUTTA* HERE!

NO GOOD. MY SOUL-SELF *FRIGHTENED* THEM ...BUT THE BROTHERHOOD HAS CAUSED THEM TO *PANIC.*

THEIR FEARS... *HURT... ME...*

...MUST *STOP* THEM ...TO GET THEM *AWAY* FROM HERE BEFORE THE PEOPLE ARE *HURT...*

...BEFORE I AM *DESTROYED* BY ALL THOSE EMOTIONS.

DERE!

SH-SHE COMES AT *ME?* WELL, SHE WILL NOT FIND ME A *STANDING TARGET.*

SO, THE LITTLE ONE *RUNS,* EH?

WELL, YOU ARE STILL WITHIN MY *GRASP!*

19

NO, FRÄULEIN -- I AM NOT --

I AM PURE PROTOPLASM... NOT AT ALL HUMAN.

YOUR SOUL CANNOT CONFINE ME.

RAVEN SCREAMS AS HER SOUL-SELF SEEMINGLY SHATTERS...

...AND SHE COLLAPSES AS IT RUSHES TO REJOIN HER.

TOO MUCH... PAIN... PLEASE... NO MORE ... NO MORE ...

HI, GUYS -- YOU HEAR THE CIRCUS IS IN TOWN AND THEY NEED A NEW FREAK SHOW?

DEY FOUND US.

OF COURSE THEY DID. DIDN'T YOU EXPECT THEY WOULD?

HURRY AND TAKE THE GIRL... SHE'S THE ONLY ONE WE WANT TODAY.

NO WAY, LADY.

DER YOUNG ONE -- DER GIRL... THIS IS HER DOING.

YOU CATCH ON QUICK, TERRA.

NOT BAD, KID.

YEAH, I KNOW. WHAT'RE YOU DOIN' TO HOLD UP YOUR END?

DID YOU HEAR THAT? THEY WANT RAVEN.

WELL, LET THEM TRY!

KOMAND'R TRIES KIDNAPPING ME... THESE FOOLS TRY TAKING RAVEN.

I'M SICK OF THESE SCUM!

20

GET RAVEN *OUT* OF HERE. I'M GOING IN FOR ANOTHER *ATTACK*.

CONSIDER HER *OUT*, STARFIRE.

WRONG, MONSIEUR FLASH.

ZE BRAIN *WANTS* HER... AND I AM TAKING HER *TO* HIM.

TOO LATE... CAN'T *TURN*.

ENTERING WARP'S *SPATIAL WARP*.

GOD, I'M *SORRY*, RAVEN... I--

SCHWEIN, YOU NEVER *LEARN*, DO YOU? YOU CANNOT STOP *ME* WITH A PUNCH.

REALLY?

YOU MEAN I CAN'T DO *THIS*?

GOOD THING YOU *TOLD* ME, GRUESOME-- NOW I'LL KNOW NEVER TO *TRY* IT.

I WOULDN'T WANT TO WASTE A PERFECTLY GOOD *SONIC BLASTER ATTACK*! NOW WOULD I?

SKRAKK

MY INSIDES! ACCHHH! VAT ARE YOU DOING?

FAILING TO *STOP* YOU. ISN'T THAT WHAT YOU *SAID* WOULD HAPPEN?

Y'KNOW, I COULD *GET OFF* ON THIS, HOUNGY, REMEMBER WHAT YOU DID TO ME THE *LAST* TIME WE MET?

IT TOOK A WHILE, CREEP, BUT MY *LEGS* FINALLY STOPPED ACHING.

L-LOGAN... GET OVER HERE-- FAST!

PAM PAM PAM

STAND BACK, FOOLS, WE ALREADY *HAVE* THE ONE WE WANT.

CONTINUE FIGHTING AND YOU WILL ALL *PERISH*.

* TITANS #15--Len.

N-NO! WE CAN'T LET YOU *GO*.

WHAT DID YOU DO TO WAL-- *FLASH*? WHERE IS HE?

THE WATER PIPES BREAK THROUGH THE SIDEWALKS... HOW IS THIS *POSSIBLE*?

21

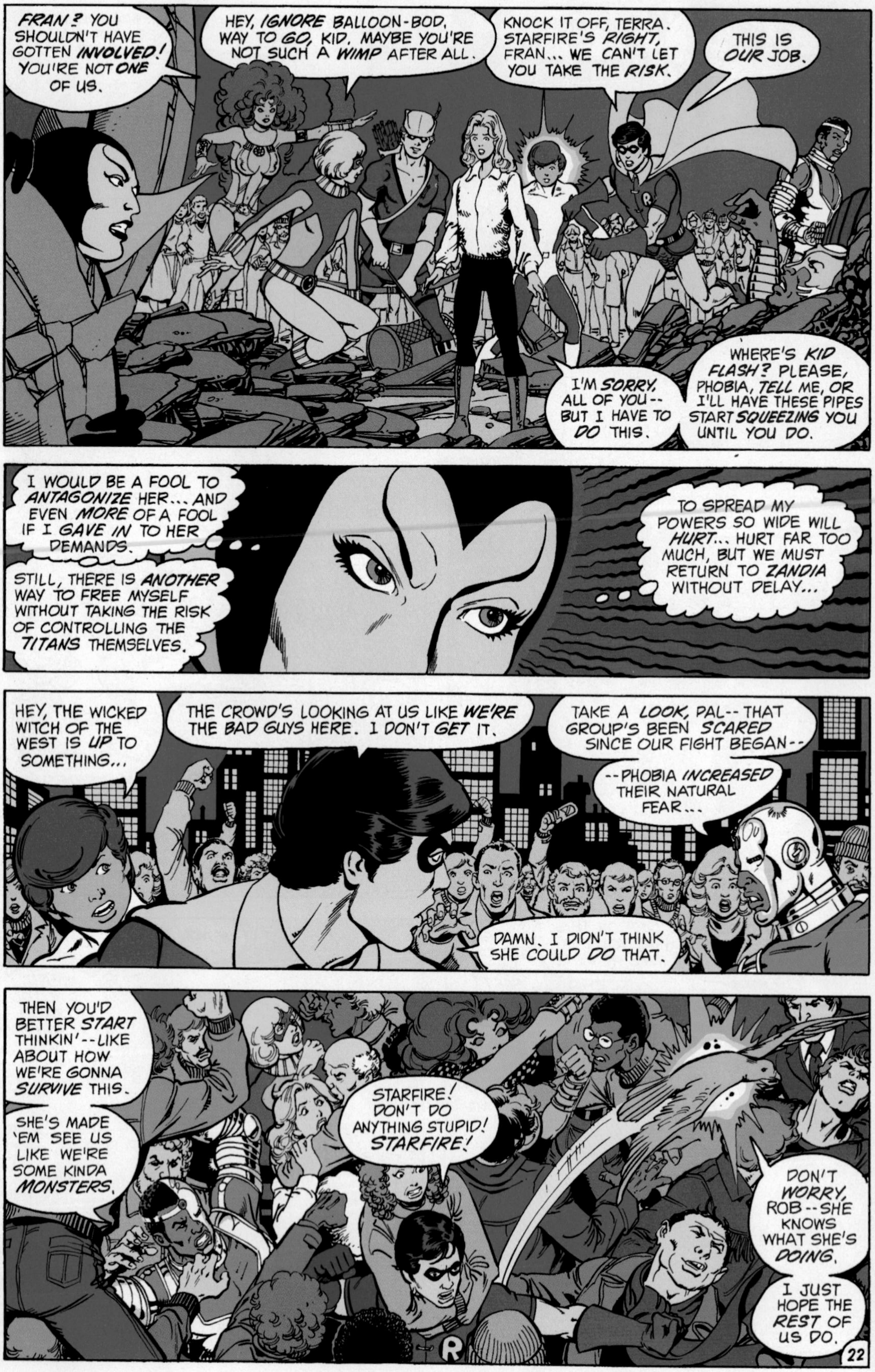
FRAN? YOU SHOULDN'T HAVE GOTTEN INVOLVED! YOU'RE NOT ONE OF US.
HEY, IGNORE BALLOON-BOD, WAY TO GO, KID. MAYBE YOU'RE NOT SUCH A WIMP AFTER ALL.
KNOCK IT OFF, TERRA. STARFIRE'S RIGHT, FRAN... WE CAN'T LET YOU TAKE THE RISK.
THIS IS OUR JOB.
I'M SORRY, ALL OF YOU-- BUT I HAVE TO DO THIS.
WHERE'S KID FLASH? PLEASE, PHOBIA, TELL ME, OR I'LL HAVE THESE PIPES START SQUEEZING YOU UNTIL YOU DO.
I WOULD BE A FOOL TO ANTAGONIZE HER... AND EVEN MORE OF A FOOL IF I GAVE IN TO HER DEMANDS.
STILL, THERE IS ANOTHER WAY TO FREE MYSELF WITHOUT TAKING THE RISK OF CONTROLLING THE TITANS THEMSELVES.
TO SPREAD MY POWERS SO WIDE WILL HURT... HURT FAR TOO MUCH, BUT WE MUST RETURN TO ZANDIA WITHOUT DELAY...
HEY, THE WICKED WITCH OF THE WEST IS UP TO SOMETHING...
THE CROWD'S LOOKING AT US LIKE WE'RE THE BAD GUYS HERE. I DON'T GET IT.
TAKE A LOOK, PAL-- THAT GROUP'S BEEN SCARED SINCE OUR FIGHT BEGAN--
--PHOBIA INCREASED THEIR NATURAL FEAR...
DAMN. I DIDN'T THINK SHE COULD DO THAT.
THEN YOU'D BETTER START THINKIN'--LIKE ABOUT HOW WE'RE GONNA SURVIVE THIS.
SHE'S MADE 'EM SEE US LIKE WE'RE SOME KINDA MONSTERS.
STARFIRE! DON'T DO ANYTHING STUPID! STARFIRE!
DON'T WORRY, ROB--SHE KNOWS WHAT SHE'S DOING.
I JUST HOPE THE REST OF US DO.
22

BEAUTIFUL, PHOBIA...WITH LUCK THE CROWD WILL *DESTROY* THEM.

IF THEY DO NOT, I VILL. I DO NOT VANT TO LEAVE NOW...THE BLACK ONE IS *MINE!*

ANOTHER TIME... MY SPELL WILL FADE AS SOON AS WE *LEAVE,* AND WE MUST RETURN TO ZANDIA -- *NOW!*

WHERE *ARE* YOU, WARP?

I HAVE *RETURNED,* MADAME... BUT I HAD TO MAKE CERTAIN ZE *RAVEN* GIRL WAS SAFELY IMPRISONED WHERE SHE COULD NOT *ESCAPE...*

...AS WELL AS RENDER HER VALIANT PROTECTOR *UNCONSCIOUS.*

NOW, MES AMIS-- HURRY -- *HURRY!* BEFORE MY POWER FADES.

WAIT! DON'T GO! RAVEN!?!

GONE...AGAIN... AND I WAS USELESS...*AGAIN.*

I JUST DON'T UNDERSTAND HOW I *FEEL...* RAVEN ALMOST *KILLED* ME-- I WANT TO *HATE* HER... I WANT TO FORGET SHE EVER *LIVED--*

BUT-- BLAST IT-- I *CAN'T!* HEAVEN HELP ME... I STILL *LOVE* HER.

WHILE, ELSEWHERE IN NEW YORK, CELEBRATING A LOVELY NEW YEAR'S EVE...

TERRY, I DON'T WANT THIS DANCE TO *END.*

I WANT IT TO GO ON *FOREVER!*

DONNA, I TRULY HOPE YOU *MEAN* THAT.

BECAUSE I WANT *US* TO GO ON FOREVER.

HONEY...I CAN'T THINK OF A BETTER TIME TO *ASK.*

TERRY? WHA--

DONNA, I *LOVE* YOU. I WANT TO TAKE CARE OF YOU. I WANT TO *BE* WITH YOU ALWAYS.

DONNA TROY, WILL YOU *MARRY* ME?

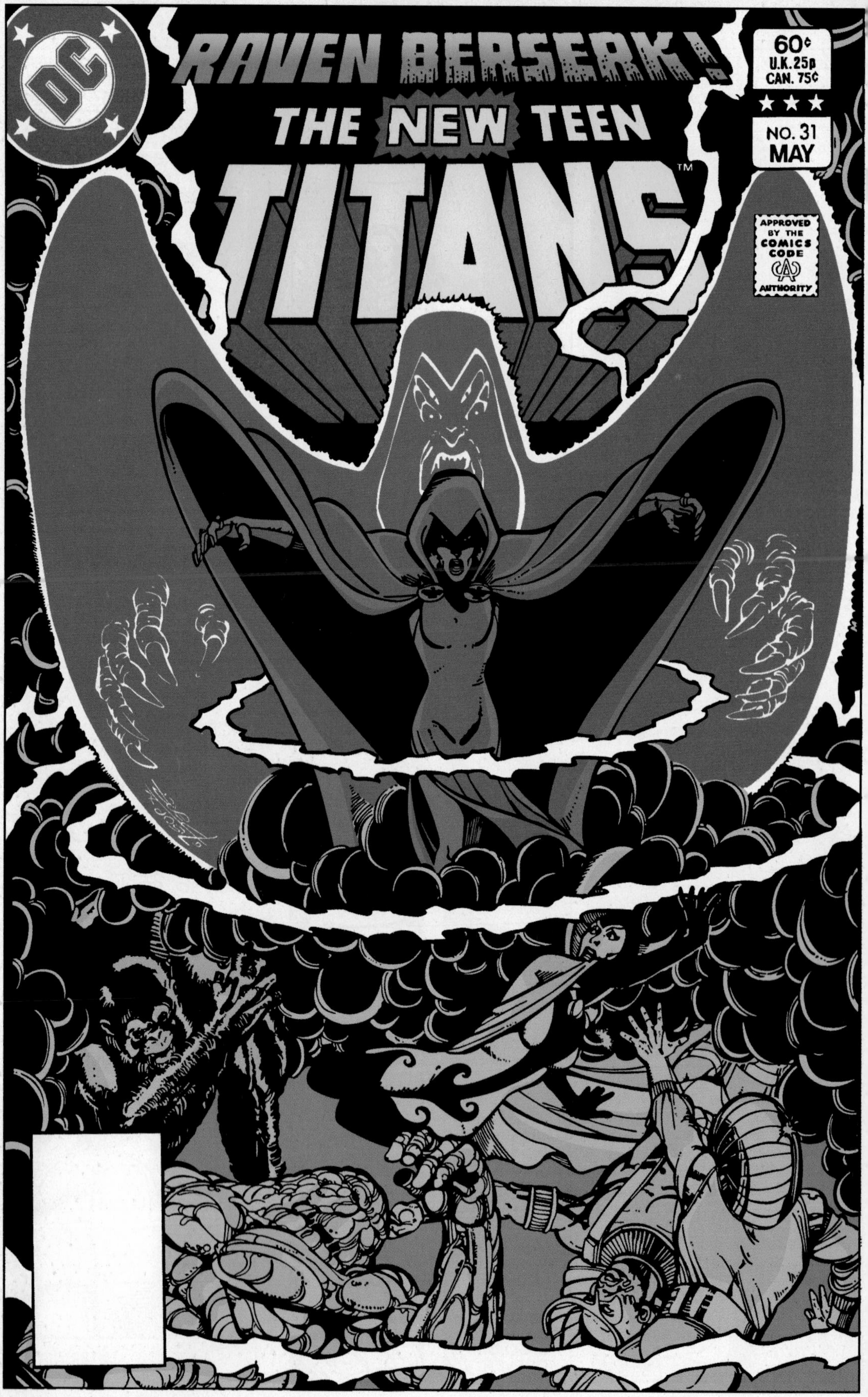
DC
RAVEN BERSERK!
THE NEW TEEN
TITANS™
60¢
U.K. 25p
CAN. 75¢
NO. 31
MAY
APPROVED BY THE COMICS CODE AUTHORITY

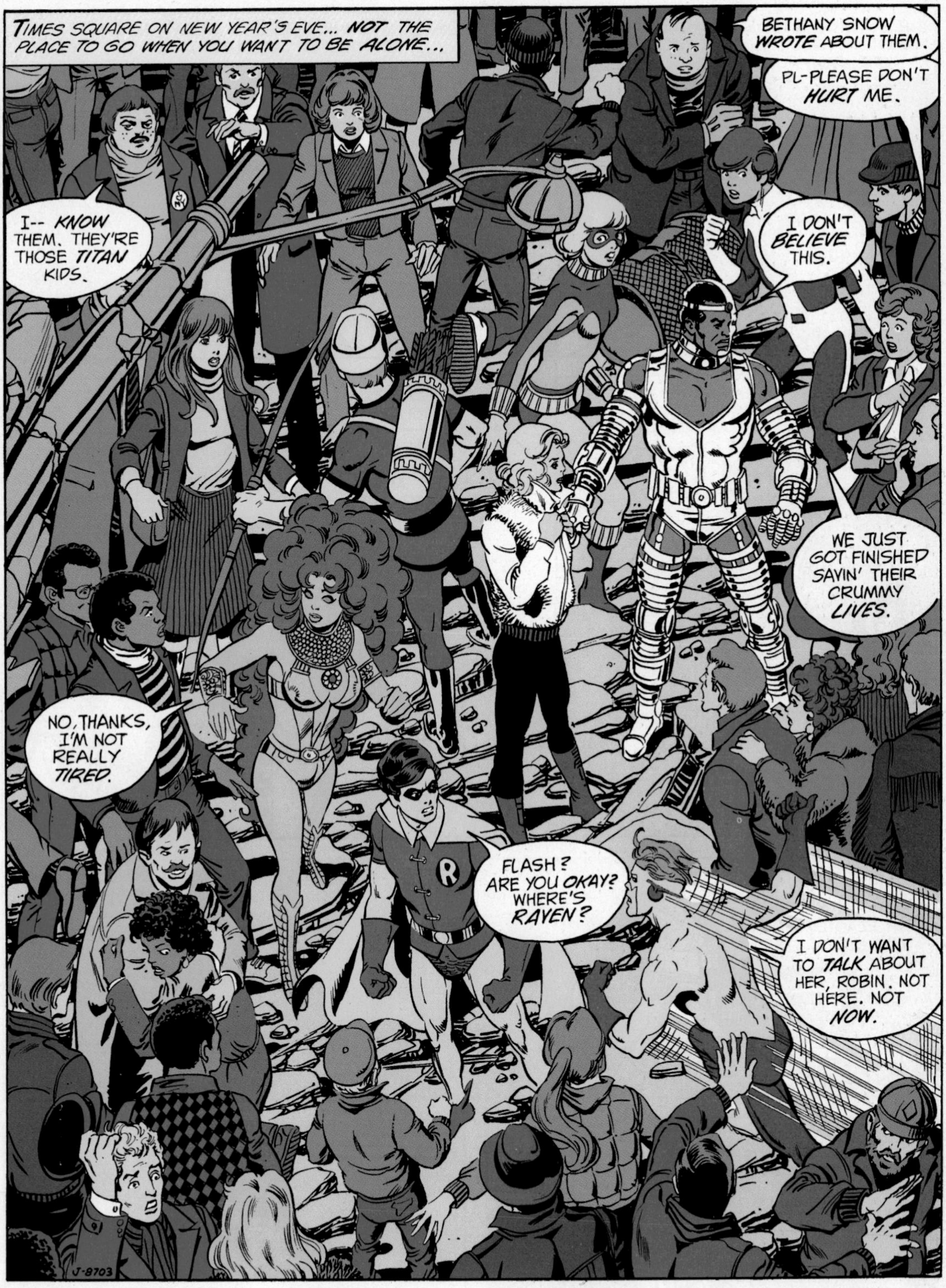
TIMES SQUARE ON NEW YEAR'S EVE... NOT THE PLACE TO GO WHEN YOU WANT TO BE ALONE...
BETHANY SNOW WROTE ABOUT THEM.
PL-PLEASE DON'T HURT ME.
I-- KNOW THEM. THEY'RE THOSE TITAN KIDS.
I DON'T BELIEVE THIS.
WE JUST GOT FINISHED SAVIN' THEIR CRUMMY LIVES.
NO, THANKS, I'M NOT REALLY TIRED.
FLASH? ARE YOU OKAY? WHERE'S RAVEN?
I DON'T WANT TO TALK ABOUT HER, ROBIN. NOT HERE. NOT NOW.
J-8703

Panel 1:

BUT *BOTH* OF YOU WERE TAKEN BY *WARP*. IS SHE *OKAY*?

STARFIRE, PLEASE. *I'LL* HANDLE THIS.

WHERE *IS* SHE?

I'M NOT *SURE*. I WAS KNOCKED OUT. LOOK, RAVEN ALMOST *KILLED* ME...

SHE'S NOT *ONE* OF US. SHE'S *NEVER* BEEN ONE OF US.

FORGET HER.

Panel 2:

WHOA THERE, FLEET-FEET. I *SAW* WHAT HAPPENED, REMEMBER?

SHE WAS TAKEN OVER BY *PHOBIA*, AND MAN -- I KNOW WHAT *THAT* FEELS LIKE.

HE'S *RIGHT*, WAL-- UH, KID FLASH. I *SAW* IT, TOO.

FRAN, PLEASE DON'T *DO* THIS TO ME.

YOU DIDN'T FEEL THE *EVIL* IN RAVEN'S SOUL-SELF. BUT I DID. AND I'M *SCARED*.

LET ME UNDERSTAND THIS, THEY'RE ALL *FRIENDS*, HUH?

UHHH... NO COMPRENDO INGLES.

LOGAN!!

WELLLL, THEY'RE *SUPPOSED* TO BE.

I *THINK*.

Panel 3:

LISTEN, SPEEDY, YOU'RE NOT A *REGULAR* TITAN, SO WHY DON'T YOU TAKE YOUR BLASTED ARROWS AND *STICK* 'EM?

DON'T *SAY* THAT. IT'S NOT *NICE*.

AHHH, JUST LIKE THE *OLD* DAYS.

NOW I REMEMBER WHY I *LEFT*.

Panel 4:

LISSEN, I DON'T CARE IF YOU TWO TEAR EACH OTHER INTO LITTLE *PIECES*--

--BUT DO IT BACK AT THE TOWER -- IN *PRIVATE*.

Panel 5:

THEY LEAVE...

...BUT NOT ONE OF THEM IS *HAPPY*.

2

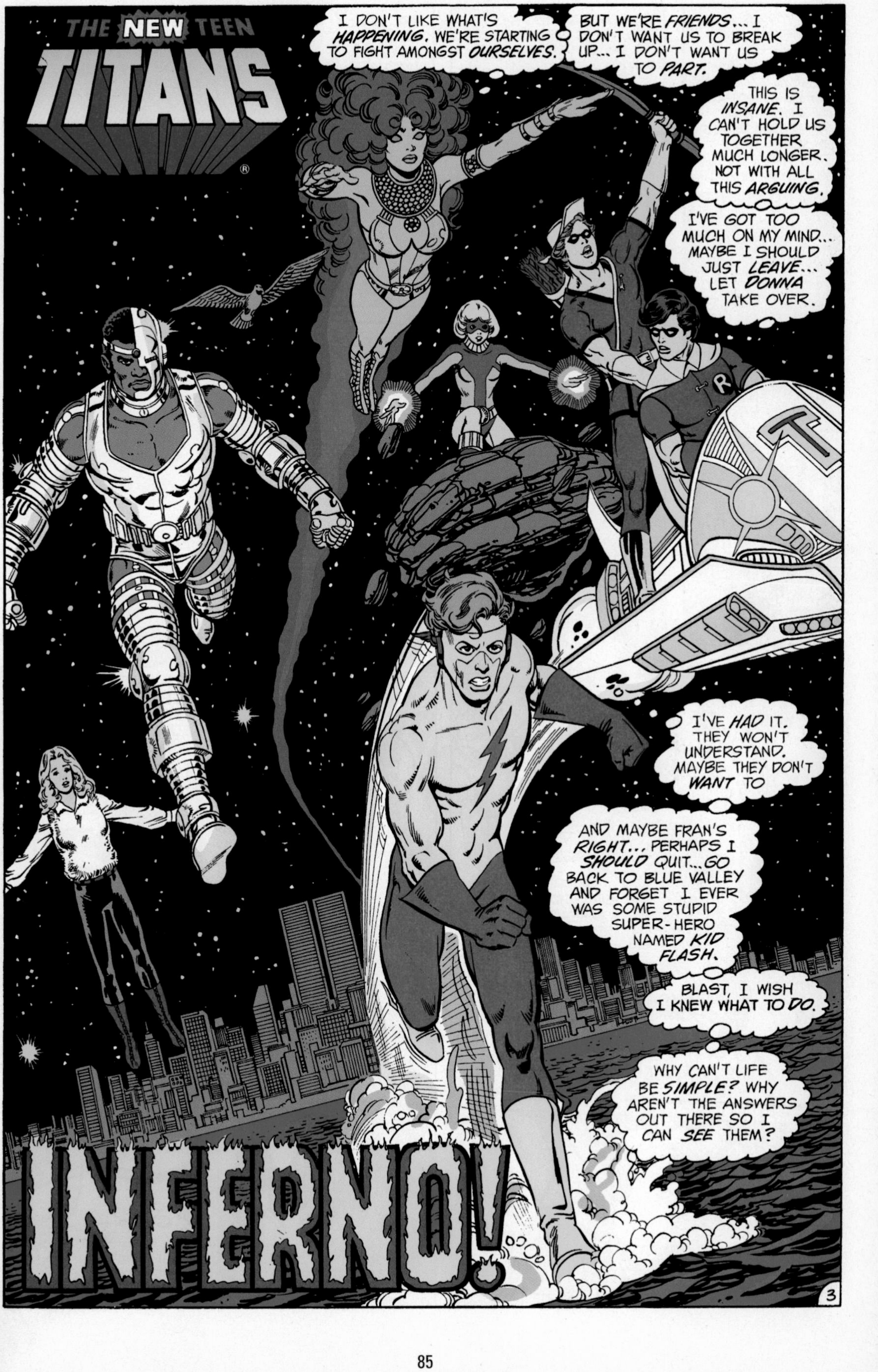
THE NEW TEEN TITANS
I DON'T LIKE WHAT'S HAPPENING. WE'RE STARTING TO FIGHT AMONGST OURSELVES.
BUT WE'RE FRIENDS... I DON'T WANT US TO BREAK UP... I DON'T WANT US TO PART.
THIS IS INSANE. I CAN'T HOLD US TOGETHER MUCH LONGER. NOT WITH ALL THIS ARGUING.
I'VE GOT TOO MUCH ON MY MIND... MAYBE I SHOULD JUST LEAVE... LET DONNA TAKE OVER.
I'VE HAD IT. THEY WON'T UNDERSTAND. MAYBE THEY DON'T WANT TO
AND MAYBE FRAN'S RIGHT... PERHAPS I SHOULD QUIT...GO BACK TO BLUE VALLEY AND FORGET I EVER WAS SOME STUPID SUPER-HERO NAMED KID FLASH.
BLAST, I WISH I KNEW WHAT TO DO.
WHY CAN'T LIFE BE SIMPLE? WHY AREN'T THE ANSWERS OUT THERE SO I CAN SEE THEM?
INFERNO!
3

FIVE TITANS, ONE RESERVIST AND ONE FRIEND... EXHAUSTED FROM THEIR BATTLE WITH THE *BROTHERHOOD OF EVIL*, THEY DRAG THEMSELVES BACK TO THEIR EAST RIVER ISLAND HEADQUARTERS...

STARFIRE IS THE *FIRST* TO ENTER, AND THE FIRST TO SPY A *FAMILIAR* RED-AND-BLUE UNIFORM...

HI, WHERE HAVE YOU *BEEN*?

WHERE HAVE *WE* BEEN? WE TRIED *CALLING* YOU.

ARE YOU *OKAY*? WHAT WAS *WRONG*?

I WAS WORRIED SOMETHING *HAPPENED*.

WELL, STARFIRE, IN A WAY I GUESS SOMETHING *DID* HAPPEN.

TERRY LONG *PROPOSED*.

HE WANTS TO *MARRY* ME.

WONDER GIRL, DIDN'T YOU HEAR THE *EMERGENCY SIGNAL*?

MARRY *YOU*?

X'HAL! THAT'S *WONDERFUL!* IT'S INCREDIBLE!

WHEN WILL IT *HAPPEN*? HOW DID HE PROPOSE? PLEASE-- DON'T LEAVE OUT *ANYTHING*.

HECK, SHE COULD HAVE BEEN *MINE*. SHE'S BEEN DYING FOR MY BONES EVER SINCE WE *MET*.

LOGAN, DON'T YOU *EVER* STOP WITH THE JOKES?

OH, NUTS-- JUST WHAT I NEED. NOW *VIC'S* FLIPPED OUT.

4

THAT'S REALLY GREAT. I'M SO GLAD FOR YOU.

YOU DIDN'T TELL US-- WHEN'S THE HAPPY DAY?

HOLD IT... I HAVEN'T GIVEN HIM MY ANSWER YET.

SOMETHING WRONG?

OH, NO-- THERE'S ABSOLUTELY NO ONE I'D RATHER SPEND MY LIFE WITH THAN TERRY--

--WE LOVE EACH OTHER. WE CARE FOR EACH OTHER. THAT'S NOT THE PROBLEM.

IT'S ME, ROBIN -- I--I ALWAYS HOPED I'D FIND OUT WHO I REALLY WAS BEFORE I GOT MARRIED...

I--I DON'T KNOW WHAT TO DO.

HEY, IT'LL WORK OUT. MAY- BE I CAN HELP, OKAY?

WELL, MY ONE-TIME HEART-THROB, IF YOU HAVEN'T GIVEN HIM AN ANSWER, REMEMBER--I'M AVAILABLE.

THANKS, PAL -- I'LL CON- SIDER YOUR OFFER.

YEAH, LET'S ALL SAY CONGRATULATIONS AND GET DOWN TO THE MATTER AT HAND.

I'M SORRY... I THINK WE ALL FORGOT.

I KNOW. RAVEN AND I WERE TELEPORTED TO ZANDIA-- THAT'S THE LAST I SAW OF HER.

IF YOU REALLY DO WANT TO FIND HER -- I'D SUGGEST WE START THERE.

MINUTES LATER THE TITANS' T-JET STREAKS ACROSS THE NEW YORK SKIES, HEADING ON A COURSE, DUE EAST...

THE SILENCE ON BOARD IS THICK AND ALMOST DEAFENING.

THERE ARE PROBLEMS THAT MUST BE WORKED OUT, PROBLEMS THAT, IF LEFT TO FESTER, COULD RIP THE TITANS ASUNDER.

MEANWHILE, ON THE BALTIC ISLAND OF ZANDIA...

5

...IN THE HEADQUARTERS OF --THE BROTHERHOOD OF EVIL...

MONSIEUR BRAIN, HAS ZE NEW BROTHERHOOD WORKED OUT AS YOU HAD *HOPED*?

AH, MONSIEUR MALLAH, THEY ARE NOT THE *ORIGINAL* BROTHERHOOD, BUT THEY WILL *DO*...

THEY ARE STILL YOUNG. THEY STILL THINK MORE WITH THEIR *HEARTS* THAN WITH THEIR *BRAINS*.

BUT THEY WILL EITHER LEARN OR THEY WILL *DIE*. ONE WAY OR ANOTHER, THINGS WILL WORK OUT.

BUT WILL ZEY INTERFERE WITH YOUR *PLANS*? YOU HAVE WORKED SO *HARD*...

DO NOT PUT THEM DOWN, MONSIEUR MALLAH. THEY ARE NEW, BUT THEY ARE *GOOD*.

THEY WILL GET ME WHAT I *WANT*--

--THE SECRET OF BROTHER BLOOD!

SHE AWAKENS. NOW WE CAN PROCEED.

LET *ME* TRY FIRST. I ALREADY KNOW HER WORST *FEAR*... I CAN USE IT TO *LOOSEN* HER TONGUE.

NO, PHOBIA--*I* WILL BE DER FIRST, DER BRAIN WANTED ME TO *WORK* WIF DIS TITAN.

AH, ZIS SHALL BE *INTERESTING*, NON? THIS ONE, SHE HAS ZE 'BEAUTE DU DIABLE' --THE BEAUTY OF THE *DEVIL*; THE BLOOM AND FRESHNESS OF YOUTH.

SHE WEEL NOT BE AN *EASY* ONE TO CRACK, NON.

6

YOU KNOW THE SECRET OF BROTHER BLOOD, TELL US, FRÄULEIN... VE ARE NOT IN DER MOOD FOR *GAMES*.

YOU ARE MAKING A *MISTAKE*, PLASMUS--

I WILL NOT PERMIT YOU TO *HURT* ME.

STOP!

THERE!--AS FOR THE *REST* OF YOU, I KNOW NOTHING OF BROTHER BLOOD.., YOUR FIGHT IS NOT WITH ME OR THE TITANS.

YOU WOULD DO WELL TO LEAVE US *ALONE*.

I AM *SORRY*, LITTLE GIRL, BUT THAT CANNOT *BE*.

MY STOMACH! IT IS BURNING UP!

MY DEAR RAVEN, I CAN *CURE* YOUR ILLS IF YOU WILL LET ME...

...OR I CAN *INCREASE* THEM IF YOU ARE STUBBORN.

MY COMPUTER FETISH CAN BE YOUR FRIEND--OR YOUR *KILLER*. WHICH SHALL IT BE?

TALK! TELL US THE SECRET OF BLOOD'S *POWER!*

I...CANNOT THINK ... THE PAIN CUTS THROUGH ME LIKE A *BLADE*.

AZAR-- WHY? WHY ARE MY HANDS, WHICH CAN SOOTHE THE PAINS OF OTHERS, SO POWERLESS TO CURE *ME*?

WHY, AZAR? WHY?

7

MONSIEUR BRAIN, IT IS AS I FEARED. ZE NEW ONES USE THEIR POWERS SO *CRUDELY.*

WAIT, MONSIEUR MALLAH--GIVE THEM A *CHANCE.* SHOULD THEY FAIL, *THEN* I WILL INTERFERE.

ALLOW THEM TO LEARN HOW BEST TO *WIELD* THEIR STRENGTHS.

IT'S NO GOOD... IF I *CONTINUE* USING THE FETISH, I WOULD *KILL* HER. WE'D LEARN *NOTHING* THAT WAY.

IT IS UP TO *YOU,* PHOBIA. DO NOT *FAIL* THE BRAIN.

IF I HAD BEEN THE FIRST, THE INFORMATION WOULD *ALREADY* BE OURS.

MY DEAR RAVEN -- ONE LAST CHANCE -- *TALK!*

I -- I KNOW *NOTHING!*

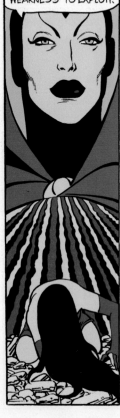

VERY WELL, IF YOU INSIST ON REMAINING SO STUBBORN, I WILL DO WHAT *MUST* BE DONE.

YOU ARE A SAD CASE, GIRL -- YOUR FEARS ARE SO *RIFE.*

THE PROBLEM WITH YOU IS NOT FINDING YOUR WEAKNESS, BUT *CHOOSING* WHICH WEAKNESS TO EXPLOIT.

YOUR FATHER *TRIGON?* NO -- I HAVE ALREADY PLAYED OUT THAT HAND.

I CAN EXPLOIT EACH FEAR ONLY *ONCE.*

PERHAPS YOUR *LUDICROUS SHYNESS...* SHALL WE PLUNGE YOU INTO THE CENTER OF A MILLION SOULS?

WAIT... WAIT, I HAVE IT. SO DELICIOUS.

YOU ARE AN *EMPATH* -- YOU THRIVE ON THE EMOTIONS OF OTHERS.

NO, PHOBIA -- *DON'T!* FOR AZAR'S SAKE, YOU DO NOT KNOW WHAT YOU COULD *UNLEASH!*

PLEASE... IF THERE IS ANY *MERCY* IN YOUR HEART -- SHOW IT *NOW!*

DO NOT *DO* THIS TO ME!

8

RAVEN CRIES OUT, FOR SHE ALREADY *SENSES* WHAT IS NEXT TO COME. THE FEAR GROWS AS THE IMAGES FORM... BEGINNING WITH TENS, GROWING ALL TOO QUICKLY TO SCORES... THEN HUNDREDS ... THOUSANDS... A MILLION SOULS AND MORE--

...THEY ALL PLEAD WITH HER, GRAB AT HER..., PULL AT HER... SCREAM AT HER!

A MILLION SOULS AND MORE RIPPING AWAY EACH PROTECTIVE BARRIER TO HER FRAGILE SOUL...

THEY ALL WANT PART OF HER ...THEY ALL WANT THAT *SAME* PART-- THE PART WHICH CAN SAVE THEM --

FOR GOD'S SAKE, RAVEN --HELP US ALL!

CURE ME!

SAVE ME!

SAVE ME!

SAVE ME!

BUT, RAVEN KNOWS, TO SAVE THEM WOULD BE TO *DESTROY* HERSELF!

AND AGAIN RAVEN SCREAMS.

THEY PICK AT HER FLESH, RIP AT HER DRESS... EXPOSE HER TO HORRORS AND SHAMES AND FEARS AND ILLNESSES AND DISEASES AND--

EVEN AS SHE PLUNGES DEEPER INTO HER NIGHT-MARE --EVEN AS HER GREATEST FEARS BECOME MANIFEST AND, IF POSSIBLE, GROW WORSE.

RAVEN SCREAMS.!

⑨

91

SHE IS NAKED TO THE WORLD...

BUT, AMIDST THE FLAME AND HEAT AND HELL, SHE FEELS... SERENE.

ALMOST WITHOUT UNDERSTANDING WHY, SHE SITS UP, CASUALLY GLANCING ABOUT HER.

AND, FOR PERHAPS THE FIRST TIME IN HER LIFE, SHE SMILES.

SHE IS ALONE, AND HER PRIVATE, PERSONAL SOUL HAS NOT BEEN VIOLATED.

THEN...

THEN, IT STARTS ALL OVER AGAIN.

AND AGAIN! AND AGAIN! AND AGAIN!

SHE CAN NEVER BE LEFT ALONE. SHE CAN NEVER ENJOY EVEN A MOMENT OF PEACE...

EMOTIONS SURROUND HER, ALWAYS ATTACKING HER, ALWAYS FEEDING UPON HER, ALWAYS DESTROYING HER!

AND AGAIN SHE SCREAMS, AND AGAIN SHE FALLS...

HER PRIVATE HORRORS EXPOSED TO ALL WHO SEE HER.

CALM?

...CRASHING INTO THE DEPTHS OF HER TORTURED SOUL.

SHE KNOWS -- SHE CRIES -- SHE PLEADS -- THE GREATEST HORRORS HAVE ONLY YET BEGUN!

⑩

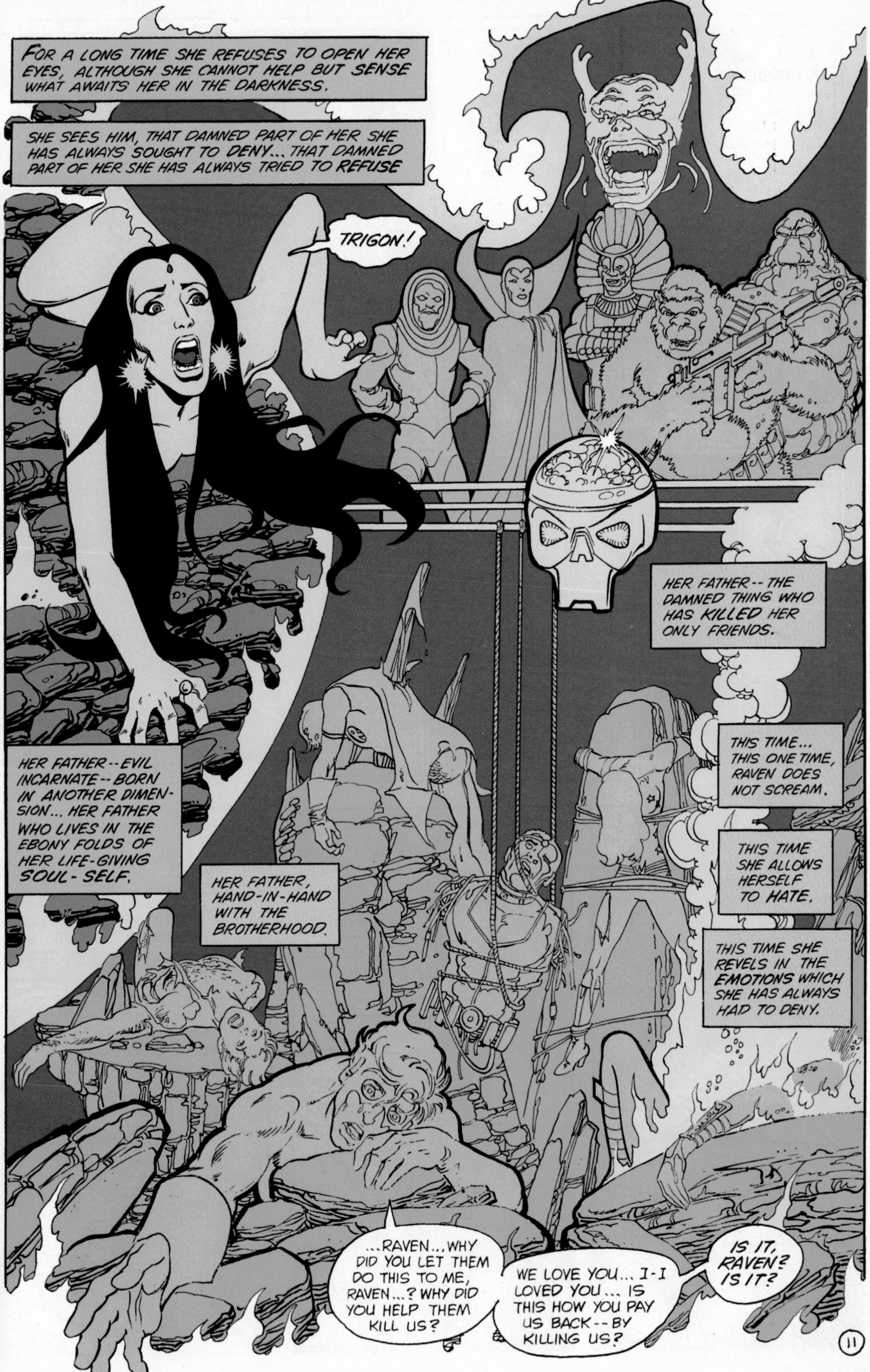
FOR A LONG TIME SHE REFUSES TO OPEN HER EYES, ALTHOUGH SHE CANNOT HELP BUT SENSE WHAT AWAITS HER IN THE DARKNESS.
SHE SEES HIM, THAT DAMNED PART OF HER SHE HAS ALWAYS SOUGHT TO DENY... THAT DAMNED PART OF HER SHE HAS ALWAYS TRIED TO REFUSE
TRIGON!
HER FATHER -- THE DAMNED THING WHO HAS KILLED HER ONLY FRIENDS.
HER FATHER -- EVIL INCARNATE -- BORN IN ANOTHER DIMENSION... HER FATHER WHO LIVES IN THE EBONY FOLDS OF HER LIFE-GIVING SOUL-SELF.
HER FATHER, HAND-IN-HAND WITH THE BROTHERHOOD.
THIS TIME... THIS ONE TIME, RAVEN DOES NOT SCREAM.
THIS TIME SHE ALLOWS HERSELF TO HATE.
THIS TIME SHE REVELS IN THE EMOTIONS WHICH SHE HAS ALWAYS HAD TO DENY.
...RAVEN... WHY DID YOU LET THEM DO THIS TO ME, RAVEN...? WHY DID YOU HELP THEM KILL US?
WE LOVE YOU... I-I LOVED YOU... IS THIS HOW YOU PAY US BACK -- BY KILLING US?
IS IT, RAVEN? IS IT?
11

T-TAKE MY HAND.

MY LIFE WILL BE PASSED ON TO YOU.

YOU WILL LIVE.

AND YOU'LL DIE, RAVEN? IS THAT IT? WILL YOU DIE?

YES... YES! TAKE MY HAND!

NO!

YOU'RE DEATH.

YOU'RE EVIL!

YOU'RE EVERYTHING THAT IS WRONG!!

I'D RATHER DIE BEFORE LETTING YOU CURE ME!

BAH! SHE IS UNCONSCIOUS. WHAT DID YOU DO TO HER?

I... DO NOT KNOW, PLASMUS. I BEGAN HER NIGHTMARE. WHERE SHE LET IT TRAVEL I DO NOT KNOW.

A SHAME. I WAS POSITIVE SHE WOULD BREAK.

HMMM. PERHAPS SHE WAS TELLING THE TRUTH. PERHAPS SHE DOESN'T KNOW ANYTHING.

IS THAT POSSIBLE?

NO, PLASMUS -- SHE KNOWS, ALTHOUGH SHE IS UNAWARE OF THAT FACT.

VERY WELL... LOCK HER AWAY. ATTACH HER TO A MIND-DAMPENER TO PREVENT HER FROM TELEPORTING TO FREEDOM.

IF I'M TO LEARN THE SECRET OF BROTHER BLOOD'S POWERS, I MUST-- THINK.

12

THERE IS SILENCE AS THE T-JET SPEEDS ACROSS A FROTHY ATLANTIC...

THE SILENCE OF CONCERN FOR A TEAMMATE...

WHAT'S *WRONG*, CAN-HEAD? SOMEONE STICK YOUR DOG IN A GARBAGE DISPOSAL?

TO USE *YOUR* WORDS, TERRA-- MIND YOUR OWN *BUSINESS*.

SOMETHING *IS* WRONG, ISN'T THERE, VIC?

GIVE YOUR GIRLFRIEND SOME HICKEYS AND LEAVE ME *ALONE*.

HEY, VIC-- C'MON. *LEVEL*.

YEAH, OKAY, LOGAN. IT'S SARAH ...I MET HER-- *FIANCE*.

OH.

MAN, I'VE BEEN A *FOOL* THINKING WE HAD SOMETHING *SPECIAL*.

HOW COULD SHE EVER CARE FOR A WALKING *JUNK PILE*?

ROBIN?

NOT *NOW*, STARFIRE.

YES--*NOW*, ROBIN, I INTEND TO TALK TO YOU. I'D LIKE TO *HELP* YOU. I WANT TO.

STARFIRE-- PLEASE...

LISTEN TO ME, ROBIN--YOU TREAT ME LIKE I'M *STUPID*.

BUT I'M *NOT*--I'M AS WELL-EDUCATED AS *ANYONE* HERE--IT'S JUST YOUR EARTH *CUSTOMS* THAT I CAN NEVER FATHOM--

...AND THE SILENCE OF PERSONAL CONCERNS AS WELL.

THEN...

IF YOU *LOVE* SOMEONE ON TAMARAN, YOU LIVE FOR THEM AND THEY FOR YOU.

YOU'RE *RIGHT*, STARFIRE--I *DO* TREAT YOU LIKE-- WELL, ALL WRONG. I'M SORRY.

BUT UNDERSTAND *OUR* CUSTOMS--SOMETIMES WHEN THINGS ARE GOING WRONG WE *PREFER* TO BE LEFT ALONE.

DO YOU UNDER-STAND?

NO, BUT I *WILL* DO WHAT YOU *WANT*.

13

MEANWHILE... COME, PHOBIA--LOOK HOW *ZE BRAIN* AND *MONSIEUR MALLAH* HANDLE THE GIRL.

PLEASE, MADEMOISELLE, YOU MUST *AID* US IN STOPPING ZIS BROTHER BLOOD.

YOU DO NOT KNOW HOW *EVIL* HE IS.

HE EES TAMPERING WITH THE *ELECTIONS* OF YOUR COUNTRY-- TRYING TO GAIN *WEAPONS* WITH WHICH HE CAN DECLARE *WAR.*

YOU DO NOT WANT HIM TO *SUCCEED,* NO?

N-NO...

MADEMOISELLE-- THIS BROTHER BLOOD WILL CAUSE MANY *DEATHS*--

--BUT THEY CAN *ALL* BE AVOIDED IF YOU HELP US FIND THE *SOURCE* OF HIS POWER.

THE BRAIN'S WORDS ARE UNNATURALLY CALMING--ALMOST REASSURING. RAVEN HAS *NO* IDEA WHY SHE *BELIEVES* HIM.

ONE IS AN *ANIMAL*--HIGHLY EVOLVED BUT STILL A *BEAST*...

THE OTHER IS A *HUMAN BRAIN* IN A *METAL CASING.*

I--I CANNOT 'READ' THESE TWO AND LEARN IF THEY SPEAK THE TRUTH, YET I *WANT* TO BELIEVE...

FASCINATING... LOOK AT THE GIRL, SHE IS *CONSIDERING* THEIR WORDS.

SHE *BELIEVES* THEM.

MAYBE ZE BRAIN *HAS* SOMETHING TO TEACH US AFTER ALL.

BUT I KNOW *NOTHING.*

NO, MADEMOISELLE, YOU *KNOW* THE TRUTH...

...BUT IT IS *BURIED* IN YOU. COME, I SHALL *EXPLAIN.*

14

WHEN YOU BATTLED BROTHER BLOOD, YOUR SOUL-SELF *ENVELOPED* HIM, AND YET HE STEPPED RIGHT *THROUGH* IT.

AT THAT MOMENT, UNKNOWN TO YOU, YOU ABSORBED *KNOWLEDGE.*

HOW DO YOU *KNOW* THIS?

I KNOW... PLEASE *TRUST* ME.

AND, RAVEN DOES... IT *MUST* BE TRUE... I AM REMEMBERING CAVERNS... DEEP *PITS...* THERE IS DARKNESS BROKEN WITH HIGH FLAMES... FLAMES THAT HOLD THE STENCH OF BRIMSTONE.

YES... YES... THAT IS IT... *LEAD* ME TO THAT PIT...

THEN BLOOD'S SECRET SHALL BE *MINE* AS WELL!

WHY DOES SHE *STOP?*

QUIET, PHOBIA... IS THERE SOMETHING *WRONG,* RAVEN?

NO... THE PIT IS *IN* THERE -- I CAN GO THERE BUT I CANNOT TAKE YOU *WITH* ME.

BAH! LEAVE DAT TO *ME!*

MY BODY IS PURE *PROTOPLASM,* IT RESPONDS TO MY EVERY COMMAND.

I CAN *BURN* A PATHWAY THROUGH THIS MOUNTAIN...

...MELTING THROUGH DIS ROCK AS IF IT WERE -- *AIR!*

I COULD *TELEPORT* AHEAD.

DERE IS A *CAVERN* AHEAD OF US.

STAY WITH US, WE SHALL BE AT MY GOAL SOON ENOUGH.

15

MEANWHILE...

SO WHAT *NOW*? DO WE TAKE IN THE *SIGHTS*?

TERRA, WE CHECK OUT BROTHER BLOOD'S *CHURCH*. THEY SHOULD KNOW WHERE THE BROTHERHOOD IS *HIDING*.

OH.

ROBIN, OF THE *TEEN TITANS*?

YES, WHAT'S *WRONG*?

BY ORDER OF ZANDIA'S PRESIDENT, PERMISSION TO LAND IN ZANDIA HAS BEEN *DENIED*.

BUT WE HAVE PROPER *CLEARANCE*.

IT HAS BEEN *REVOKED*, AS YOU KNOW, OUR 'CITIZENS' ARE ALL FORMER *CRIMINALS*.

YOUR PRESENCE HERE *WORRIES* THEM.

WE DO NOT WANT TROUBLE. YOU WILL LEAVE-- *NOW*.

NO!

OUR WEAPONS --THEY *FLOAT AWAY*?!?

WE'RE NOT GOING WITH-OUT OUR *FRIEND*.

BE *CAREFUL*, FRAN.

WAY TO *GO*, SKINNY.

GENTLEMEN...

...MY POWERS ARE NOT SO BENIGN. DO NOT FORCE ME TO *USE* THEM.

LET US *THROUGH*!

16

IN ONE OF THE DEEPER CAVERNS BENEATH BROTHER BLOOD'S CHURCH...

MOTHER MAYHEM, OUR INNER PERIMETERS HAVE BEEN *BREACHED.*

ACCESS TO THE *REGEN-ERATION CHAMBER* IS IMMINENT.

AND THE *MAJORITY* OF OUR FORCES ARE IN AMERICA WITH OUR *MASTER.*

BUT I SEE OUR *BACK-UP* FORCE HAS ARRIVED

GET ME *CAPTAIN HERNANDEZ* AT THE AIRPORT,

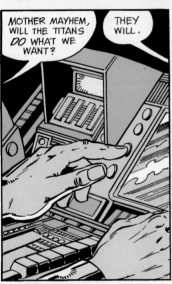

MOTHER MAYHEM, WILL THE TITANS *DO* WHAT WE WANT?

THEY *WILL.*

CAPTAIN HERNANDEZ -- A TELEPHONE MESSAGE -- FROM *BROTHER BLOOD.*

BLOOD?

CAPTAIN, ALLOW OUR GUESTS TO PASS THROUGH. WE *WANT* THEM HERE.

DO NOT WORRY. *WE* WILL DEAL WITH OUR FAIR PRESIDENT.

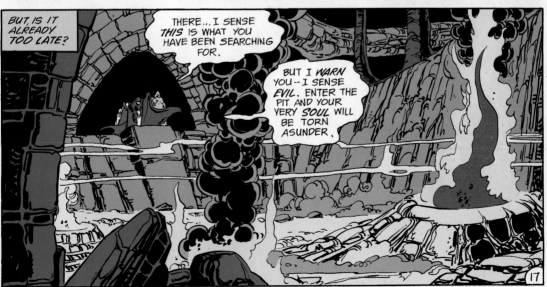

BUT, IS IT ALREADY *TOO LATE?*

THERE... I SENSE *THIS* IS WHAT YOU HAVE BEEN SEARCHING FOR.

BUT I *WARN* YOU -- I SENSE *EVIL.* ENTER THE PIT AND YOUR VERY *SOUL* WILL BE TORN ASUNDER.

17

SOUL? IF SUCH A THING EVER EXISTED, I LONG AGO *LOST* MINE.

MADEMOISELLE, YOUR WORDS DO NOT FRIGHTEN US. GO.

TREAD *CAREFULLY,* MY FRIENDS -- THE *EXISTENCE* OF THE SOUL IS NOT SOMETHING TO TAKE *LIGHTLY.*

I DO NOT FEAR ITS *LOSS,* BUT IT--

WHAT? THE GROUND SHAKES?!?

AFTER EVERYTHING I'VE DONE -- THEY'VE COME?!!

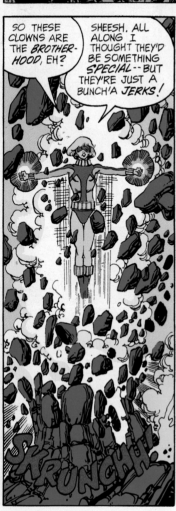

SO THESE CLOWNS ARE THE *BROTHER-HOOD,* EH?

SHEESH. ALL ALONG I THOUGHT THEY'D BE SOMETHING *SPECIAL* -- BUT THEY'RE JUST A BUNCH'A *JERKS!*

I SEE *RAVEN*... THANK X'HAL THEY HAVEN'T *HURT* HER.

WATCH YOURSELF -- THEY'RE NOT GOING TO GIVE HER UP WITH-OUT A *STRUGGLE.*

GOOD. I'M *NOT* VERY HAPPY, AND I WANT THEM TO *KNOW* THAT.

THIS IS *IT?* WE'RE ACTUALLY *HERE?*

FRAN, IF YOU'RE FRIGHTENED, YOU CAN *WAIT* FOR US.

NO. I HAVE TO *DO* THIS.

THEN *WATCH* YERSELF. WE HAVEN'T GOT THE TIME TO FIGHT THEM WHILE *NURSEMAIDIN'* YOU.

18

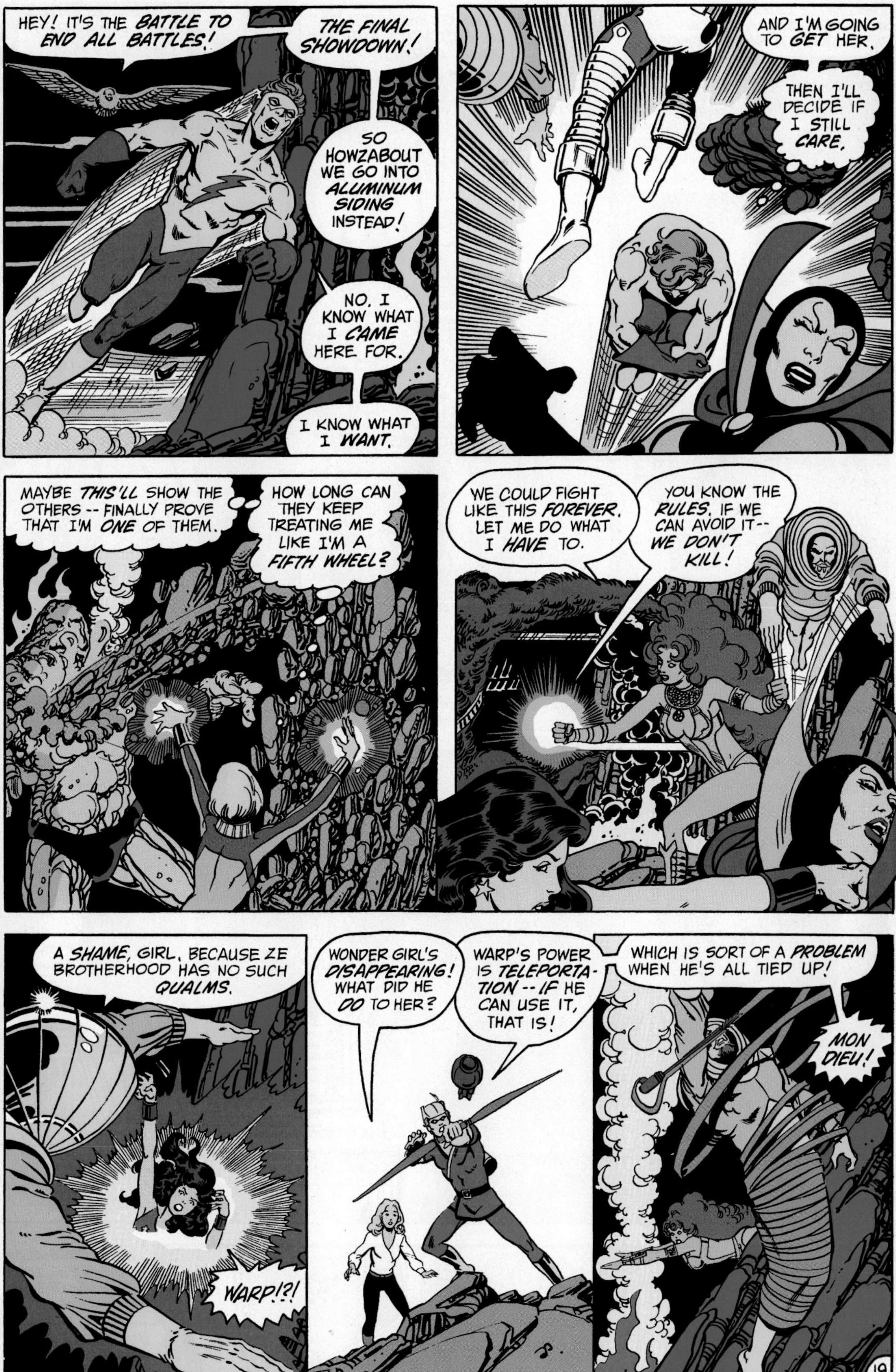
HEY! IT'S THE BATTLE TO END ALL BATTLES!
THE FINAL SHOWDOWN!
SO HOWZABOUT WE GO INTO ALUMINUM SIDING INSTEAD!
NO. I KNOW WHAT I CAME HERE FOR.
I KNOW WHAT I WANT.
AND I'M GOING TO GET HER.
THEN I'LL DECIDE IF I STILL CARE.
MAYBE THIS'LL SHOW THE OTHERS -- FINALLY PROVE THAT I'M ONE OF THEM.
HOW LONG CAN THEY KEEP TREATING ME LIKE I'M A FIFTH WHEEL?
WE COULD FIGHT LIKE THIS FOREVER. LET ME DO WHAT I HAVE TO.
YOU KNOW THE RULES. IF WE CAN AVOID IT-- WE DON'T KILL!
A SHAME, GIRL, BECAUSE ZE BROTHERHOOD HAS NO SUCH QUALMS.
WARP!?!
WONDER GIRL'S DISAPPEARING! WHAT DID HE DO TO HER?
WARP'S POWER IS TELEPORTATION -- IF HE CAN USE IT, THAT IS!
WHICH IS SORT OF A PROBLEM WHEN HE'S ALL TIED UP!
MON DIEU!
19

THE BATTLE EBBS AND FLOWS LIKE AN OCEAN TIDE, FOR STARFIRE THERE COMES A PAINFUL *DEFEAT...*

...AS SHE HELPLESSLY CRUMBLES BEFORE THE COMPUTERIZED VOODOO OF HOUNGAN.

MEANWHILE, ALL *RAVEN* CAN DO IS WATCH IN HORROR AND PRAY TO *AZAR...*

RELIEVED, SHE WATCHES AS *VICTORY* IS SNATCHED FROM DEFEAT...

...AND, FOR THE MOMENT, RAVEN IS *PLEASED...*

SKRAMMM!

YET...SHE KNOWS BETTER THAN TO ASSUME *SUCCESS* IS AT HAND.

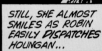

STILL, SHE ALMOST SMILES AS ROBIN EASILY *DISPATCHES* HOUNGAN...

...AND CHANGELING DEFEATS *MALLAH.*

SHE SENSES AND LIVES HER TEAM-MATES' JOYS...

BUT, SOMETHING *BOTHERS* HER...

SHE IS BEGINNING TO BASK IN THEIR PHYSICAL VICTORIES.

SHE IS *ENTHRALLED* BY THE VIOLENCE.

SHE ANXIOUSLY *ANTICIPATES* THE CONFRONTATIONS.

AND SHE IS *FRIGHTENED.* ALL HER LIFE SHE HAS BEEN TRAINED IN *PASSIVITY...* IN NON-VIOLENCE...

WHY DOES SHE NOW *REVEL* IN EVERYTHING SHE DOES NOT BELIEVE?

20

THEN, ONCE AGAIN, SHE FEELS THE EBBING TIDE...

THE BATTLE IS ABOUT TO *CHANGE.*

AND ONE...

...BY ONE...

...BY ONE...

...THE TITANS FALL...

...DEFEATED.

AND STILL ALL RAVEN CAN DO IS WATCH IN HORROR.

HER TEAM-MATES SEEM *DEAD.* SHE FEELS THE HEAT SURROUNDING HER.

SHE IS MIRED IN PURGATORY...

...A HELL SHE HAS WALKED BEFORE...

HER NIGHTMARE! HER PREMONITION!

IT HAS TRAGICALLY ALL COME TRUE!

AND RAVEN SCREAMS!

21

103

WHILE ALL HELL BREAKS LOOSE!

YOU HAVE GONE TOO FAR.

YOU WILL HAVE TO PAY!

MON DIEU! WHAT HAS *HAPPENED* TO HER?

I-I CANNOT BELIEVE IT! *LOOK!*

SHE HAS BECOME *HIM*... THAT DAMNED PART OF HER SHE HAS ALWAYS SOUGHT TO *DENY*... THAT DAMNED PART OF HER SHE HAS ALWAYS TRIED TO *REFUSE*.

TRIGON!

HER FATHER--EVIL INCAR-NATE--BORN IN ANOTHER DIMENSION... HER FATHER WHO LIVES IN THE EBONY FOLDS OF HER LIFE-GIVING SOUL-SELF.

HER FATHER, HAND IN HAND WITH THE BROTHERHOOD,

HER FATHER--THE DAMNED THING WHO HAS *KILLED* HER ONLY FRIENDS.

22

THIS TIME...THIS ONE TIME, RAVEN DOES NOT SCREAM.

THIS TIME SHE ALLOWS HERSELF TO HATE.

THIS TIME SHE REVELS IN THE EMOTIONS WHICH SHE HAS ALWAYS HAD TO DENY.

GREAT HERA-- NO! RAVEN-- DON'T!

YOU DON'T KNOW WHAT YOU'RE DOING!

NO GOOD, SHE'S NOT LISTENING...

THANK HERA I GOT BACK IN TIME--BUT IS THERE ANY WAY I CAN--

NO! SHE DOESN'T RECOGNIZE ME. SHE'S NO LONGER HERSELF.

EVEN THE WAY SHE'S STANDING--SO CONFIDENT...SO MUCH IN CONTROL OF HER POWER.

THAT'S NOT RAVEN--BUT IT REMINDS ME OF--

GREAT HERA!!!

NO!

23

IF TRIGON'S *CONTROLLING* HER, WE COULD ALL BE IN DANGER.

I'VE GOT TO *STOP* HIM -- GOT TO FORCE HIM *OUT* OF HER.

LISTEN TO ME, RAVEN -- FOR GOD'S SAKE -- *LISTEN!*

GET AWAY FROM ME, *HUMAN!* AWAY BEFORE I *DESTROY* YOU!

TRIGON WOULD *KILL* ME IF HE COULD -- NOT JUST THREATEN ME. IT'S NOT *TOO LATE.*

NO -- I WANT RAVEN... *RAVEN!* PLEASE... HEAR ME... DEEP IN YOUR SOUL -- HEAR ME. *LISTEN TO ME!*

YOU ARE *NOT* YOUR FATHER -- YOU ARE NOT TRIGON. YOU CAN *FIGHT* HIM!

RESIST HIM!

IF YOU DON'T -- YOU'LL *MURDER* ALL YOUR FRIENDS!

NO!

I WILL NOT KILL! I WILL NOT KILL! I WILL *NOT KILL!*

AND...

WH- WHAT *HAPPENED?*

IS RAVEN *ALL RIGHT?*

SHE TRIED TO *KILL* US... DIDN'T SHE?

N... NO... GOD PITY HER AND HELP HER --

-- SHE TRIED TO KILL *HERSELF!*

BUT YOU'RE WITH YOUR *FRIENDS* NOW, RAVEN... EVERY-THING WILL BE ALL RIGHT...

EVERYTHING WILL BE ALL RIGHT!

106

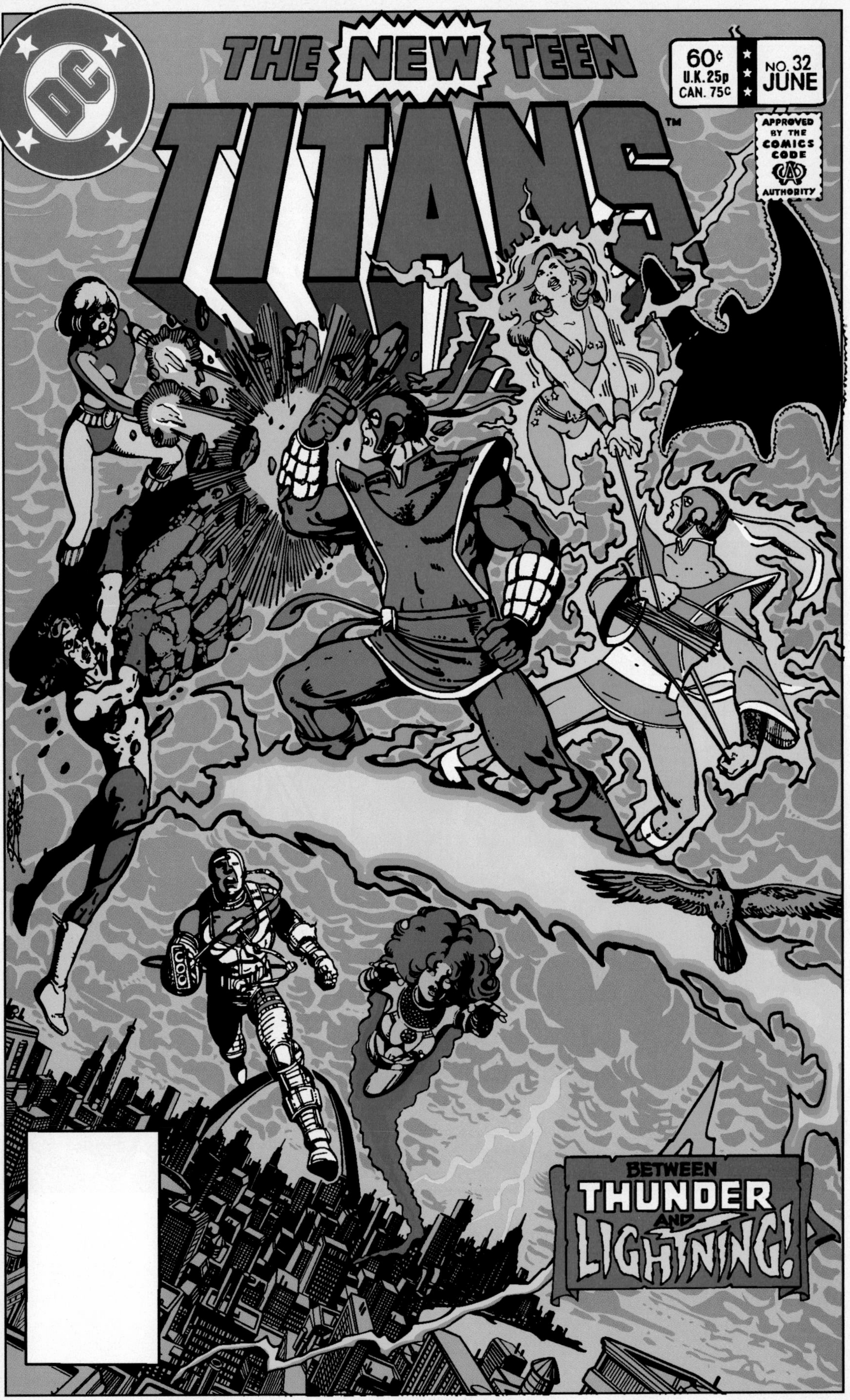
DC
THE NEW TEEN
TITANS™
60¢
U.K. 25p
CAN. 75¢
NO. 32
JUNE
APPROVED BY THE COMICS CODE AUTHORITY
BETWEEN THUNDER AND LIGHTNING!

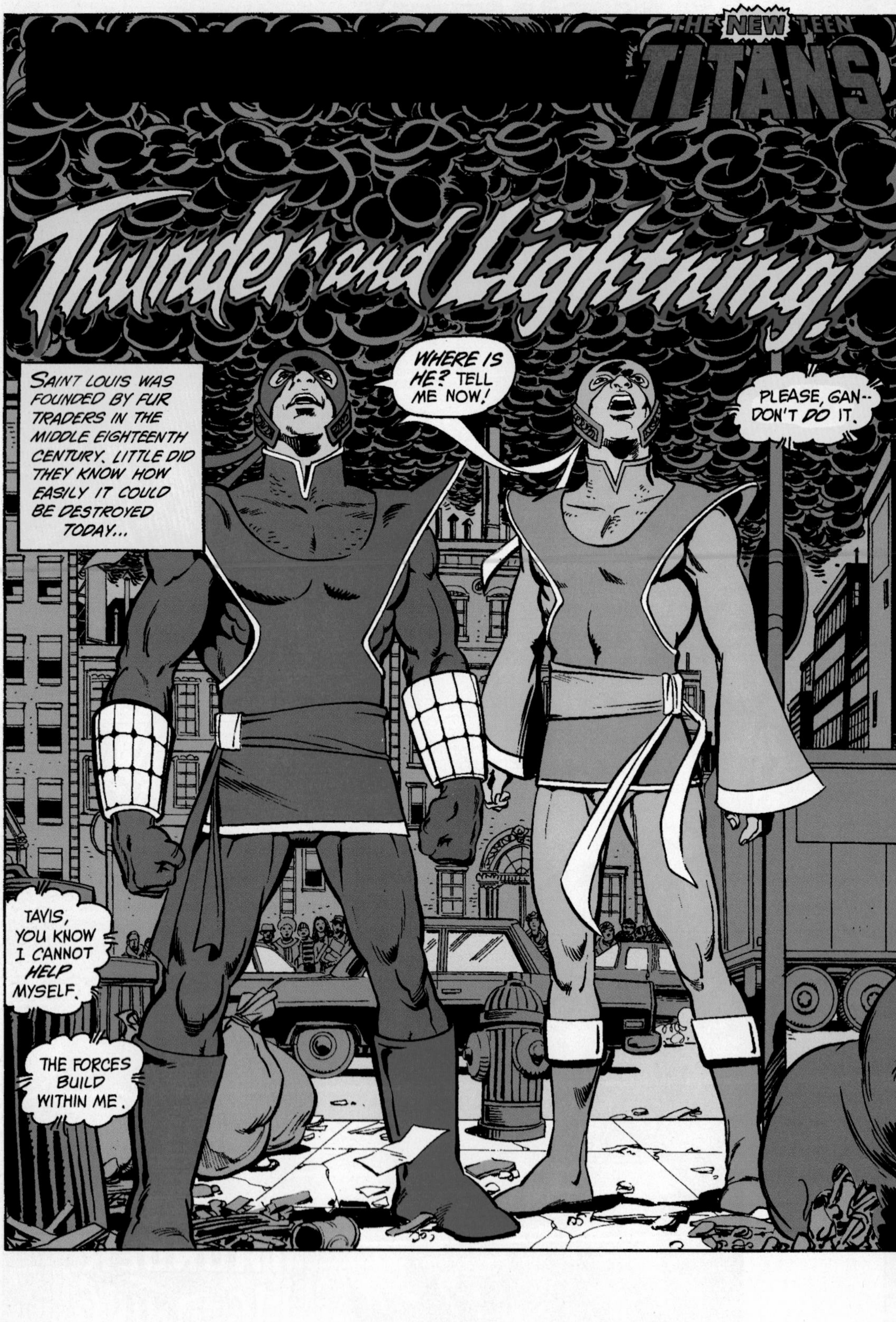
[redacted]
THE NEW TEEN TITANS
Thunder and Lightning!
SAINT LOUIS WAS FOUNDED BY FUR TRADERS IN THE MIDDLE EIGHTEENTH CENTURY. LITTLE DID THEY KNOW HOW EASILY IT COULD BE DESTROYED TODAY...
WHERE IS HE? TELL ME NOW!
PLEASE, GAN-- DON'T *DO* IT.
TAVIS, YOU KNOW I CANNOT *HELP* MYSELF.
THE FORCES BUILD WITHIN ME.

PLEASE-- TELL US WHERE HE *IS*. I DON'T KNOW IF I CAN HOLD BACK MY BROTHER MUCH *LONGER.*

GET *OUTTA* HERE. WE ALREADY TOLD YA HE'S NOT *HERE.*

HE MOVED WEEKS AGO.

WHERE? TELL US WHERE HE HAS GONE?

YOU MUST *CONTROL* YOURSELF.

I CANNOT...IT IS *TOO LATE.*

HURRY, GAN -- LET'S GET *AWAY* FROM HERE

NO. NOT UNTIL I GET *ANSWERS.* WE'VE SEARCHED TOO LONG *ALREADY.*

LOOK, WE TOLDA YA -- NOBODY *KNOWS.* HE DIDN'T SAY *NOTHIN!*

LEAVE US *ALONE!*

I-I CANNOT!

AT FIRST IT SOUNDS LIKE THE ROAR OF DISTANT DRUMS. THEN THE RUMBLING DRAWS *CLOSER...*

RRRRRRRRRRRRRR

CLOSER...

DO YOU *SEE* IT? YOU HAVE NO CHOICE NOW -- *RUN!* LEAVE YOUR BUILDING -- *RUN!*

RRRRRRRRRR

STORM *CLOUDS?* BUT IT'S SUPPOSED TO BE *SUNNY.*

THEY DID IT -- THOSE *KIDS!*

2

109

DIDN'T YOU FOOLS HEAR ME? *RUN! RUN!*

ONCE THE *CHAIN REACTION* BEGINS-- OUR POWERS CAN'T BE *STOPPED!!*

WE'RE AS MUCH *VICTIMS* AS YOU ARE! *RUN!*

I'M GETTIN' *OUTTA* HERE!

WH- WHAT ARE THEY *DOING?*

THE CRASH OF THUNDER DEAFENS THE FRIGHTENED MISSOURIANS, AS LIGHTNING CUTS A JAGGED SWATH ACROSS THE CLOUD-BLACKENED SKIES...

IN AN INSTANT, THE APARTMENT HOUSE IS GONE, CRUMBLED TO SO MUCH WORTHLESS *RUBBLE*...

THEY *RUN* THEN, HID-ING IN THE DARKNESS, AS FRIGHTENED AS ANY OTHER BY THE TERRIBLE DISPLAY OF THEIR AWESOME POWER...

IT *HURTS,* GAN?

NO, THAT'S THE THING OF IT.... IT FEELS *GOOD* NOW.

CHAN TI WAS *RIGHT.* I ALMOST *WANT* TO USE MY POWERS... I WANT TO FEEL THE *CALM* THEY GIVE ME.

IT *FRIGHTENS* ME, TAVIS-- I THINK I *HAVE* TO USE MY POWERS NOW.

I KNOW WHAT YOU MEAN.... *I* AM FEELING THOSE SENSATIONS AS WELL.

DEEP INSIDE I *WANT* TO HURT. I WANT TO *DESTROY.*

WE MUST FIND HIM BEFORE WE DO.

WHERE IS HE, BROTHER--?

WHERE IS HE?

3

THEIR MISSION IN ZANDIA IS OVER AND THE TITANS ARE TIRED. FOR MOST, THIS IS A TIME TO *REST*...

HE WON'T EVEN TELL ME WHAT'S *WRONG*, DICK -- DON'T YOU UNDERSTAND? -- I'D *LIKE* TO HELP. WE ALL WOULD.

GOD, IT'S GETTING TO BE *TOO MUCH*. I CAN'T *HACK* IT ANY LONGER.

MAYBE I NEED A *BREAK*... SOME TIME OFF TO *THINK*.

HE HELPED CONVINCE *RAVEN* TO TELL US WHAT WAS WRONG WITH HER. WHY WON'T HE TAKE HIS OWN *ADVICE*?

I'VE LIVED SO MANY *LIVES*. THE FLYING GRAYSONS. BATMAN. THE TITANS. COLLEGE. MY *OWN* ADVENTURES. NOW -- CONSIDERING WHAT'S *HAPPENED*...

MAYBE I SHOULD *QUIT* THE TITANS --! BLAST! I WISH I KNEW WHAT TO *DO*.

I'M SO HAPPY YOU'RE *BACK* WITH US, RAVEN. BUT WHY DID YOU *LEAVE* IN THE FIRST PLACE?

YOU HAVE *SEEN* ME, KORIAND'R -- I CANNOT *CONTROL* WHAT I AM.

I COULD *KILL* -- I ALMOST *DID*. I -- SHOULD NOT BE A *MEMBER* OF THIS GROUP.

I'LL *SECOND* THAT MOTION.

FLASH...

YEAH? WHAT *IS* IT, FRAN?

HAVE YOU *DECIDED* YET? DO YOU WANT TO COME BACK WITH ME TO *BLUE VALLEY*?

I DON'T *KNOW*.

I NEED *HELP*. I LOVE BEING WITH THE TITANS -- I REALLY *DO* --

-- BUT SO MUCH OF ME DOESN'T *BELONG* HERE. I STILL THINK I NEED TIME TO BE IN *SCHOOL*. I NEED TIME TO *GROW UP*.

TRYING TO JUGGLE *TWO BALLS* AT ONCE IS SOMETHING *I* CAN'T DO.

4

111

THEN WHAT IN BLAZES ARE YA *DOIN'* THIS FOR?

I KNOW WHY *I'M* IN IT. ALL THOSE SUPER-HERO *GROUPIES* OUT THERE.

WHAT A WAY TO SPEND A *CAREER.*

Y'KNOW, I NEVER *INTENDED* TO BE A HERO --IT WAS AN *ACCIDENT.*

"I WAS VISITING MY UNCLE'S LABORATORY WHEN *LIGHTNING* SHATTERED HIS CHEMICALS.

"THEY SPILLED OVER ME-- *CHANGED* ME... I FOUND THAT I WAS GIVEN SUPER-SPEED... LIKE *THE FLASH* HIMSELF.

"AT FIRST I WORE A *COSTUME* LIKE HIS-- THEN I GOT MY *OWN* UNIFORM.

"IN THE BEGINNING, I LOVED IT. BUT NOW... I DON'T KNOW."

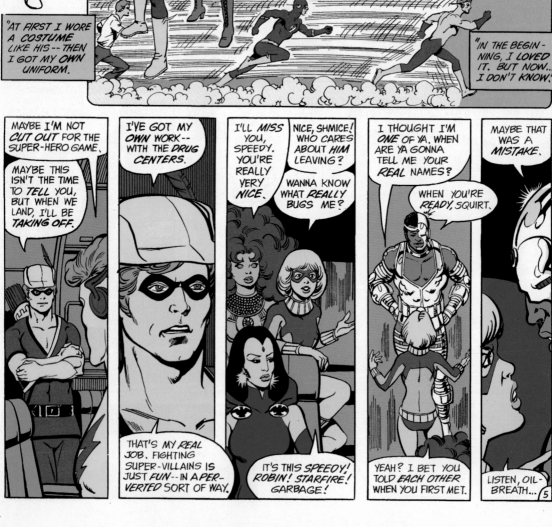

MAYBE I'M NOT *CUT OUT* FOR THE SUPER-HERO GAME.

MAYBE THIS ISN'T THE TIME TO *TELL* YOU, BUT WHEN WE LAND, I'LL BE *TAKING OFF.*

I'VE GOT MY *OWN* WORK-- WITH THE *DRUG CENTERS.*

THAT'S MY *REAL* JOB. FIGHTING SUPER-VILLAINS IS JUST *FUN--* IN A *PER-VERTED* SORT OF WAY.

I'LL *MISS* YOU, SPEEDY. YOU'RE REALLY *VERY NICE.*

NICE, SHMICE! WHO CARES ABOUT *HIM* LEAVING?

WANNA KNOW WHAT *REALLY* BUGS ME?

IT'S THIS *SPEEDY!* ROBIN! STARFIRE! GARBAGE!

I THOUGHT I'M *ONE* OF YA. WHEN ARE YA GONNA TELL ME YOUR *REAL* NAMES?

WHEN YOU'RE *READY,* SQUIRT.

YEAH? I BET YOU TOLD *EACH OTHER* WHEN YOU FIRST MET.

MAYBE THAT WAS A *MISTAKE.*

LISTEN, OIL-BREATH...

5

NOW, NOW, LET'S BE *GOOD* LITTLE BOYS 'N' GIRLS, SHALL WE?

LOGAN, GET THOSE *SCALES* OFF ME OR YOU'RE *DEAD MEAT.*

WOTTA WAY TO *DIE,* EH? C'MON, ADMIT IT-- YOU *LOVE* THIS.

I'D RATHER CUDDLE WITH A SACK'A *SLIME!*

ROBIN, ARE WE NEAR *HOME* YET?

ABOUT TO *LAND,* STARFIRE.

TRYING TO KEEP THIS LOONEY TUNE TAG-TEAM TOGETHER IS *GETTING TO ME.*

I WONDER IF IT'S *WORTH* IT.

LISSEN, SQUIRT--ROBBIE HAS TIES TO *THE BATMAN.* WONDER GIRL WITH *WONDER WOMAN.* KID FLASH WITH *FLASH.*

IF WE TELL YOU *OUR* NAMES, WE'D BE TELLIN' YOU *THEIR* SECRET *ID'S* TOO.

NOW YA UNDERSTAND?

WHY DON'TCHA GO OUT IN THE RAIN AN' *TARNISH?*

KNOCK IT OFF BACK THERE. AND TAKE YOUR SEATS. WE'RE *LANDING.*

JUST IN *TIME,* TOO. I COULDN'T TAKE ANOTHER *MINUTE* OF THIS NONSENSE.

SHORTLY, INSIDE TITANS' TOWER...

LISTEN, I'VE GOT OTHER WORK, SO I'LL SEE YOU PEOPLE IN A *WEEK OR TWO.*

ROBIN, CAN WE *SPEAK?*

HE WALKED RIGHT *BY* ME?!?

DON'T *HOVER* OVER HIM, KORY--EITHER HE'LL COME AROUND...

...OR HE'S *NOT* THE ONE YOU REALLY SHOULD *LOVE.*

MAYBE YOU'RE *RIGHT.* MAYBE HE *DOESN'T* CARE ABOUT ME.

THESE DAYS I WONDER IF HE CARES ABOUT *ANYONE.*

YOU'RE REALLY *GOING,* FRAN? I THOUGHT.

THAT I'D *STAY?* NO. THIS LIFE ISN'T FOR *ME.*

IS IT FOR *YOU?*

6

I'M REALLY STARTING TO *WONDER*.

I'M GOING TO *MISS* YOU, FRAN.

YOU DON'T HAVE TO, YOU CAN STILL COME *WITH* ME.

WELL, I GUESS THIS IS IT. WHOSE GONNA BE THE FIRST TO KISS ME *GOOD-BYE*?

AND I DON'T MEAN *YOU*, LOGAN.

NO *TAKERS*? WELL, THEN IT'S UP TO *ME*.

COME *HERE*, YOU TAWNY *VIXEN!*

MMMFMM FFMMF MM

SKREEEE

WHAT IN THE WORLD--?!?

THIS IS *PRICELESS*. SOMEONE, GET ME A *POLAROID*.

OOPS. I'M *SORRY*. YOU TOOK ME BY *SURPRISE*.

DON'T *APOLOGIZE*, HONEY. I ALWAYS WANTED TO DO THAT TO HIM *MYSELF*.

NOW Y' WANNA TRY THAT WITH *ME*?

UHH, NO, THANKS, TERRA. I THINK I'LL JUST *SAY* MY GOOD-BYES.

OKAY, EVERYONE-- THAT'S *IT*. LET'S GET *OUT* OF HERE.

WE'VE ALL GOT *REAL* LIVES TO LIVE.

7

SAINT LOUIS...

GET BACK, ALL OF YOU.

WE CAN'T CONTROL OURSELVES MUCH LONGER.

MY BROTHER IS RIGHT. PROVOKE US AND YOU WILL SUFFER.

SIR? WHAT DO WE DO?

YOU SAW WHAT THEY DID TO THAT APARTMENT BUILDING.

YOU EVER PLAY POKER? THERE'S TWO OF THEM AGAINST ONE HUNDRED OF US.

I THINK WE CAN PULL OFF A SUCCESSFUL BLUFF.

GENTLEMEN, I SUGGEST YOU SURRENDER NOW OR WE WILL BE FORCED TO OPEN FIRE!

THAT'S A MISTAKE, GENERAL!

YOUR LAST MISTAKE.

YOU WILL LEARN HOW POWERFUL ARE THUNDER AND LIGHTNING!

THE SKY GROWS THICK AND BLACK AS THE NIGHT AS ELECTRICITY SPLITS THE DEEPENING DARK...

THEN COMES THE CLARION CALL OF DEATH ITSELF -- THE HEAVENS ROAR AS THUNDER BELLOWS WITH ANGER...

THOUGH NONE DIE, AT THIS MOMENT ALL WISH THEY HAD.

8

THE WINTER SKIES OVER NEW YORK CITY ARE GRAY AND BLEAK, OFFERING LITTLE HOPE TO THOSE WHO VENTURE OUT...

BETTER TO STAY INSIDE, OR AT LEAST THAT'S WHAT *VICTOR STONE* BELIEVES...

WHAT ARE *YOU* DOING HERE, PAL? THE *RATS* FORCE YOU OUTTA YOUR PLACE?

NAH, JUST THOUGHT I'D TAKE IT *EASY*, CATCH ON SOME *READING*. WHAT'S *UP*?

TARA AND ME ARE GOING TO A MOVIE.

"FRIDAY THE THIRTEENTH, PART THIRTEEN." *EVERYONE* DIES IN THIS ONE.

WANNA *COME*?

NAH. I THINK I'LL WAIT FOR THE NEW *STAR WARS* PIC INSTEAD.

I THINK YOU'RE RIGHT, DONNA-- I'M NOT GOING TO *BOTHER* WITH *DICK* ANY MORE.

GOOD FOR YOU. IF HE *REALLY* CARES, HE'LL LET YOU KNOW.

YOU *AGREE*, RAVEN?

I ... I DO NOT *KNOW*.

I AM ILL AT EASE WITH *SOCIAL PROTOCAL*.

BUT I'M STILL *WORRIED* ABOUT HIM.

I KNOW, BUT WE'VE *ALL* ASKED HIM WHAT'S WRONG AND HE WON'T *TELL*.

WE CAN'T KEEP *CHASING* HIM. IT'S UP TO *HIM* NOW.

THE *EMERGENCY ALARM* SIGNALS IN EVERY ROOM, AND...

SOME-THING *WRONG* SPEEDY?

YEAH. I THINK YOU'LL WANNA *HEAR* THIS.

THERE'S SOMETHING ON THE *WIRE-SERVICE* YOU SHOULD KNOW ABOUT.

SOME KINDA *SUPER-BADDIE TROUBLE* DOWN IN ST. LOUIS.

THANKS, WE'LL PICK YOU UP ON OUR WAY *DOWN*.

SORRY, *GORGEOUS*, BUT NO CAN *DO*.

I'M ON A *SPECIAL ASSIGNMENT* DOWN IN WASHINGTON -- SO, GOOD LUCK, GUYS.

LEMME *KNOW* HOW IT PANS OUT.

SECONDS LATER...

WELL, YOU *WANTED* TO BE A TITAN.

I ALSO WANTED TO SEE A *MOVIE*. GUESS WHICH *WINS*?

RAYEN, YOU LOOK SO SAD. CAN I *HELP* YOU?

I DO NOT *THINK* SO, STARFIRE, BUT THANK YOU.

REALLY, I *WANT* TO HELP.

I KNOW WE'RE *DIFFERENT*. MY BACKGROUND *JUSTIFIES* VIOLENCE, YOURS *SHUNS* IT AT ALL COSTS--

--AND I KNOW WE HAVEN'T BEEN ALL THAT *CLOSE*...

...BUT I *REALLY* DO *LIKE* YOU.

AND I KNOW YOU'VE BEEN *HURT*...

KORIAND'R....STARFIRE... WHAT I *AM* IS WHAT HURTS ME. THERE CAN BE NO *SIMPLE* SOLUTION.

...DON'T KNOW WHERE *DICK* RAN OFF TO...SO I GUESS THAT LEAVES *YOU* IN CHARGE.

ME? WHY NOT *YOU*?

I *HATE* THIS, LOGAN.

DON'T WE HAVE A DAY *OFF*?

'CAUSE THE WAY I'VE BEEN FEELIN' LATELY, I'D MARCH US RIGHT INTO A *DEATH TRAP*.

WHAT'S *UP*?

I MET SARAH'S *FIANCE*. ANY LAWS AGAINST ME *SQUEEZIN'* HIM--*REAL HARD*?

AT LEAST ONE OR TWO.

I'M SORRY TO *HEAR* ABOUT THAT, VIC. NOW I UNDER-STAND WHY YOU SOUNDED SO *STRANGE* WHEN I MENTIONED TERRY'S PROPOSAL.

SO YOU *ARE* MARRYIN' 'IM?

I--I *WANT* TO, BUT I HAVEN'T SAID *YES* YET.

STRANGE, ISN'T IT? I DON'T FLINCH AT TAKING ON CREEPS LIKE *BROTHER BLOOD*--

--BUT WHEN IT COMES TO MARCHING DOWN THE AISLE, I *FREEZE*.

10

DON'T YOU UNDERSTAND US *YET?*

SEND A *THOUSAND* SOLDIERS AGAINST US AND IT *STILL* WON'T MATTER.

TAVIS, IT IS BECOMING IMPOSSIBLE TO *RESTRAIN* MYSELF.

DO SOMETHING BEFORE IT IS TOO LATE.

WE WANT *HIM!* FIND HIM FOR US OR ELSE!

SORRY, BOYS, BUT I THINK YOU'VE WAITED *TOO LONG.*

MAYBE. THE *MILITARY* CAN'T STOP YOU, BUT THEY *CAN!*

I *SEE* THEM. LET'S *GO!*

YOU'RE THE *TITANS?* I THOUGHT THE *JUSTICE LEAGUE* WAS COMING.

DON'T WORRY, WE'LL DO JUST *FINE.*

THEY'RE THE PROBLEM?

BET YOUR SWEET-- UH, YEAH, THEY'RE *IT!* THEY CALL THEMSELVES *THUNDER AND LIGHTNING.*

THEY'RE NOT *GOING* ANYWHERE, WONDER GIRL. I'VE *GOT* THEM.

I *AGREE* WITH YOU, BROTHER ....WE CAN WAIT *NO LONGER.*

GOOD! THE ENERGIES THAT FLOW THROUGH ME ARE *READY* TO EXPLODE!

I MUST *RELEASE* THEM.

11

118

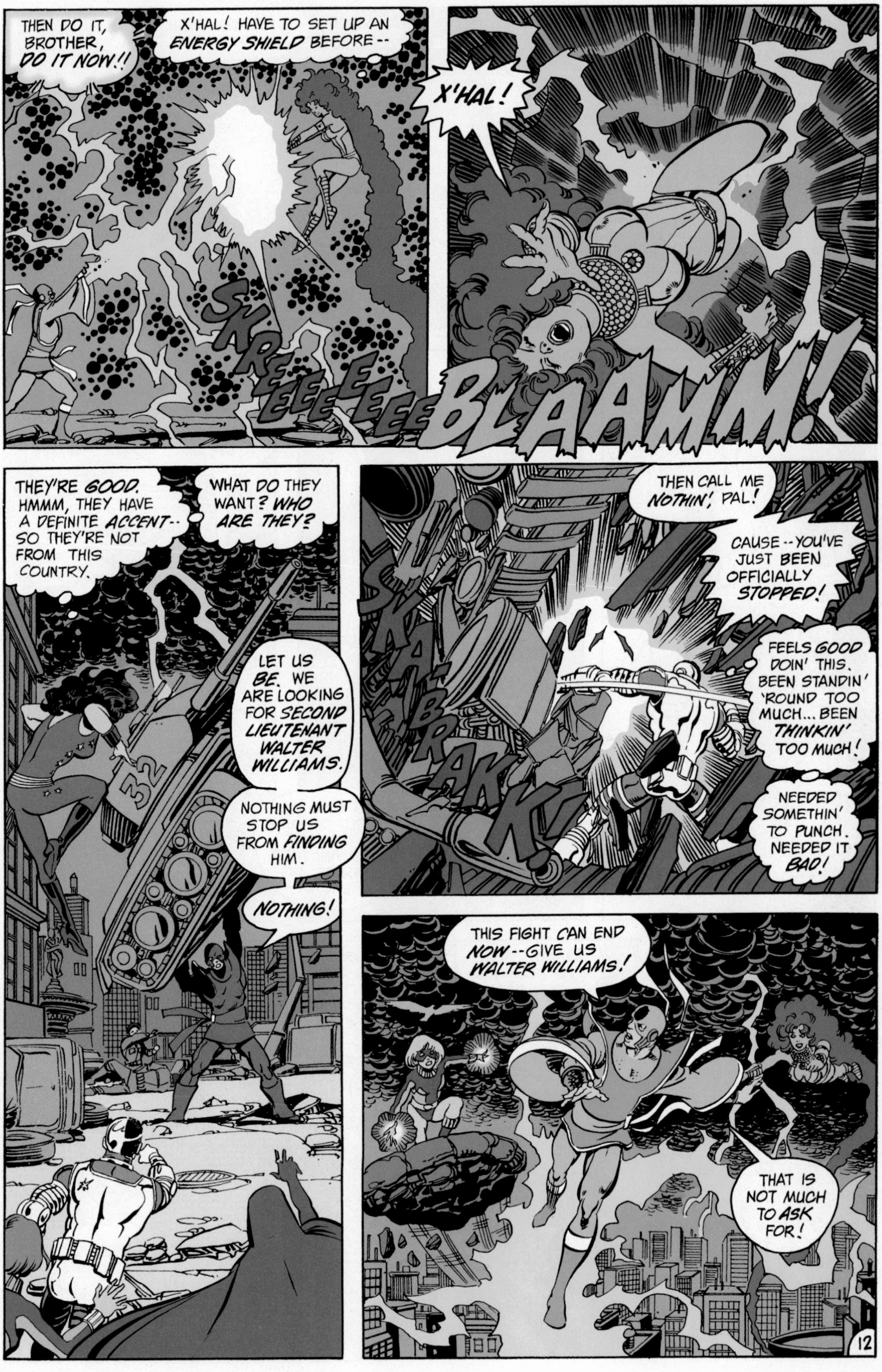
THEN DO IT, BROTHER, DO IT NOW!!
X'HAL! HAVE TO SET UP AN ENERGY SHIELD BEFORE --
X'HAL!
SKREEEEEEEEEBLAAMM!
THEY'RE GOOD. HMMM, THEY HAVE A DEFINITE ACCENT-- SO THEY'RE NOT FROM THIS COUNTRY.
WHAT DO THEY WANT? WHO ARE THEY?
LET US BE. WE ARE LOOKING FOR SECOND LIEUTENANT WALTER WILLIAMS.
NOTHING MUST STOP US FROM FINDING HIM.
NOTHING!
THEN CALL ME NOTHIN', PAL!
CAUSE -- YOU'VE JUST BEEN OFFICIALLY STOPPED!
SKA-BRAKK!
FEELS GOOD DOIN' THIS. BEEN STANDIN' 'ROUND TOO MUCH... BEEN THINKIN' TOO MUCH!
NEEDED SOMETHIN' TO PUNCH. NEEDED IT BAD!
THIS FIGHT CAN END NOW -- GIVE US WALTER WILLIAMS!
THAT IS NOT MUCH TO ASK FOR!
12

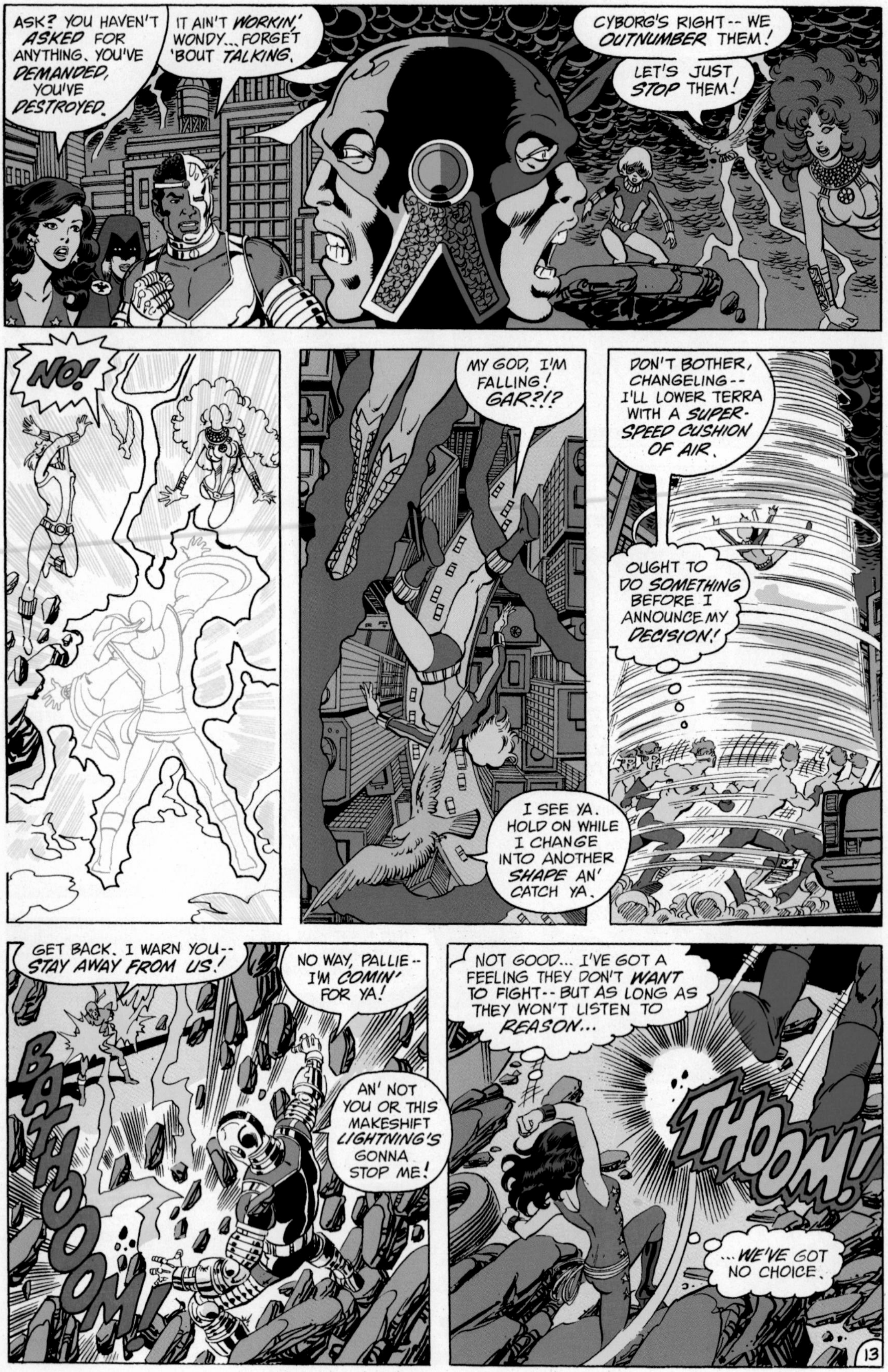
ASK? YOU HAVEN'T ASKED FOR ANYTHING. YOU'VE DEMANDED, YOU'VE DESTROYED.
IT AIN'T WORKIN', WONDY... FORGET 'BOUT TALKING.
CYBORG'S RIGHT -- WE OUTNUMBER THEM!
LET'S JUST STOP THEM!
NO!
MY GOD, I'M FALLING! GAR?!?
I SEE YA. HOLD ON WHILE I CHANGE INTO ANOTHER SHAPE AN' CATCH YA.
DON'T BOTHER, CHANGELING -- I'LL LOWER TERRA WITH A SUPER-SPEED CUSHION OF AIR.
OUGHT TO DO SOMETHING BEFORE I ANNOUNCE MY DECISION!
GET BACK. I WARN YOU -- STAY AWAY FROM US!
NO WAY, PALLIE -- I'M COMIN' FOR YA!
BATHOOOM!
AN' NOT YOU OR THIS MAKESHIFT LIGHTNING'S GONNA STOP ME!
NOT GOOD... I'VE GOT A FEELING THEY DON'T WANT TO FIGHT -- BUT AS LONG AS THEY WON'T LISTEN TO REASON...
THOOM!
...WE'VE GOT NO CHOICE.
13

IT'S LIKE TRYING TO MOVE A 747... BUT IF I KEEP APPLYING *CONSTANT PRESSURE,* HE'LL GIVE IN.

AS STRONG AS *THUNDER* IS, I'M *STRONGER...*

WONDER GIRL-- *DON'T!* I SENSE HIS *POWER BUILDING.*

LEAVE-- *LEAVE HIM!*

YOU *HEARD* HER... MOVE AWAY OR YOU'RE *DEAD!*

NO. WE *TALK!*

KRASH!

NO! I AM *THROUGH* TALKING. WE HAVE WASTED *YEARS* TALKING...

IT IS NOW TIME FOR *ACTION!*

FOOM!

SO ACTION IT *IS.*

HE WASN'T *EXPECTING* THAT... I THINK I CAN KEEP HIM *OFF-BALANCE* ... MOVE SO FAST HE'LL NEVER *TOUCH* ME.

UH-OH-- *VIC!* BEHIND YOU!

THANKS, BUT MY *INTERNAL AMPLIFIERS* ALREADY TOLD ME HE WAS SKULKING THERE.

HAD PLENTY A' TIME TO GET MY *WHITE SOUND BLASTER* IN PLACE.

WE *WARNED* YOU... WE *PLEADED* WITH YOU.

BUT NO MORE. NOW WE FIGHT TO *KILL.*

YEAH, YEAH, THAT'S WHAT THEY *ALL* SAY.

GOD, YOU'D THINK YOU JERKS COULD COME UP WITH *SNAPPIER DIALOGUE.*

WHY DON'TCHA GET YERSELF A *JOKE-WRITER* ...LIKE *ME.*

14

BE CAREFUL, GAN... HE MOVES TOO SWIFTLY TO *TOUCH*.

I *KNOW* THAT, TAVIS, AND I AM *PREPARED*.

COME, FAST ONE -- I AM NOT *DONE* WITH YOU.

YOU MAY AS WELL BE, *JERKO*...

...CAUSE YOU'RE NOT GETTIN' THE *CHANCE* TO DO ANYTHING *ELSE*.

TERRA?!?

SHOOOM

IN THE *COSTUME*, FLEET-FEET. NOT *BAD*, AM I?

BLAM!

ACHH!

LOGAN -- THE *LIGHTNING* GOT 'IM!..

CYBORG, HOW *IS* HE?

SKREEEEE

BREATHING, THANK GOD... GET THE *WITCH* OVER HERE, HE *NEEDS* HER.

GAN, HELP ME!

TAVIS?

THE FEMALE'S BLAST.... IT *HURTS*...HURTS *BADLY*...PLEASE HELP ME.

THAT IS IT. THE BATTLE IS *OVER*.

MY BROTHER *NEEDS* ME.

IT'S ABOUT TIME. NO ONE HAS TO *DIE*.

15

DIE? WE WILL *BOTH* DIE IF WE DO NOT FIND SECOND LIEUTENANT WALTER WILLIAMS.

YOU STILL HAVEN'T TOLD US-- *WHY* DO YOU WANT HIM?

IS THAT *IMPORTANT*, WONDER GIRL? THE BOY IS BADLY *HURT.*

QUESTIONS CAN WAIT FOR LATER. LET ME *HELP...*

DON'T, RAVEN -- WITH YOUR *POWERS* THE WAY THEY'VE BEEN, YOU CAN'T TAKE THE *CHANCE.*

BUT HOW CAN I *IGNORE* HIM? I AM AN *EMPATH.* I MUST--

YOU CAN'T, RAVEN -- NOT NOW... NOT UNTIL WE *KNOW* WHY YOU HAVEN'T BEEN ABLE TO CONTROL YOURSELF.

GAN...IT IS ...ALL RIGHT... I WAS ONLY *STUNNED.*

I ...FEEL MY STRENGTH *RETURN.*

YOUR BROTHER WILL BE ALL RIGHT. I *KNOW* HE WILL.

THEN YOU DON'T KNOW WHAT YOU'RE TALKING ABOUT. HE'S *DYING...* JUST AS I AM.

IT BEGAN AT THE *BEGINNING* OF THE VIETNAMESE WAR. YOUR COUNTRY SENT "ADVISORS" TO MINE. ONE OF THOSE "ADVISORS" MET A NATIVE WOMAN.

THEY FELL IN LOVE AND FOR SEVERAL MONTHS THEY THOUGHT THEY WOULD NEVER PART. BUT THEN HE WAS ASSIGNED ELSEWHERE...

AND THEY *NEVER* SAW EACH OTHER AGAIN.

16

123

"THE WOMAN WAS *OSTRACIZED* FOR CARRYING HIS CHILD, AND WAS SENT FROM HER VILLAGE FOR THIS *CRIME*. IN TEARS SHE *LEFT* VIETNAM, BUT WHEREVER SHE WENT, SHE WAS REFUSED. THEN SHE FOUND THE FABLED LAND OF *HSUAN* IN THE NORTH CHINA SEA...

"HSUAN, WHERE ONCE THE DEAD WAS RETURNED TO LIFE. HSUAN, THOUGHT A MYTH BUT WAS REALITY, A *PHANTOM ISLE* WHERE THIS BANISHED WOMAN GAVE BIRTH TO *SIAMESE TWINS*...

"*CHAN TI* WAS A WISE MAN WHO SOME SAY WAS DESCENDED FROM THE GREAT *EMPEROR WU TI* HIMSELF. HE PERFORMED HIS CEREMONIES AND APPLIED THE JADE HERBS AND ANCIENT INCENSE.

"THE CHILDREN WERE *SEPARATED*... AS IF BY MAGIC, BUT ALL SENSED THEY WERE *DIFFERENT*. ONE COULD CALL UPON THE *THUNDER*--AND THE OTHER COULD WIELD THE VERY *LIGHTNING* ITSELF.

17

WE ARE THOSE CHILDREN, BORN OF *AMERICAN* BLOOD MINGLED WITH *VIETNAMESE.*

AND NOW WE SEARCH FOR SECOND LIEUTENANT WALTER WILLIAMS -- *OUR FATHER.*

THERE ARE TIMES WHEN OUR POWERS CANNOT BE *CONTROLLED.* AT THESE TIMES OUR PAIN IS *GREAT.*

CHAN TI SAYS WE NEED OUR FATHER -- HIS *BLOOD* IS OUR ONLY SALVATION.

WE ASKED YOUR GOVERNMENT, BUT THEY SAY THERE IS NO *RECORD* OF A SECOND LIEUTENANT WALTER WILLIAMS.

THEY WILL NOT *HELP,* AND TIME IS GROWING *SHORT.*

OH, WOW.

THERE'S GOT TO BE SOME *MISTAKE.*

WE'LL *HELP* THEM, WON'T WE?

WE'LL DO WHAT WE *CAN.*

I KNOW SOMEONE IN *ARMY INTELLIGENCE.* SHE'LL GET US THE INFORMATION.

YOU DON'T *NEED* TO. WE HAVE A *COMPUTER READ-OUT...* WILLIAMS' LAST KNOWN ADDRESS IN A FISHING VILLAGE IN *MAINE,* BUT...

WE CANNOT *WAIT.*

NOW, TAVIS,... LET US *GO!*

WAIT!

STOP THEM! WILLIAMS HAS A SPECIAL GOVERNMENT CODE -- YOU WON'T *FIND* HIM.

18

THEY WON'T GET AWAY, I'LL *FOLLOW* THEM.

DON'T BOTHER, STARFIRE. WE *KNOW* WHERE THEY'RE GOING.

RAVEN-- I WILL MEET YOU AT THE *VILLAGE* AND I WILL TRY TO KEEP THINGS *PEACEFUL* UNTIL YOU ARRIVE.

LET'S JUST HOPE YOU *CAN.*

OKAY, WHAT DO WE DO *NOW?* FOLLOW THEM AND START *ANOTHER* FIGHT?

WHAT DO YOU *MEAN?*

THEY'RE IN *TROUBLE.* CAN'T WE *HELP?*

I *THINK* SO.

AND I HAVE AN *IDEA.* LISTEN...

MAINE...

...ON A NIGHT WHEN NONE SHOULD STRAY FROM HOME.

FAITH!

19

THE SKY EXPLODES WITH THUNDER'S SCREAM AND LIGHTNING'S CALL...

AND EVEN A WEATHER-WEARY VILLAGE KNOWS WHEN THINGS ARE NOT AS THEY SHOULD BE.

THEY'RE AFRAID, EVERYONE HERE... AND THEIR FEARS ARE, AS EVER, PAINFUL.

YET, I CAN 'FEEL' IT... EVEN ABOVE ALL THESE OTHERS.

I FEEL THEIR PAIN!

WHERE IS HE? WHERE IS OUR FATHER?!?

PLEASE STOP... DO NOT DO THIS. I UNDERSTAND YOUR PAINS... I UNDERSTAND YOU.

IF YOU CONTINUE LIKE THIS, YOU WILL NOT BE ABLE TO STOP!

YOU CAN'T UNDERSTAND. WE NEED OUR FATHER.

SOAK!

AND YOUR GOVERNMENT WON'T KEEP US FROM HIM.

NO ONE WILL KEEP US FROM FINDING HIM.

20

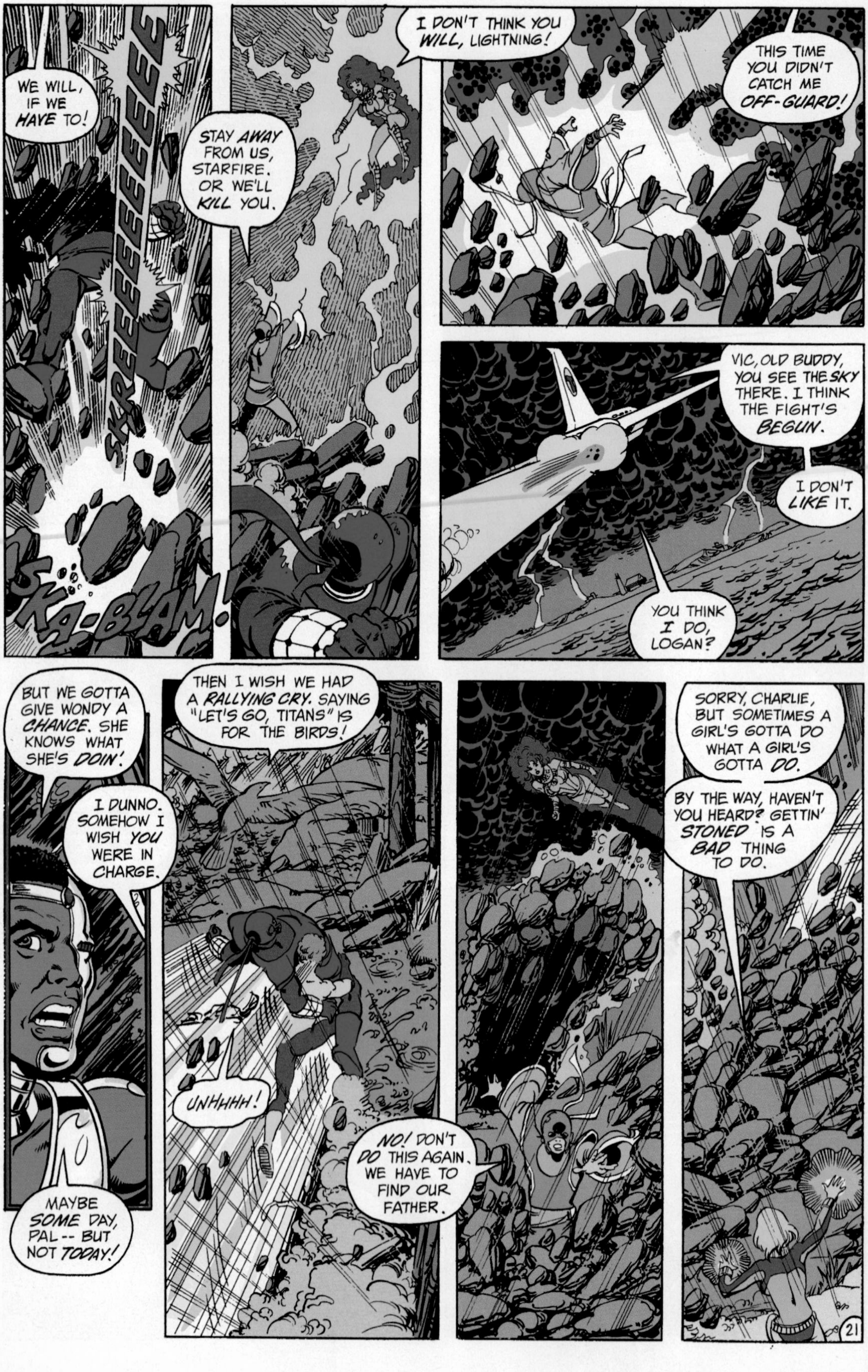

WE WILL, IF WE HAVE TO!
SKREEEEEEEE
SKA-BLAM!
STAY AWAY FROM US, STARFIRE. OR WE'LL KILL YOU.
I DON'T THINK YOU WILL, LIGHTNING!
THIS TIME YOU DIDN'T CATCH ME OFF-GUARD!
VIC, OLD BUDDY, YOU SEE THE SKY THERE. I THINK THE FIGHT'S BEGUN.
I DON'T LIKE IT.
YOU THINK I DO, LOGAN?
BUT WE GOTTA GIVE WONDY A CHANCE. SHE KNOWS WHAT SHE'S DOIN'.
I DUNNO. SOMEHOW I WISH YOU WERE IN CHARGE.
MAYBE SOME DAY, PAL -- BUT NOT TODAY!
THEN I WISH WE HAD A RALLYING CRY. SAYING "LET'S GO, TITANS" IS FOR THE BIRDS!
UNHHHH!
NO! DON'T DO THIS AGAIN. WE HAVE TO FIND OUR FATHER.
SORRY, CHARLIE, BUT SOMETIMES A GIRL'S GOTTA DO WHAT A GIRL'S GOTTA DO.
BY THE WAY, HAVEN'T YOU HEARD? GETTIN' STONED IS A BAD THING TO DO.
21

TAVIS, ARE YOU *ALL* RIGHT?

I... AM. MY *LEGS* HURT... MY *ARMS* ARE IN PAIN. PERHAPS WE SHOULD *CEASE* ALL FIGHTING.

NO! WE MUSTN'T. THEY WON'T HELP US.

WE WILL *NEVER* BE DEFEATED.

YOU'RE *WRONG*, GRANITE-BREATH! FIRST FLOOR, LADIES LINGERIE, MEN'S CLOTHES AND JANITOR-IN-A-DRUM, GOING *DOWWNNN*.

WHOMP!

SPAK!

PAL...

...THAT WAS A *BIG* MISTAKE!

SPOOOM!

FLASHER! PITCH COMIN' TO *FIRST!*

GOT 'IM, CYBORG. HE'S SPINNING OUT... GOING... GOING... GOING...

ISN'T HE *GONE* YET?

YOU WANT ME TO SET HIM FREE?

ON SECOND THOUGHT...

22

THEN THEY'VE *BOTH* BEEN STOPPED.

I DON'T THINK THIS ONE IS GOING TO MOVE FOR A *LONG* TIME.

RAVEN, ARE YOU *ALL RIGHT?* YOU LOOK AWFUL.

I AM NOT *USED* TO PHYSICAL VIOLENCE, TERRA.

THUNDER'S PUNCH *HURT* ME. TERRA, I MUST SPEAK WITH --

EVERYONE, PLEASE-- *STOP!*

IT'S ALREADY OVER. WE'VE *WON.*

BUT JUST FOR *NOW.* LET ME LAND. I HAVE *INFORMATION.*

I JUST FINISHED CHECKING WITH *WASHINGTON.*

YOU'VE FOUND OUR *FATHER?*

NO...BUT I DID LEARN *SOMETHING.* THERE'S NO RECORD OF HIM BEING IN VIETNAM BECAUSE LEGALLY HE *WASN'T.*

HE WAS A *MILITARY* SCIENTIST DOING GENETIC EXPERIMENTS WHICH SOMEHOW AFFECTED *HIS* GENES AND THEREFORE *YOURS.*

WHERE IS HE *NOW?*

THERE WAS *ACCIDENT* HERE A MONTH AGO, IN HIS LABORATORY ...WHEN THEY CLEARED THE *RUBBLE,* ALL THE BODIES HAD *VANISHED.*

THEN THERE ARE NO FURTHER *CLUES.*

THEN *WE ARE DOOMED.*

IT IS OVER... ALL *OVER.* 23

WE SHOULD RETURN HOME... IF WE ARE TO DIE...

NO, DON'T *THINK* THAT, GAN... THERE'S ALWAYS *HOPE.*

HE'S RIGHT...WE CAN CHECK *S.T.A.R.* LABS...

MAYBE THE SCIENTISTS *THERE* CAN HELP.

AT LEAST IT'S WORTH A *TRY.*

AND LATER...

WHAT A *SHAME.* IF ONLY THEIR FATHER HADN'T *DIED.*

HE *DIDN'T,* STARFIRE. I NEVER SAID HE *DID.*

BUT YOU SAID...

THEY NEVER WOULD HAVE STOPPED THEIR DESTRUCTIVE WAVE IF THEY THOUGHT HE WAS *ALIVE.*

HE WAS A *MILITARY SCIENTIST* IN VIETNAM, BUT FOR SOME REASON EVERYTHING WENT *WRONG* FOR HIM. ONE DAY HE *DISAPPEARED...*

...FLEW TO *AMERICA.* AND HE'S BEEN WANTED BY THE GOVERNMENT EVER SINCE THE '60'S...

...BUT NOT EVEN MY SISTER, WITH HER *ACCESS* TO PENTAGON COMPUTERS, COULD FIND OUT *WHAT* HE DID, *WHY* HE RAN OR, MORE IMPORTANTLY-- *WHERE* HE IS NOW.

HE'S BEEN DECLARED *TOP SECRET...* SOMETHING'S *WRONG* HERE, GUYS... SOMETHING'S *VERY* WRONG.

AND WE'RE GOING TO HAVE TO FIND OUT *WHAT!*

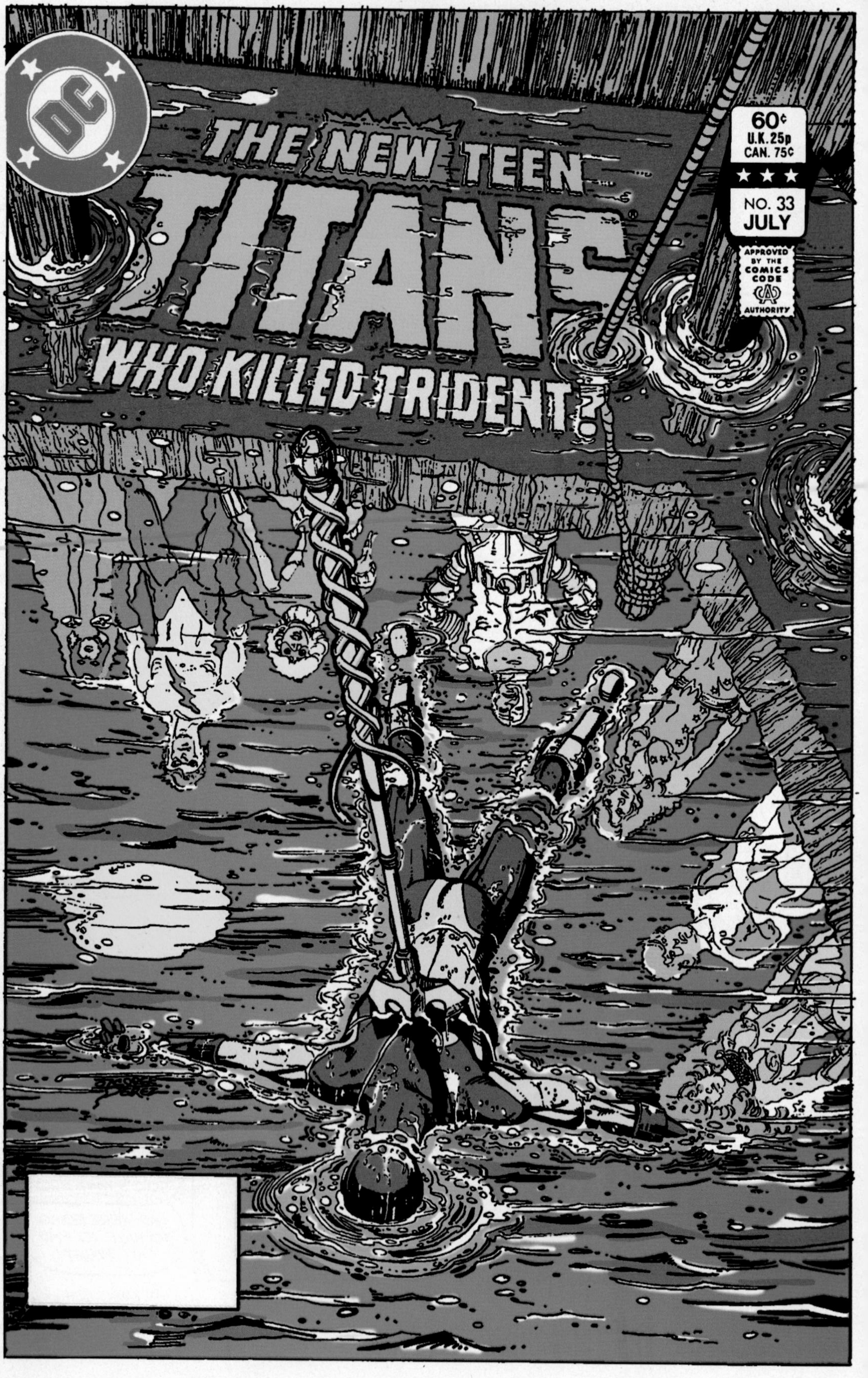

DC
THE NEW TEEN
TITANS
WHO KILLED TRIDENT?
60¢
U.K. 25p
CAN. 75¢
NO. 33
JULY
APPROVED BY THE COMICS CODE AUTHORITY

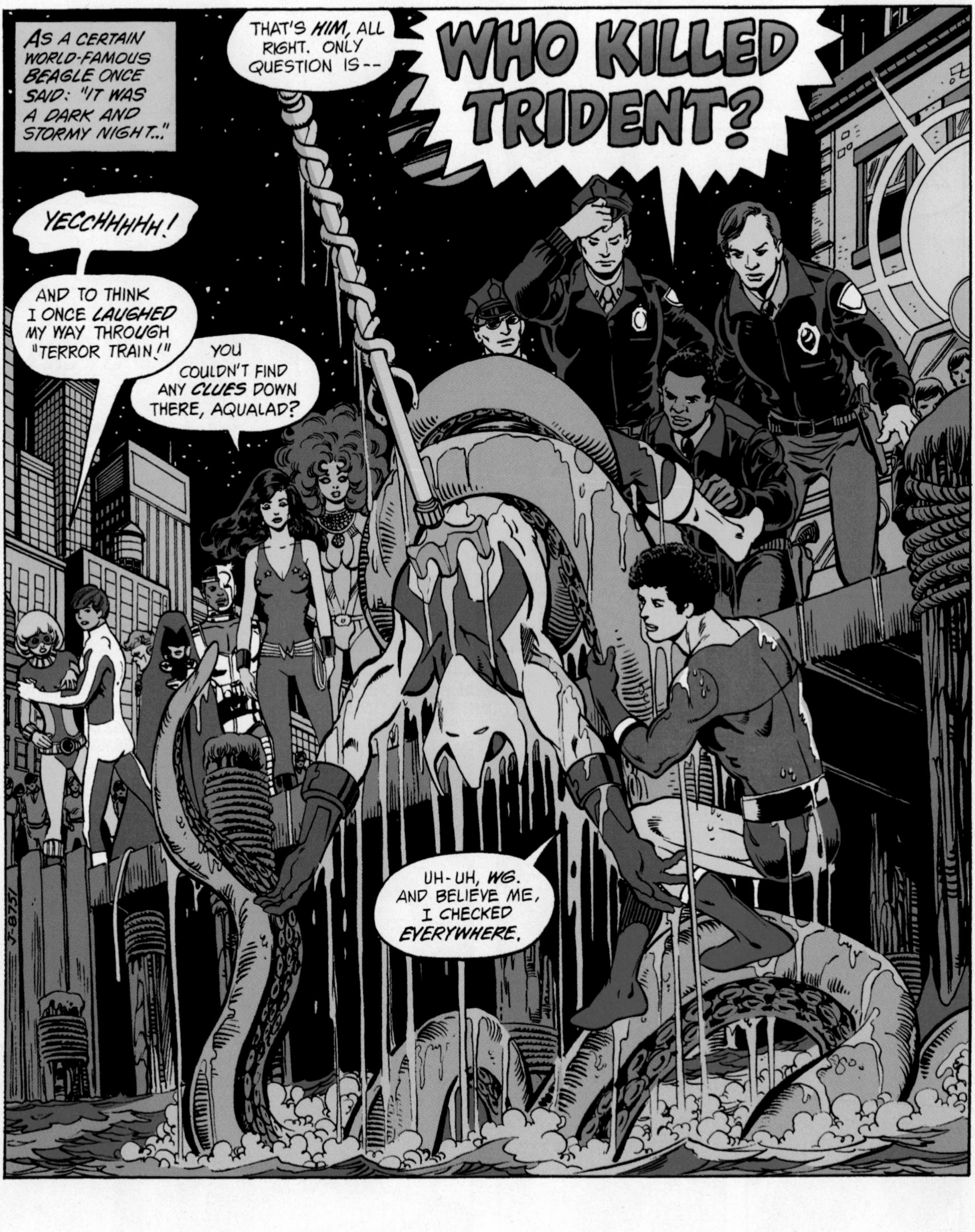

AS A CERTAIN WORLD-FAMOUS BEAGLE ONCE SAID: "IT WAS A DARK AND STORMY NIGHT..."
THAT'S HIM, ALL RIGHT. ONLY QUESTION IS--
WHO KILLED TRIDENT?
YECCHHHHH!
AND TO THINK I ONCE LAUGHED MY WAY THROUGH "TERROR TRAIN!"
YOU COULDN'T FIND ANY CLUES DOWN THERE, AQUALAD?
UH-UH, WG. AND BELIEVE ME, I CHECKED EVERYWHERE.

YOU KNOW I LOVE OCCASIONALLY *JOINING* YOU ON A TITANS' CASE, BUT NEXT TIME--

--GIVE ME A LESS *GRISLY* TASK.

SORRY, I HOPE OUR NEXT *MURDER CASE* WILL BE PRETTIER.

I DON'T UNDERSTAND. WHO COULD HAVE KILLED *HIM* WITH HIS OWN *WEAPON?*

GOOD QUESTION, STARFIRE. I THOUGHT WE WERE GETTING A *LEAD* ON TRIDENT, THEN *THIS* HAPPENS.

FRANKLY, I'M *STUMPED.*

WE'LL RUN A *MAKE* ON HIM DOWNTOWN, BUT DO YOU *RECOGNIZE* HIM, MISS?

SORRY. STRANGE, I DIDN'T *PICTURE* HIM LOOKING LIKE THAT.

HE SEEMED SO *SOFT* WHEN WE FOUGHT.

SOFT? FORGET IT, WONDER *GIRL.* HE'S *SOLID MUSCLE.*

LISTEN, WE CAN'T DO ANYTHING MORE *HERE.* LET'S CHECK HIM OUT ON THE *COMPUTERS* BACK IN THE TOWER.

WHICH IS THE *PERFECT* TIME FOR ME TO SAY "SO LONG"!

YOU'VE GOT TO GO *ALREADY?*

YOU KNOW IT. DUTIES IN *ATLANTIS* AWAIT... ALSO THIS *GORGEOUS* YOUNG MERMAID TYPE.

TAKE CARE, AQUALAD-- AND *THANKS.*

SEEYA, PALS.

②

ON A PRIVATE ISLAND LOCATED IN MANHATTAN'S EAST RIVER...

WELL, WHATTAYA THINK? YOU LIKE IT?

IT'S BEAUTIFUL, VIC. HOW DID YOU DO IT?

HOLOGRAPHICS. WE CAN SET THE COMPUTER TO SIMULATE ANY BACKGROUND.

YOU WANT THE ARCTIC? PARIS? YOU NAME IT, YOU GOT IT!

IT'S LOVELY AS IT IS, BUT I CAN'T THINK ABOUT HOLOGRAMS RIGHT NOW.

I STILL WANT TO KNOW WHO KILLED TRIDENT.

FORGET IT. HE'S DEAD. SO WE SCRATCH ONE SUPER-VILLAIN.

WHAT'S THE DIFFERENCE?

THE DIFFERENCE, FLASHER, IS WE'GOT A MURDERER FREE OUT THERE.

SO, LIKE FLEET-FEET SAYS -- WHO CARES?

SAVES US THE PROBLEM.

TERRA, WE WOULD NOT HAVE KILLED HIM.

GREAT! WE'VE GOT A MYSTERY AND ROBBIE'S GONE. HE'D FIGGER THIS OUT IN A SEC.

WELL, HE AIN'T HERE, SALAD-HEAD -- SO IT'S UP TO US.

YEAH, AND SINCE WE SAW HIM FIRST, I'LL BEGIN.

BUT, BEFORE GAR LOGAN SPEAKS, VICTOR STONE REMEMBERS...

3

WHY DIDN'T YOU *SPEAK* TO SARAH WHEN SHE CALLED?

LOGAN, MIND YER OWN *BUSINESS.*

C'MON, VIC-- WE'RE *FRIENDS...*

LOOK, I *DON'T* WANNA SPEAK TO HER. SHE'S GOT HER LIFE, I GOT MINE. SO *BUTT OUT!*

MEMORIES COME TO AN *ABRUPT* END AS...

SO WHATTAYA *WAITIN'* FOR, GREENIE? START TALKING. JUST DON'T *BORE* US.

"BORE YOU?" OKAY, LADY, YOU *ASKED* FOR THIS.

TA DA DA DA DA DA DA DA DA...♪

I ASKED FOR A *STORY,* SO WHATTA I GET? *"JAWS 3-D!"*

STAND BACK, EVERYONE. THIS ONE'S ON *ME!*

WOP!

YAGHHH!

MY *NOSE!* MY *BEAUTIFUL NOSE!*

YOU *BROKE* IT! I'LL *SUE* YOU FOR EVERY CENT YOU'VE GOT.

GO RIGHT AHEAD, BOZO-BREATH. YOU STILL WON'T HAVE *CHANGE* FOR A DIME!

WONDY, IS IT AGAINST TITANS' BY-LAWS TO *KILL* A NEW MEMBER?

OKAY, OKAY, I'M *SORRY.*

PLEASE DON'T THROW ME OUTTA THE GROUP... PLEASE.

DON'T WORRY, TARA -- WE'VE *ALL* WANTED TO BOP LOGAN.

NOW, IF HE WON'T MIND *STARTING* HIS STORY... ④

YEAH, YEAH, OKAY, IT BEGAN WHEN I WAS *VISITIN'* WHAT'S-HIS-JUNKPILE OVER THERE...

...TRYIN' TO *EXPLAIN* TO HIM THE "GREEN EXPERIENCE!"

"THAT'S WHEN EVERYTHING WENT *KABLOOEY!*"

SKROOOOM!

WHAT IN THE *WORLD?* YOU *HEAR* THAT?

NO. I'M COMPLETELY *DEAF!* OF COURSE I HEARD IT, YOU JERK.

AN *EXPLOSION...* SOMEPLACE *UPTOWN!*

"WELL, IT DIDN'T TAKE LONG FOR ME TO FLY THERE WHILE SALVAGE-SIDES *LEAPED* UP TO THE EIGHTIES, WHERE..."

IF YA *VALUE* YER LIVES—*STAY BACK* WHILE I *SPLIT!*

THEN NO ONE ELSE GETS *HURTS!*

WELL, LOOKEE HERE, RUSTHEAD—A JERK WITH AN OVERSIZED *COCKTAIL FORK!*

TITANS?

FOOOSHH

I WAS *WONDERIN'* IF EITHER YOU CREEPS OR THAT *FIREHEAD* CHARACTER WOULD SHOW UP TO STOP ME.

Y'SEE, I'VE BEEN *ITCHIN'* TA TRY OUT THIS *GIZMO!*

"*ITCHING?*" THEN YOU'VE UNSIGHTLY *DRY SCALP...* PROBABLY A SIGN OF *DANDRUFF!*

YOU REALLY OUGHTTA TRY THAT *SHAMPOO,* THEN MAYBE THAT CUTE *SECRETARY* IN THE ELEVATOR WILL NOTICE YA.

5

YOU FINISHED *JOKING?* THAT CLOWN'S GETTING AWAY.

NO, LOOK-- WE CAN STILL *GET* HIM. C'MON.

JOIK! YA KNOCKED ME *OVER,* JOIK!

I'LL SUE YA FER EVERY CENT YA *STOLE!*

PUT A *CORK* IN IT, BIMBO!

POLICE LINE

NOW, IS THAT ANY WAY TO SPEAK TO A *LADY?*

BE A NICE GUY, TRIDENT. GO BACK AND *APOLOGIZE,* HUH?

ONLY THING I'M *SORRY* ABOUT, IS FER NOT *KILLIN'* YA WHEN I HAD THE CHANCE!

BUT ONE'A THESE *CONTROL* GIZMOS WILL MORE'N MAKE UP FOR THAT MISTAKE.

ICE?

SPOOOM!

MY WINGS'VE FROZEN... I-I C-CAN'T FLY!

VIC? I COULDN'T *CHANGE* IN TIME ... THOUGHT I WAS A *GONER!*

JUST DON'T TELL THE *OTHERS* I SAVED YOU. THEY MAY *NEVER* FORGIVE ME.

DON'T *SWEAT* IT, MISTER-- YOU AIN'T *SAVED* HIM YET!

6

FACT IS, YOU AIN'T EVEN SAVED YERSELF!

SKROOOOMM!

HE'S BLASTED THE GIRDERS ...THEY'RE *FALLIN'!*

NO TIME TO MOVE... AND GAR'S STILL *OUT* OF IT...

GOTTA HOPE DAD MADE THIS BODY STRONG ENOUGH TO *WITHSTAND* THAT SORT'A WEIGHT SMASHIN' ONTO IT.

"VIC SPUN HIS MOLYB- DENUM STEEL-PLATED BODY, PROTECTING YOURS TRULY FROM A TON OF ALMOST CERTAIN DEATH..."

KEEP STILL, LOGAN-- AN' CROSS YOUR *FINGERS!*

I-I HEARD VIC CRY OUT, EVEN IF HIS HEAD *IS* AS THICK AS HIS BODY, IT STILL HURT.

BUT HE *SAVED* ME ANYWAY.

WHAT *ELSE* COULD I DO? HE STILL OWED ME *FIVE BUCKS.*

ONLY *TRIDENT* GOT AWAY WITH MORE THAN $125,000.

ANYONE SEE *STARFIRE?*

YEAH, SHE WENT TO LOCATE *DICK.*

SHE FIGURED THIS CASE WAS UP *HIS* ALLEY.

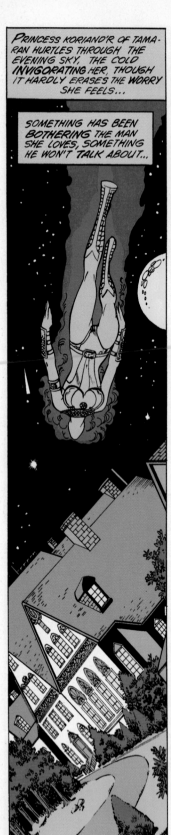

PRINCESS KORIAND'R OF TAMARAN HURTLES THROUGH THE EVENING SKY, THE COLD *INVIGORATING* HER, THOUGH IT HARDLY ERASES THE *WORRY* SHE FEELS...

SOMETHING HAS BEEN BOTHERING THE MAN SHE LOVES, SOMETHING HE WON'T *TALK* ABOUT...

JUST OUTSIDE GOTHAM CITY...

...AT STATELY *WAYNE MANOR*...

MASTER JASON, ANSWERING THE DOOR-BELL IS MY JOB.

SO? WITH BRUCE AWAY, IT'S *BORING* HERE. LET ME DO--

--SOME-THING??

OBOY.

HI. I--UH...

UHHHHH...

AND *NOW* SHE'LL GET HER ANSWERS...

MISS STARFIRE, PLEASE, COME *IN*...

IS IT *ALL RIGHT*, ALFRED?

YES, YOUNG *JASON TODD* KNOWS MASTER BRUCE'S SECRET.

I CAME TO SEE *DICK*.

BUT HE *MOVED OUT* WHEN MASTER BRUCE TOOK ON MASTER JASON AS HIS NEW *WARD*.

DICK'S *MOVED OUT?* HE DIDN'T TELL THE *TITANS*.

I'VE *GOT* TO FIND HIM.

THANKS, ALFRED. AND NICE MEETING *YOU*, JASON. 'BYE.

SIGHHH! AM I *TOO YOUNG* TO BE A TITAN, *TOO?*

8

ANYONE FOR *HOT CHOCOLATE?*

HEY, GUACOMOLE-BREATH, MAKE ME A *DOUBLE.*

SURE, AS LONG AS I WAS ASKED SO *SWEETLY.*

... THAT ALL HAPPENED YESTERDAY *MORNING.* RAVEN AND I FOUGHT HIM IN THE *AFTERNOON.*

AN' FLEET-FEET AND I TRASHED 'IM THAT *NIGHT,* WHILE HE WAS *SNEEZING* LIKE THAT STUPID *DISNEY DWARF.*

VIC, ARE YOU *SURE* HE STOLE A HUNDRED THOU? I DIDN'T GET THAT *IMPRESSION* FROM HIM.

FRANKLY, I FOUND HIM *CONFUSED...UNCERTAIN...*

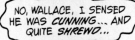

NO, WALLACE, I SENSED HE WAS *CUNNING...* AND QUITE *SHREWD...*

"FOR US, IT BEGAN WHEN *WONDER GIRL* ASKED ME TO WALK WITH HER..."

YOU'VE HAD *SEVERAL* ATTACKS LATELY -- FOR YOUR OWN SAKE, RAVEN, LET US *HELP* YOU.

ON PARADISE ISLAND WE HAVE CERTAIN *MACHINES...*

I AM SORRY, BUT THEY CANNOT *CHANGE* WHAT I AM.

I AM *TRIGON'S* CHILD, AND ONE WAY OR ANOTHER THAT *DEVIL* INTENDS TO POSSESS ME.

RAVEN, PLEASE -- YOU CAN'T CONTINUE TO BE *TORTURED* LIKE YOU'VE BEEN. TRUST US, WE'RE YOUR *FRIENDS.*

"WE WALKED THROUGH THE MUSEUM OF *NATURAL HISTORY* AND I WAS FASCINATED BY THE EXHIBITS. BUT THEN..."

GET *OUTTA* HERE. *RUN!*

THERE'S A *CRAZY GUY* IN THERE!

FOR GOD'S SAKE -- DON'T *PANIC.*

9

DO A QUICK *SCAN* OF THE PLACE...

I'VE GOT A HUNCH THIS COULD BE THE *SAME* GUY CYBORG AND CHANGELING FOUGHT.

LET US *HOPE*, WITH OUR POWERS, HE CANNOT *ESCAPE*.

WHAT?

I SAW THE *LOOK* IN HER *EYES*... SHE IS *WORRIED* ABOUT ME. BUT THERE WAS NO NEED FOR *CONCERN*.

I *CONTROL* MY *ACTIONS*. I AM IN *FULL COMMAND* OF MY POWERS.

YES, THERE HE IS -- AS VICTOR AND GARFIELD *DESCRIBED*.

WHO? HMMM. I *RECOGNIZE* HER... SHE IS ONE OF THE *TEEN TITANS*. FASCINATING.

IF *ONE* IS ABOUT, THEN THERE MIGHT WELL BE *OTHERS*.

I CANNOT *DELAY*.

BE *CAREFUL*, GIRL -- PERMIT ME TO LEAVE IN PEACE OR SOMEONE WILL BE *HURT!*

SKROOOOMM!

YOU'RE RIGHT ABOUT *THAT*, TRIDENT--

WHAT?

10

142

--ONLY THAT SOMEONE IS GOING TO BE *YOU!!*

NO MATTER. THERE IS A SIMPLE WAY TO *DEAL* WITH YOU.

FOOOSH!

WONDER GIRL *TOO?* ARE THE *OTHERS* HERE AS WELL?

NOTE MY *TRIDENT.* A RATHER *INGENIOUS* DEVICE, WOULDN'T YOU SAY?

THE *CENTER* TINE SHALL CREATE ALL THE *DAMAGE* NEEDED TO DETAIN YOU.

NO! FIRE SPREADING EVERYWHERE...

MAYBE ALL THOSE YEARS LIVING ON PARADISE ISLAND MAKE ME MORE *AWARE* OF THEIR VALUE--

--BUT I SIMPLY *CAN'T* LET THOSE ANTIQUES BE *DAMAGED.*

MUCH BETTER. NOW I HAVE A CLEAR PATH *OUT* OF HERE...

UNHH! NERO'S TREASURES WEIGH ALMOST AS MUCH AS THE *MAN* DID HIMSELF!

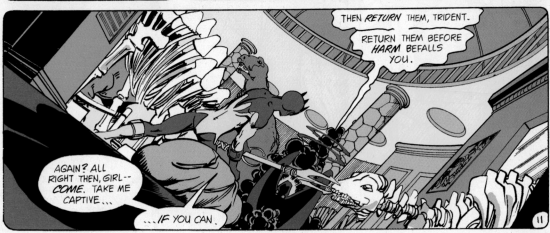

THEN *RETURN* THEM, TRIDENT.

RETURN THEM BEFORE *HARM* BEFALLS YOU.

AGAIN? ALL RIGHT THEN, GIRL-- *COME.* TAKE ME CAPTIVE...

....IF YOU CAN.

11

PLEASE, DO NOT MAKE ME USE MY *POWERS*. I DO NOT KNOW IF THEY CAN BE *CONTROLLED*.

THAT DOESN'T *MATTER*, RAVEN, GO AHEAD-- TAKE ME *PRISONER*.

MY HAND?!? IT--

WENT *THROUGH* ME? PERHAPS... *FASCINATING*, ISN'T IT?

STILL, MY *TANGIBILITY* IS THE LEAST OF YOUR WORRIES.

YOUR *CLOAK*, RAVEN-- LOOK AT IT.

HURRY, GIRL, REMOVE IT BEFORE IT BECOMES YOUR *FUNERAL PYRE*.

NO!

HE'S *PLAYING* WITH US... WELL, I'LL GIVE HIM ALL THE *ROPE* HE WANTS, AND THEN GLADLY TIGHTEN THE *NOOSE*.

THIS IS TOO *SIMPLE*. HOW CAN YOU CATCH--

"-- WHAT IS NO LONGER THERE?"

GONE? BUT CYBORG DIDN'T SAY HE COULD *TELEPORT.*

BLAST! WHAT'S HE UP TO?

HEY, WHERE DID THAT GUY GO? HE JUST *VANISHED?*

I--I DO NOT *KNOW.*

DID YOU *SENSE* ANYTHING *STRANGE* ABOUT HIM?

NOTHING... HE WAS AN *ORDINARY* MAN--YET I CAN SAY *THIS*, WONDER GIRL--

MY HAND DID NOT GO *THROUGH* HIM. HE SIMPLY WAS *NOT* WHERE MY HAND TOUCHED.

⑫

HE *GOT AWAY*, SIMPLE AS THAT!

WHAT WAS *WRONG*, RAVEN? YOUR POWERS GO *CRAZY* AGAIN?

C'MON. BE *FAIR*. *I* COULDN'T STOP HIM, EITHER.

THE ONLY THING RAVE *DID* *WRONG* WAS MAKE HIM SOUND *TOO* SMART.

THAT GUY'S BRAIN WAS LEFT ON *SPIN-CYCLE*.

LOOK, AT LEAST *HE* COULD WALK AND CHEW GUM AT THE SAME TIME. CAN *YOU*?

I DID NOT *EXAGGERATE*, NOR COULD I HAVE *STOPPED* HIM.

HE POSSESSES GREAT ABILITIES AND UNDER-STANDS HOW BEST TO *USE* THEM.

SORRY, RAVEN, BUT FOR ONCE SALAD-HEAD'S *RIGHT*. TRIDENT EATS SOUP WITH A *FORK*.

Y'KNOW, *ROBBIE* WOULD FIGGER THIS ALL OUT IN *FIVE* SECONDS.

SO NATCH, THE *ONE* TIME WE NEED HIM, HE'S *OUT* SOMEWHERE. PROBABLY SAVING A *CAT*.

NOT EXACTLY. FOR AT THIS VERY MO-MENT ROBIN IS ON THE EASTERN TIP OF LONG ISLAND, WHERE...

I DON'T *UNDERSTAND*, CHASE. WE HAD ANTHONY SCARAPELLI CAUGHT RED-HANDED. HOW COULD HE BE *FREED*?

ASK ME SOMETHING I CAN *ANSWER*, KID. HE GOT TO SOMEONE WHO'S *SOFT* ON CRIME, OR ON HIS PAY-ROLL, OR A THOUSAND *OTHER* POSSIBILITIES.

BUT I'LL TELL YOU *THIS*, I *HATE* IT. I MAKE A *TEXT-BOOK* ARREST...

...BUT BECAUSE OF SOME STUPID *TECHNICALITY* A CREEP LIKE SCARAPELLI WHO PUSHES DRUGS TO KIDS GETS AWAY WITHOUT EVEN SPENDING A *NIGHT* BEHIND BARS.

ONLY, IF THE INFO I GOT TONIGHT PANS OUT, SCARAPELLI ISN'T *STAYING* FREE.

Y'KNOW, KID -- SOMETIMES I *ENVY* YOU AN' THE BATMAN. YOU *DON'T* HAVE TO FOLLOW THE BOOK LIKE *I* DO.

WELL, YOU *READY*?

AS I'LL *EVER* BE.

LET'S GO.

13

WALL AHEAD. YOU GOT THAT THING?

ONE *BATARANG* COMING UP.

CLEAR SAILIN', KID.

NOW, STAY BACK. IT'S UP TO *ME.*

HE SLIPS AHEAD, CLUMSILY CRISS-CROSSING THE IMMACULATELY MANICURED GROUNDS...

THEN...

DON'T MOVE OR YER *DEAD.*

OKAY, OKAY, DON'T SHOOT. I *GIVE.*

WHO *ARE* YA? WHATTAYA *DOIN'* HERE?

JUST TAKING MY EVENING CONSTITUTIONAL. YOU DON'T *MIND,* DO YOU?

NAH, *I* DON'T THINK HE MINDS.

RIGHT?

WHAP!

YOU'RE NOT *HALF BAD,* KID.

TRUSS 'IM UP AN' LET'S GO.

14

MEANWHILE...

FLASHER, PUT A *HOLD* ON YOUR STORY. I DON'T WANNA *MISS* ANY OF IT WHILE I ANSWER THE PHONE.

RRINNGG!

AND...

THAT WAS THE *POLICE.* THEY GOT A *MAKE* ON TRIDENT. HIS NAME'S *SAMMY JAYE,* KNOWN MUSCLE FOR THE *H.I.V.E.**

I WAS WONDERING WHY WE HAVEN'T *HEARD* FROM THOSE CREEPS IN A WHILE.

WHAT'S THE *H.I.V.E.?*

A CRIMINAL GANG RUN BY *SCIENTISTS.* THAT WOULD EXPLAIN HIS *TRIDENT* WEAPON.

*HIERARCHY FOR INTERNATIONAL VENGEANCE AND EXTERMINATION. --Len.

BUT *BANK ROBBERY* ISN'T TYPICAL *H.I.V.E.* BUSINESS. IT DOESN'T MAKE *SENSE.*

YOU SAID THEY WERE *CRIMINALS.* ISN'T THAT GOOD ENOUGH?

YOU HAVE A LOT TO *LEARN,* TARA. ORGANIZATIONS LIKE THE *H.I.V.E.* AREN'T INTERESTED IN *MONEY.* THEY WANT *POWER.*

HOLD ON, GUYS... I FOUND OUT SOMETHING ABOUT DI-- I MEAN, *ROBIN.*

CRIPES. HERE WE GO AGAIN, HIDIN' YOUR SECRET *ID'S* ON ME. I'M TELLIN' YA-- *I HATE IT!*

HE ISN'T AT HOME AND HE ISN'T REGISTERED IN ANY *COLLEGE DORMITORY.*

BUT LISTEN TO *THIS...*

15

147

DON'T WORRY, ROBIN CAN *HANDLE* HIMSELF!

I WOULDN'T BE SO SURE. YOU SEE THE WAY HE'S BEEN *ACTING* LATELY?

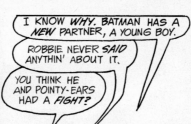

I KNOW *WHY.* BATMAN HAS A *NEW* PARTNER, A YOUNG BOY.

ROBBIE NEVER *SAID* ANYTHIN' ABOUT IT.

YOU THINK HE AND POINTY-EARS HAD A *FIGHT?*

LISSEN, NOBODY CARES ABOUT THAT. WE'VE GOT *TITANS* BUSINESS. SPEED-FREAK WAS GONNA TELL *OUR* STORY.

WITH MY PARENTS VACATIONING IN *BERMUDA,* I STUCK AROUND AFTER MOST OF YOU LEFT. THAT'S WHEN TERRA AND I HEARD TRIDENT HAD STRUCK *AGAIN* -- AT A JEWELRY STORE ON 83RD STREET.

WE HURRIED, BUT TRIDENT WAS *GONE.* WE FINALLY FOUND HIM UP BY THE *CROSS-BRONX EXPRESSWAY...*

SPEEDO, THIS SURE BEATS RIDIN' *ROCKS.* YOU THIS FAST WITH *EVERYTHING?*

WE'RE NOT HERE TO *CHIT-CHAT.* AND FRANKLY, I DIDN'T EVEN *WANT* YOU WITH ME.

I DON'T KNOW WHAT THE *OTHERS* THINK, BUT I DON'T BELIEVE *ANYTHING* YOU TOLD US.

OKAY, SO MAYBE I *STRETCHED* A POINT HERE OR THERE, BUT I WASN'T *LYING.*

YOU DON'T KNOW WHAT IT WAS LIKE-- DAD'S WIFE *HATED* ME AN' I COULDN'T STAY IN MARKOVIA.

THEN WHEN I WAS HELD BY THESE *TERRORISTS,* THEY KEPT ME DRUGGED SO I COULDN'T *ESCAPE.*

I USED TO GO TO BED *CRYING,* I-I WANTED TO KILL MYSELF BUT I WAS ALWAYS SO *SCARED.*

PLEASE, THIS IS MY *BIG CHANCE*--DON'T SAY ANYTHING THAT'LL GET ME THROWN OUTTA THE TITANS, PLEASE.

"TERRA AND I CHIT-CHATTED WHILE WE SEARCHED, THEN FINALLY FOUND HIM HIDING IN THAT BIG *DRIVE-IN.*"

16

W-WELL, LOOK WHO'S ≷SNIFF≷ HOT ON MY TRAIL.

Y-YEW DIDN'T S-SUFFER ENOUGH THE *LAST* TIME, DID YA?

BOY, IS HE *GREEDY.* IF *I* STOLE OVER A HUNDRED THOU--

--I'D BE TAKIN' IT EASY ON THE *RIVIERA* BY NOW,

AITCHOOOO

HIS KIND IS *ALWAYS* TAKING, THAT'S WHY *WE'RE* NEEDED.

SO, YEW SAY I SKEDADDLED WITH A HUNDRED G'S, EH?

WELL, MEBBE ME AN' MY MONEY OUGHT NOT TO BE *PARTED.* BE *SEEIN'* YEW, SON.

HUH? I--RAN *THROUGH* HIM.

AND I-I'M *ON FIRE!?!*

IT'S BURNING THROUGH MY *COSTUME...*

GOT TO PUT IT OUT BEFORE IT *SCORCHES* ME.

HEY, "SUGAR-FREE"-- WHY DON'T YA PICK ON SOMEONE *HALF* YOUR SIZE--

--LIKE *ME!*

"*TERRA WAS EXCELLENT! SHE USED HER EARTH- SHIFTING POWERS--*

"--AND THE GROUND FAIRLY CAME ALIVE!

"LIKE HOMING MISSILES, ROCK AND STONE HURTLED THROUGH THE AIR TOWARD THEIR PREY...

"BUT...

FOOSH

AITCHOO! ≷SNIFF≷ NOT BAD, LI'L GIRL--

17

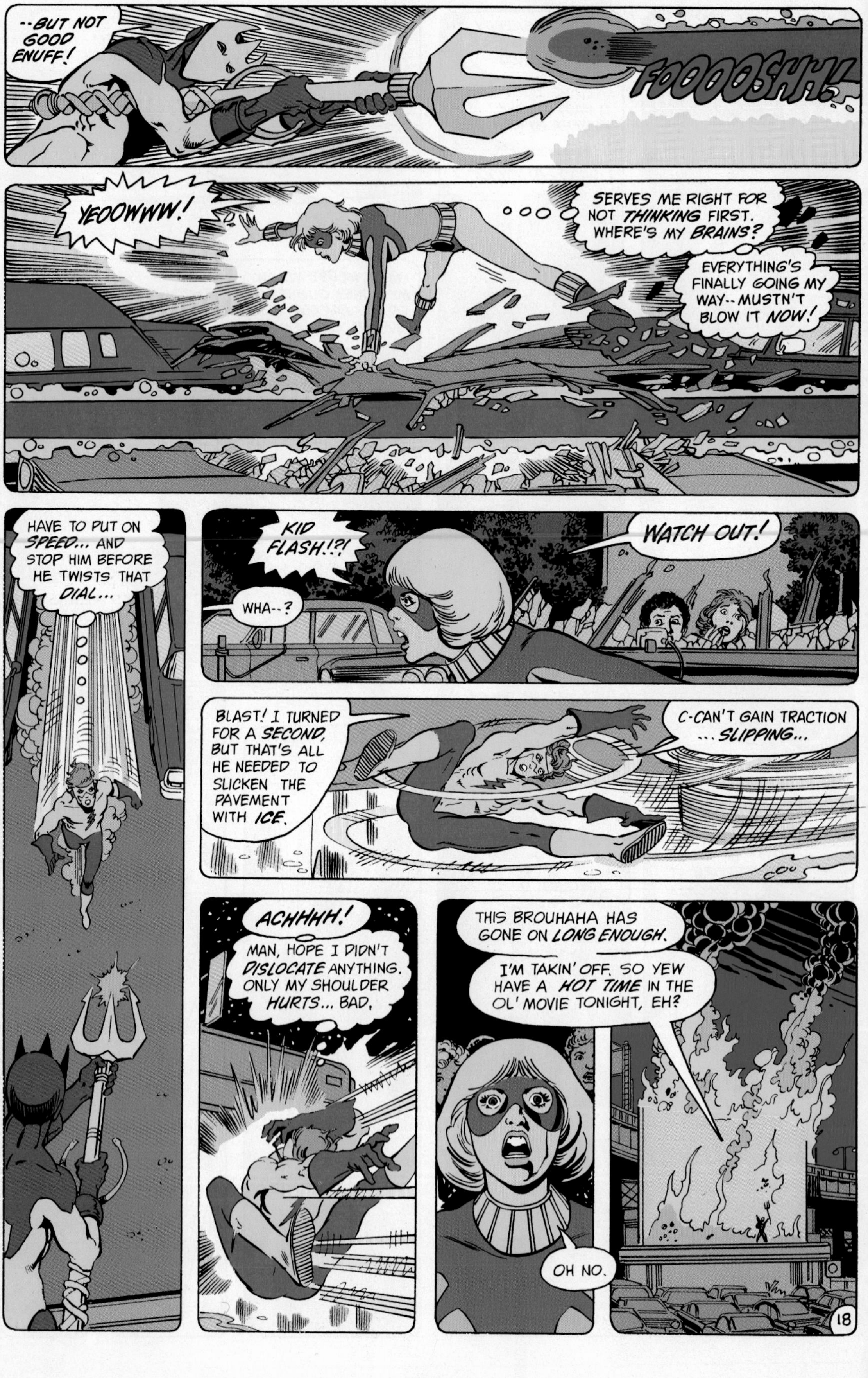
--BUT NOT GOOD ENUFF!
FOOOOSHH!
YEOOWWW!
SERVES ME RIGHT FOR NOT THINKING FIRST. WHERE'S MY BRAINS?
EVERYTHING'S FINALLY GOING MY WAY--MUSTN'T BLOW IT NOW!
HAVE TO PUT ON SPEED... AND STOP HIM BEFORE HE TWISTS THAT DIAL...
KID FLASH!?!
WATCH OUT!
WHA--?
BLAST! I TURNED FOR A SECOND, BUT THAT'S ALL HE NEEDED TO SLICKEN THE PAVEMENT WITH ICE.
C-CAN'T GAIN TRACTION ...SLIPPING...
ACHHHH!
MAN, HOPE I DIDN'T DISLOCATE ANYTHING. ONLY MY SHOULDER HURTS... BAD.
THIS BROUHAHA HAS GONE ON LONG ENOUGH.
I'M TAKIN' OFF. SO YEW HAVE A HOT TIME IN THE OL' MOVIE TONIGHT, EH?
OH NO.
18

"I HAVE TO SAY THIS, TERRA THOUGHT FAST AND ACTED JUST AS QUICKLY...

"SHE BLEW OUT AN UNDERGROUND *WATER MAIN* WHICH PUT OUT THE FIRE BEFORE THERE WAS ANY PANIC.

WHATEVER I'VE THOUGHT OF HER IN THE PAST, SHE'S *PROVED* HERSELF.

UNFORTUNATELY, THOUGH, TRIDENT *ESCAPED*.

I DUNNO. DOESN'T SOUND LIKE THE GUY *I* FOUGHT.

SO WHAT'S THE *PROBLEM?*

LOOK, *I* DIDN'T FIGHT THIS TRIDENT, BUT IT SEEMS *OBVIOUS* TO ME--

--YOU ALL MET *DIFFERENT* PEOPLE.

SHEESH. JUST 'CAUSE SHE WON THE 'GOLDEN GLOBES' AWARD, SHE THINKS SHE'S GOT AN *I.Q.*

GIRL, YOU MAY *FIGHT* OKAY--

-- BUT YOU GOT YOUR-SELF ONE *LOUSY* PERSONALITY.

WE MAY *JOKE* AMONGST OURSELVES, BUT *NOT* LIKE THAT.

PLEASE DON'T FIGHT. SOMETIMES I THINK *MOST* OF YOU THINK THE SAME ABOUT ME.

BUT IT'S NOT TRUE. THE *ONLY* THINGS I'M IGNORANT OF ARE YOUR PLANET'S *CUSTOMS*.

YOU KNOW, THERE ARE TIMES I REALLY PREFER *MY* WORLD, WHERE *LOVE* IS WHAT'S IMPORTANT.

-- NOT YOUR DEGREE OF *EDUCATION*.

19

I'M SORRY I HAD TO GET *ANGRY*, BUT YOU'RE MY *FRIENDS*--

AND WE WEREN'T *ACTING* LIKE IT. NO, YOU'RE RIGHT, HONEY--

AND I ALSO THINK YOU'RE RIGHT ABOUT *TRIDENT*--

I GOT AN IDEA. SOMEONE GET ME HIS *PIG-STICKER*.

I THINK I CAN FIND US OUR *BAD GUYS*.

SOON, IN A DILAPIDATED HIGHRISE IN NEW YORK'S WEST EIGHTIES...

SNIFF WHAT'RE YEW SO *UPSET* ABOUT, PROF? NOW WE SPLIT THE LOOT *TWO WAYS!* AITCHOOO

THE IDEA OF SLAYING TRENT STILL *REPELS* ME.

HEY, C'MON-- HE WAS *HOLDING OUT* ON US.

TOLD US THAT BANK JOB ONLY GOT US *50* GRAND WHEN HE PULLED IN OVER *HUNDRED* THOU.

MAN, HE DESERVED GETTING IT STUCK TO HIM. *AITCHOO!*

BLAST IT. YOU'RE SO GOOD *INVENTING* STUFF, DO SOMETHIN' ABOUT *COLDS*, HUH?

IF I COULD, I'D GO *STRAIGHT*.

BUT ALL I'VE EVER BEEN USEFUL FOR IS INVENTING *WEAPONS* FOR THE *H.I.V.E.*

NO MORE OF THAT, EH? NOW WE'RE *FREELANCE!* AND WE'RE DOIN' JUST *FINE*.

YOU WOULDN'T WANNA *BET* ON THAT, WOULDJA, *GOOFBALL*?

WH-WHAT?

OH, MY--

AW, THEY CAN'T FIGGER OUT HOW WE *FOUND* 'EM.

YEAH, RUSTY TRACED YOU THROUGH THE *RADIO-WAVES* IN THAT DEAD-GUY'S *PITCHFORK*.

IT'S *OVER*, BOYS. YOU MAY AS WELL COME *PEACEFULLY*.

WATCH OUT, ONE OF THEM'S GOING FOR HIS *WEAPON!*

20

THAT'S WHAT I *NEEDED*.

BUDDY, IT'S ALL *OVER!*

STAY BACK. I WARN YOU. WE HAVE CAPABILITIES YOU KNOW *NOTHING* OF.

I'VE HEARD HOW *POWERFUL* YOU ARE. I CAN'T WAIT TO SEE IF IT'S *TRUE*.

BECAUSE IF IT ISN'T, YOU'RE GOING TO SEE HOW POWERFUL *I* CAN BE.

AN *ICE BLAST?*

HARDLY EFFECTIVE AGAINST SOMEONE WHO'S *POWER* COMES FROM THE *SUN!*

NOW, COME HERE...

SKRAAK!

TOO LATE, BEAUTIFUL-- *WONDY'S* GOT 'IM.

YOU'RE WRONG... WHEN I'M PREPARED, I CAN'T BE *TOUCHED*.

JUST LIKE I THOUGHT WHEN I EXAMINED THAT *TRIDENT*. YOU'RE *NOT* GOING THROUGH HIM.

SOMETHIN' ONLY *I* CAN SEE WITH MY *INFRARED* EYE.

HE'S GOT NO *SPECIAL POWERS*--

21

--HE'S JUST *PROJECTING* HIS IMAGE, FROM *BEHIND* YOU.!

HERA! HE SEEMS SO *REAL*...

YOU GOTTA BE CRAZY. *I* DON'T SEE ANYTHING.

WHERE *IS* HE?

DON'T LET YOUR *LETTUCE WILT*, LOGAN-- I'LL *SHOW* YA.

KRUNCH!

WITHOUT HIS TRIDENT BLOCKING ONE IMAGE WHILE *CREATING* ANOTHER--

--HE BECOMES *VISIBLE* AGAIN.

THAT HE DOES, RUSTY. HI, GUY. MY NAME'S *CHANGELING*.

YOU'RE GONNA TELL US *EVERYTHING.*

AREN'T YA?

YES, YES, DON'T *EAT* ME. I WILL TALK.

HOW COULD YOU *SLAY* A FRIEND FOR *MONEY?*

HEY, HE *LIED*... WHAT ELSE COULD WE ... WE ... WE ...

AITCHOOO!

YOU COULD TAKE YOUR-SELF *SOME COLD PILLS*, AND GET A NICE *LONG* REST...

...FOR ABOUT *TEN TO TWENTY YEARS.*

PROLOGUE:

THEY CREEP ACROSS THE GREAT LAWN, SILENT AS BIRDS IN FLIGHT, THEN PAUSE BENEATH THE PICTURE WINDOW...

NO WORDS ARE EXCHANGED...

...YET EACH KNOWS WHAT THE OTHER IS THINKING.

THEY WAIT...

THEN...

NOW!!

SKRASSHH!

155

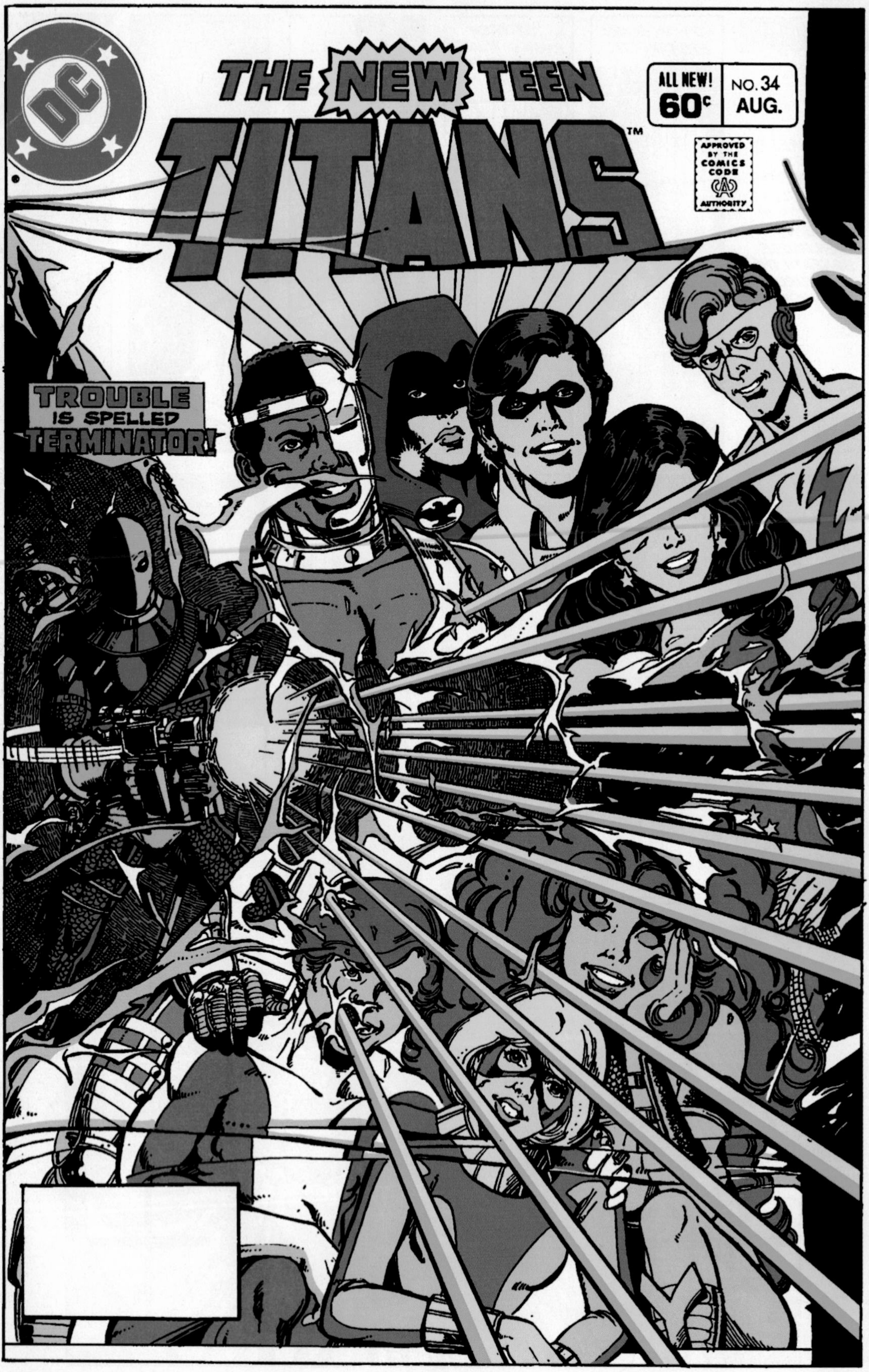

THE NEW TEEN
TITANS™
ALL NEW! 60¢
NO. 34 AUG.
APPROVED BY THE COMICS CODE AUTHORITY
TROUBLE IS SPELLED TERMINATOR!

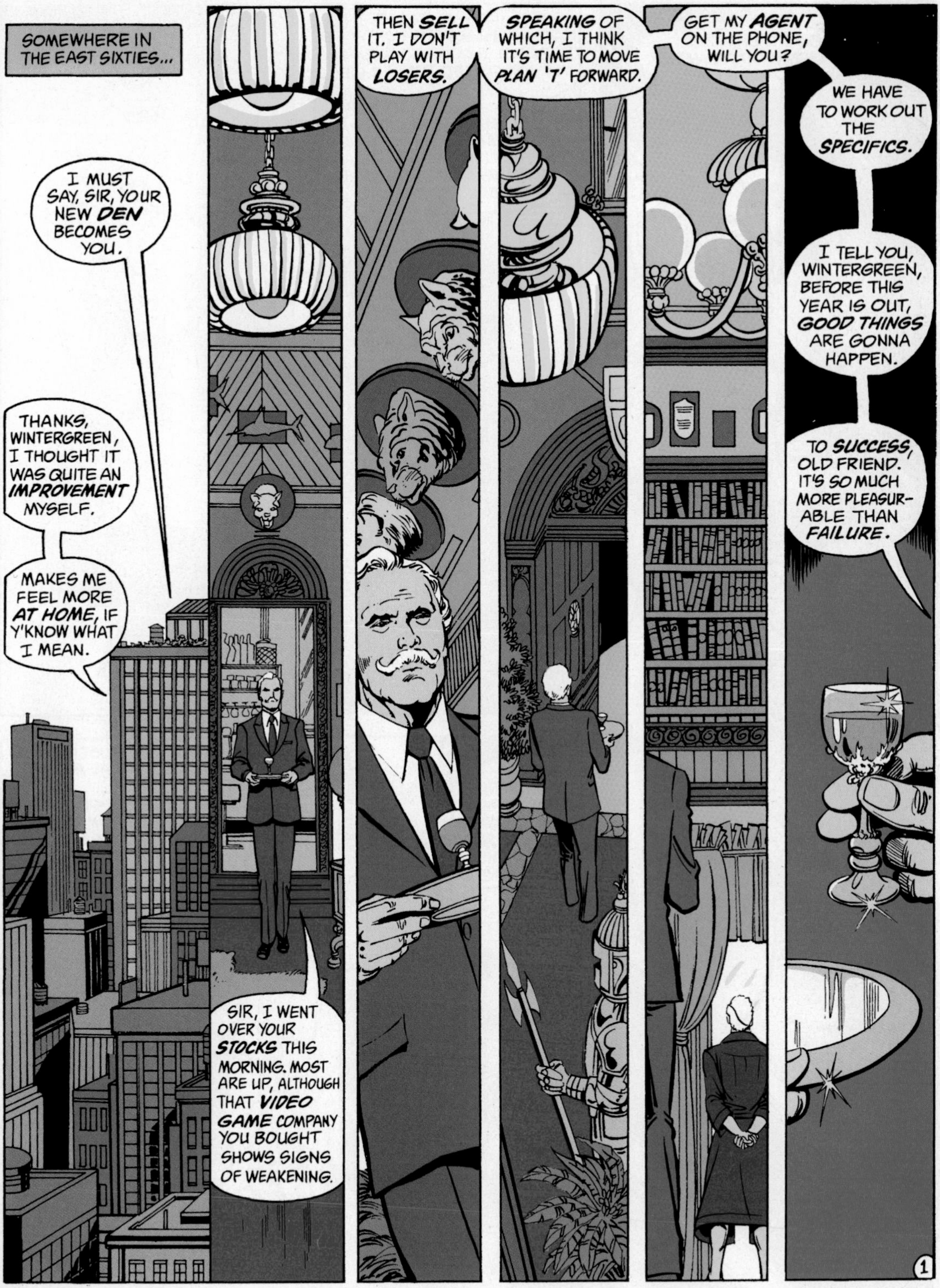
SOMEWHERE IN THE EAST SIXTIES...
I MUST SAY, SIR, YOUR NEW DEN BECOMES YOU.
THANKS, WINTERGREEN, I THOUGHT IT WAS QUITE AN IMPROVEMENT MYSELF.
MAKES ME FEEL MORE AT HOME, IF Y'KNOW WHAT I MEAN.
SIR, I WENT OVER YOUR STOCKS THIS MORNING. MOST ARE UP, ALTHOUGH THAT VIDEO GAME COMPANY YOU BOUGHT SHOWS SIGNS OF WEAKENING.
THEN SELL IT. I DON'T PLAY WITH LOSERS.
SPEAKING OF WHICH, I THINK IT'S TIME TO MOVE PLAN 'T' FORWARD.
GET MY AGENT ON THE PHONE, WILL YOU?
WE HAVE TO WORK OUT THE SPECIFICS.
I TELL YOU, WINTERGREEN, BEFORE THIS YEAR IS OUT, GOOD THINGS ARE GONNA HAPPEN.
TO SUCCESS, OLD FRIEND. IT'S SO MUCH MORE PLEASUR-ABLE THAN FAILURE.
1

BUT THEN, *THE TERMINATOR* NEVER FAILS!

HIS NAME IS *SLADE WILSON,* SEEMINGLY A BUSINESSMAN UPON WHOM SUCCESS ALWAYS SEEMS TO SHINE. BUT WILSON'S STOCK-IN-TRADE IS NEITHER TANGIBLE GOODS NOR INFORMATIONAL SERVICES. FOR YOU SEE, SLADE WILSON IS A *MERCENARY,* AND HE IS THE VERY *BEST* AT WHAT HE DOES.

AS YOU KNOW, WINTERGREEN, I HAVE SEVERAL *NEW* CONTRACTS TO BEGIN, THOUGH I HAVEN'T YET COMPLETED THE H.I.V.E. AFFAIR.

THE TEEN TITANS ARE STILL *ALIVE,* AND AS LONG AS THEY LIVE, THEY'LL BE A *BLEMISH* ON MY OTHERWISE SPOTLESS REPUTATION.

THEN YOU'LL BE NEEDING YOUR *UNIFORM?*

OF COURSE.

AH, WINTERGREEN, SOMETIMES I FEEL I MAY BE GETTING *OLD...* I KEEP THINKING OF ADELINE. THOSE WERE *GOOD* DAYS, WEREN'T THEY?

THE *BEST,* SIR. MRS. WILSON WAS AN EXCELLENT WOMAN.

NOT TO MENTION ONE HELLUVA *MARKSMAN.* OH WELL, THE *PAST* IS.... PAST.

WE MUST ALL LIVE FOR THE *FUTURE.*

STILL, SOMETIMES IT IS GOOD TO *REMEMBER.*

2

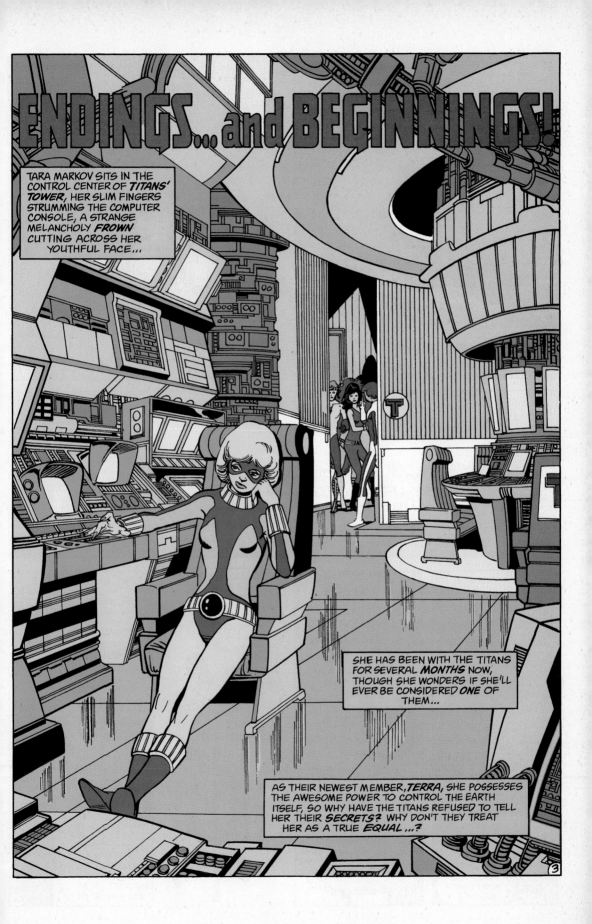

ENDINGS... and BEGINNINGS!

TARA MARKOV SITS IN THE CONTROL CENTER OF *TITANS' TOWER,* HER SLIM FINGERS STRUMMING THE COMPUTER CONSOLE, A STRANGE MELANCHOLY *FROWN* CUTTING ACROSS HER YOUTHFUL FACE...

SHE HAS BEEN WITH THE TITANS FOR SEVERAL *MONTHS* NOW, THOUGH SHE WONDERS IF SHE'LL EVER BE CONSIDERED *ONE* OF THEM...

AS THEIR NEWEST MEMBER, *TERRA,* SHE POSSESSES THE AWESOME POWER TO CONTROL THE EARTH ITSELF, SO WHY HAVE THE TITANS REFUSED TO TELL HER THEIR *SECRETS?* WHY DON'T THEY TREAT HER AS A TRUE *EQUAL*...?

TERRA?

YEAH? WHATTAYA WAN--?

WHAT IN BLAZES--?

SWEET SIXTEENTH, HONEY.

♪ HAPPY BIRTHDAY TO YOU, HAPPY BIRTHDAY HAPPY BIRTHDAY, DEAR TARA, HAPPY BIRTHDAY TO YOU!

GOOD EVENING, FRIENDS!

FOR ME? I-I'VE NEVER HAD A BIRTHDAY PARTY BEFORE.

I--I DON'T KNOW WHAT TO SAY.

THAT'S A FIRST.

WE THOUGHT YOU'D LIKE IT.

I HAD MY DAD'S CHEF PREPARE THE CAKE. YOU'LL LOVE IT.

SO WHAT'S BUGGIN' YA, SQUIRT?

OH, NOTHIN'S WRONG. I WAS JUST...THINKING OF SOMETHING.

HEY, THIS IS MY PARTY, RIGHT?

OKAY. THEN STAND BACK.

FESTIVITIES CONTINUE, THEN FINALLY...

HEY, WASN'T THAT GREAT? SEE, YOU'RE ONE OF US!

YEAH? THEN HOWCUM I DON'T HAVE MY OWN CHAIR IN THE MEETIN' ROOM OR HOWCUM YOU HAVEN'T TOLD ME WHO YOU REALLY ARE?

MEBBE YOU SAY I'M A TEEN TITAN, BUT I'LL BE DARNED IF YOU SHOW IT.

4

MEANWHILE, ON THE EASTERN TIP OF LONG ISLAND...

WHAM!

THUD!

BLAM

I DON'T LIKE THIS ONE BIT. WE HAD *NO RIGHT* BREAKING IN HERE...

CERTAINLY NO *LEGAL* RIGHT, NO MATTER HOW SCUMMY SCARAPELLI AND HIS THUGS MAY BE.

YET, CHASE *IS* A DISTRICT ATTORNEY, HE MUST KNOW WHAT HE'S *ALLOWED* TO DO...

...ASSUMING HE HASN'T GONE OVER THE *EDGE.*

YOUR GOONS ARE *USELESS,* SCARAPELLI.

NOTHING'S GOING TO KEEP YOU OUT OF PRISON-- *NOTHING!*

FOOM!

FATSTUFF, YOU'RE GOING TO *PAY* FOR YOUR CRIMES.

YOU GOT NO *RIGHT* BEING HERE.

YOU'RE TALKING ABOUT RIGHTS? MISTER, YOU'RE *SICK!*

KANK!

WHAT ABOUT THE RIGHTS OF ALL THOSE *KIDS* YOU PEDDLED YOUR DAMN *DRUGS* TO?

I-I DON'T KNOW WHAT YOU *MEAN,* CHASE. I'M AN *IMPORTER.*

I DON'T *PUSH* THAT STUFF. BUT THAT DON'T *MATTER*--YOU'RE INVADIN' MY HOME. I GOT THE *RIGHT* TO BLAST YOU.

YOU'RE *SHAKING,* SCARAPELLI...YOU USUALLY HAVE YOUR *GOONS* DO YOUR DIRTY WORK?

THAT'S IT FOR *BOTH* OF YOU. THE FIGHT'S *OVER.*

HEY!?!

BAM

SPIN

⑤

GET *OUTTA* HERE, CHASE. YOU DON'T HAVE NO *SEARCH* WARRANT.

WARRANT? YOU WANT A *WARRANT?* AMAZING HOW YOU CREEPS WANT ALL THE *LAWS* OBEYED WHEN *YOU'RE* IN TROUBLE.

HERE'S YOUR WARRANT.

Y-YOU STILL CAN'T *ARREST* ME, CHASE. YOU'RE NO *COP.*

YOU'RE RIGHT, *I'M* NOT,,,

...BUT ROBIN HERE IS *LEGALLY DEPUTIZED*...THAT'S WHY I BROUGHT HIM *WITH* ME.

ROBIN, YOUR *COLLAR*...

WHAT?

WE'LL TALK ABOUT THIS *LATER,* CHASE.

YOU'VE GOT *NOTHING* ON ME.

WRONG, TUBS, THE WARRANT'S FOR ANY *ILLEGAL GUNS.* I CHECKED, YOU DON'T HAVE A *LICENSE.*

YOU'RE *DEAD* CHASE ...YOU'RE A *DEAD* MAN!

WHEN YOU *PULLED* THAT PISTOL, YOU PUT YOURSELF IN *BIG TROUBLE.*

I'M *QUIVERIN'*, TUBS --ALL THE WAY DOWN TO MY *BOOTIES.*

WHILE, IN TITANS' TOWER,,,

Y'GOTTA UNDERSTAND, I DON'T *FEEL* LIKE I'M ONE OF YOU.

BUT YOU *ARE*, TERRA... WE REALLY *LIKE* YOU.

STARRY, YOU LIKE *EVERYONE.*

LOOK, Y'GOTTA REMEMBER WHAT I'VE *GONE* THROUGH THESE PAST COUPLE'A YEARS,,,

6

WE KNOW YOUR *PARENTS* WERE KILLED, BUT THAT'S NOT *UNIQUE* IN THIS GROUP.

MEBBE NOT, BUT HOW MANY OF *YOU* LIVED WITH TERRORISTS?

I WAS A *SLAVE* FOR ALMOST FIVE YEARS.

TERRA, WE HAVE *ALL* SURVIVED DIFFICULTIES.

THE WITCH IS *RIGHT,* KID.

YA GOTTA *ROLL* WITH THE BLOWS.

HEY, WHY DON'T WE JUST FILL HER IN ON *ALL* TITANS' STUFF?

WE *WILL*... SOON ENOUGH. AH, I'VE GOT TO *GO.*

ARE YOU MEETING *TERRY?*

I AM.

ARE YOU GOING TO *MARRY* HIM?

HONEY, I THINK I SHOULD LET *HIM* KNOW THAT FIRST.

BUT DON'T PUT AWAY THE *CHAMPAGNE.*

KID FLASH, HOW COME *YOU* DIDN'T JOIN US? TERRA DOESN'T TURN SIXTEEN *EVERY* DAY.

I DIDN'T *FEEL* LIKE IT, WONDER GIRL.

STILL HAVING PROBLEMS DECIDING WHAT TO *DO?*

NO. I THINK I'VE MADE UP MY *MIND.*

FRAN WAS RIGHT-- I DON'T *BELONG* HERE NOW. MAYBE I WILL LATER ON, BUT NOT *NOW.*

I'M GONNA *LEAVE.*

FL--WALLY, I THINK YOU'VE MADE THE *RIGHT* DECISION FOR YOU.

YOU'RE WELCOME TO COME BACK AT *ANY* TIME.

THANKS, DONNA... Y'KNOW, I ALWAYS ENJOY *TALKING* TO YOU.

YOU ALWAYS SEEM TO *KNOW* WHAT TO SAY AND DO.

7

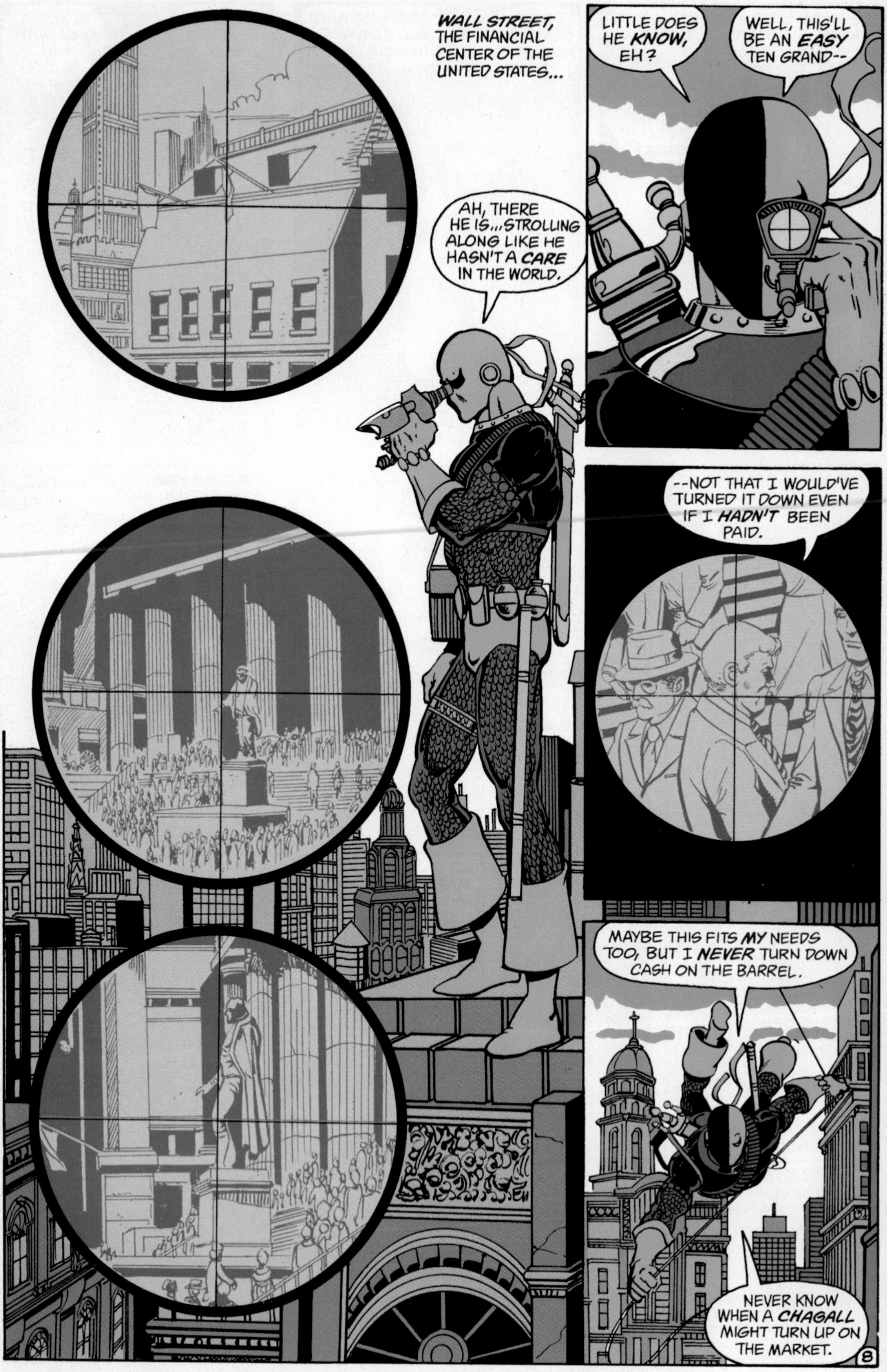
WALL STREET, THE FINANCIAL CENTER OF THE UNITED STATES...
LITTLE DOES HE KNOW, EH?
WELL, THIS'LL BE AN EASY TEN GRAND--
AH, THERE HE IS...STROLLING ALONG LIKE HE HASN'T A CARE IN THE WORLD.
--NOT THAT I WOULD'VE TURNED IT DOWN EVEN IF I HADN'T BEEN PAID.
MAYBE THIS FITS MY NEEDS TOO, BUT I NEVER TURN DOWN CASH ON THE BARREL.
NEVER KNOW WHEN A CHAGALL MIGHT TURN UP ON THE MARKET.
8

CITY COMMUNITY COLLEGE...

THE OTTOMAN RULE OVER *GREECE* IN THE EIGHTEENTH CENTURY CREATED MANY CHANGES.

THE TURKS SHIFTED THE PEOPLE AROUND THEIR EMPIRE AND THAT CAUSED MANY GREEKS TO *FLEE* TURKISH RULE AND RELOCATE IN *ITALY...*

BING4!

OKAY, THAT'S IT. CHAPTERS NINE AND TEN FOR *WEDNESDAY.*

AND REMEMBER, YOUR *PAPERS* ARE DUE THE END OF THE MONTH.

PROFESSOR LONG?

OH, SALLY... WHAT *IS* IT?

WELL, PROFESSOR, I'M HAVING A REAL *HARD TIME* WITH THIS AND WELL, I WAS WONDERING--

--DO YOU DO ANY *PRIVATE* TUTORING?

Uhhh... *PRIVATE*--?

YOU KNOW--YOU AND ME. OH, AND THE *GREEKS*, OF COURSE.

I'M *SORRY*, SALLY, I REALLY AM, BUT I MAKE IT A PRACTICE *NEVER* TO--

TERRY...

D-DONNA?

OH?

HI, HONEY.

YOU'RE WEARING THE RING.

THE *RING?*

DONNA, YOU'VE MADE ME THE *HAPPIEST* GUY IN THE WORLD.

SHORTLY... SO WHEN DO YOU WANT TO **DO** IT? WE CAN GET MARRIED **NOW** OR IN THE **FALL.**

HOW ABOUT **TOMORROW?**

WE CAN FLY TO **LAS VEGAS** TONIGHT.

STOP ME IF I'M MAKING A **FOOL** OF MYSELF.

IF YOU ARE, YOU'RE THE MOST **WONDERFUL** FOOL I'VE EVER KNOWN.

IT'S JUST THAT I DON'T WANT TO GET MARRIED **RIGHT AWAY.**

I NEED A **LITTLE** TIME TO SEE IF I CAN **FIND** MY TRUE PARENTS.

JUST A **FEW MONTHS?** PLEASE?

DONNA, AS LONG AS YOU NEED IS OKAY WITH **ME.**

YOU SEE, TIME ISN'T **IMPORTANT** NOW. WE'VE MADE A REAL **COMMITMENT** TO EACH OTHER THAT TIME WON'T CHANGE.

MISS TROY, I LOVE YOU TODAY, AND I'LL LOVE YOU TOMORROW, AND **WHATEVER** YOU WANT I'LL GO ALONG WITH IT... HAPPILY.

MEANWHILE, BACK AT THE TOWER...

CRIPES, NONE OF YOU **UNDERSTAND** ME.

I WANT A **DECISION NOW.** EITHER I'M A TITAN AND GET TO KNOW EVERYTHING, OR I **WALK.**

MEBBE I'LL SET UP A STOREFRONT AND **SELL** MY POWERS TO WHOEVER **PAYS** THE MOST.

I DON'T GIVE A **HOOT** ABOUT HOW YOU DID THIS OR THAT.

C'MON, BE **SERIOUS,** TERRA. GIVE US SOME **TIME...**

10

OKAY, YOU GOT ONE WEEK.

IF YOU BOZOS DON'T THINK I'M GOOD ENOUGH TO BE A TITAN BY THEN-- *I WALK!*

MEBBE THE JLA'LL HIRE ME.

TARA, YOU'RE THE *FIRST* NEW MEMBER WE'VE HAD SINCE WE BEGAN...

WE DON'T HAVE ANY *RULES* ABOUT ADDING PEOPLE.

AND YOU HAVE REFUSED TO ANSWER CERTAIN *QUESTIONS.*

LOOK WHO'S *TALKING.* YOU ALMOST *KILLED* YOUR BOYFRIEND--

--NOT TO MENTION ATTACKING EVERYONE ELSE, LADY, IF *ANYONE'S* HIDIN' SOMETHIN'--IT'S *YOU.*

KNOCK IT OFF. Y'KNOW, UNTIL YOU CAME ALONG WE *NEVER* FOUGHT...

IS *THAT* IT? YOU *WANT* ME TO LEAVE, DON'T YOU?

IT'S *ALWAYS* THE SAME. NOBODY EVER *WANTS* ME.

LORD, I CAN'T *TAKE* IT ANY MORE. I'VE BEEN KICKED OUTTA EVERYTHING I EVER REALLY WANTED.

TARA...LOOK, I'M *SORRY* I SAID THAT.

LOGAN, LEMME ALONE...

...PLEASE.

BZZZZ

SAVED BY THE PHONE BUZZER.

WHY DO I GET THE DREAD FEELING *EVERYTHING'S* FALLING APART?

I'M SURE *WALLY'S* GONNA LEAVE, RAVEN'S GOING *PSYCHO,* DICK HASN'T CALLED IN FOR *DAYS*...

TEEN TITANS HQ. BAD GUYS DON'T STAND A *CHANCE* WITH US!

OH, SARAH,,,. HOW'M *I?* HEY, WHEN YOU'RE PERFECTION ITSELF, THINGS DON'T *DARE* GO WRONG. WHAT'S *UP?*

GAR, PLEASE LET ME SPEAK TO VICTOR. IT'S *IMPORTANT.*

HOLD ON. I'LL BUZZ HIM IN THE *GYM.*

11

VIC, IT'S *SARAH*. SHE SAYS IT'S IMPORTANT.

I DON'T WANT TO *TALK* TO HER.

C'MON, RUSTHEAD, YOU TWO WERE TIGHTER'N CHARO'S *PANTS*.

SO WHY DIDN'T SHE TELL ME SHE WAS *ENGAGED?* FERGET IT, LOGAN--

--TELL HER I'M *BUSY*. TELL HER I'M OUT SAVIN' THE *WORLD*.

MY LIFE'S LOUSY ENUFF WITHOUT HEARIN' ANY MORE *LIES*.

ER, SARAH--I CAN'T GET VIC ON THE LINE. HE'S...UH... IN THE *LITTLE ROBOTS' ROOM*.

I'LL TELL HIM YOU *CALLED*.

YEAH, TAKE CARE OF *YOUR-SELF*, TOO.

AND, IN THE WEST-SIDE APARTMENT OF SARAH SIMMS...

WHO WERE YOU *CALLING?*

PLEASE, MARK--I'VE ASKED YOU TO GO.

YOU WERE CALLING THAT *BLACK* GUY, RIGHT? FORGET HIM, SARAH. WE'RE *ENGAGED*.

NO, WE'RE *NOT*--I CALLED THAT OFF *LAST* YEAR ...LONG BEFORE I MET *VIC*.

MARK, *LET GO* OF ME....

SINCE WE WERE *KIDS*, EVERYONE KNEW WE WERE GOING TO GET MARRIED.

YOU *CAN'T* CALL IT OFF.

WE *LOVE* EACH OTHER, SARAH.

FAM!

MARK, I WON'T *PUT UP* WITH THIS ANY LONGER. *LET GO!*

12

WE'RE *FINISHED*, MARK, AND IT'S BEEN FINISHED FOR OVER A YEAR.

DO ME A FAVOR, PLEASE--*STAY OUT OF MY LIFE!*

SARAH, I LOVE YOU.

SLAM

TOUGH COOKIE, EH?

NO, NOT SO TOUGH.

TITANS' TOWER...

OKAY, OKAY... I WON'T *QUIT* RIGHT AWAY.

BUT YOU DON'T UNDERSTAND WHAT BEING ACCEPTED AS A TITAN *MEANS* TO ME.

AS GREAT AS I AM, BEING *ALONE* STILL SCARES ME.

I KNOW WHAT IT MEANS TO *ME.*

TOO MANY PEOPLE I'VE CARED ABOUT HAVE DIED.

JUST THEN...

TEEN TITANS' *HEADQUARTERS?* I SURE HOPE I'VE GOTTEN THROUGH.

HUH? THE *VIEW SCREEN...* IT SUDDENLY BLINKED ON.

HIM?

TERMINATOR!

UHH, WHAT'S THE *WHO*'SINATOR?

THAT'S *TERMINATOR,* GIRL-- AS IN TERMINATING YOUR LIFE. DYING. KAPUT. DAISY PUSHING TIME.

SPEAKING OF WHICH, LOGAN, I SEE *YOU'VE* RECOVERED FROM OUR LAST MEETING.

SERVES ME RIGHT FOR NOT MAKING *SURE* YOU WERE DEAD.

WHICH IS PARTIALLY THE *REASON* FOR THIS CALL.

13

Y'SEE, I TOOK OUT A **CONTRACT** WITH THE **H.I.V.E.** TO KILL YOU. SO FAR I'VE--FAILED. I DO **HATE** THAT WORD FAILED.

ANYWAY, I'M ARRANGING A **TRADE.** YOU TITANS FOR THIS PITIFUL **STOCKBROKER.** I EITHER **KILL** YOU OR HIM.

WHO WILL IT **BE?**

YOU FILTH. I'LL TEAR YOU--

NO.

I'VE BEEN **LOOKING** FOR A WAY TO PROVE MYSELF.

ACKK!

WHAM!

I'M GONNA TAKE ON THIS CREEP--**ALONE!**

INSTANTS LATER, A WEDGE OF EARTH SOARS SKYWARD...

...AS TERRA'S FACE TURNS **GRIM,** THINKING ABOUT THE IMPORTANT MISSION AT HAND.

WHERE'S **SHE** OFF TO? MAYBE SHE'S FOUND SOMEONE SHE HASN'T **INSULTED** TODAY.

STRANGE KID.

HELP! STOP HER! DON'T LET HER **GO!**

LOGAN?

SOMETHING'S **WRONG.**

14

WALL STREET...

ACTUALLY, MY FRIEND, CONSIDER YOURSELF *LUCKY.*

IF THIS WERE AN *ORDINARY* HIT, YOU WOULD HAVE BEEN DEAD *LONG AGO.*

BUT, YOU SEE, I *NEED* YOU. DOESN'T IT FEEL *GOOD* TO BE NEEDED?

SOUNDS FROM *OUTSIDE?* I DO BELIEVE THEY'VE *COME.*

YOU HAVEN'T GUESSED *WRONG,* MISTER.

MEET --THE *NEWEST* TEEN TITAN.

FWAM!

KRASH!

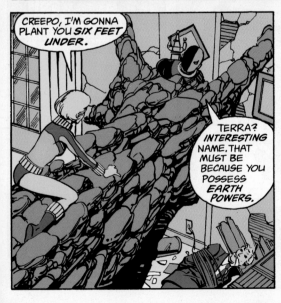

CREEPO, I'M GONNA PLANT YOU *SIX FEET UNDER.*

TERRA? INTERESTING NAME, THAT MUST BE BECAUSE YOU POSSESS *EARTH POWERS.*

THEY COULD PROVE QUITE *FORMIDABLE,* GIRL--

--*IF* I LET YOU *LIVE.*

FWAMM!

BUT THERE'S NO CHANCE OF *THAT!*

15

BUT...

THAT MOUNTAIN OF EARTH *LIFTED* YOU OUT OF THE WAY. NOT *BAD*--

GIRL, YOU'RE *BETTER* THAN I EXPECTED YOU'D BE--

--MEBBE EVEN BETTER THAN THOSE *OTHER* TITANS. BUT THAT WON'T *SAVE* YOU.

WANNA *BET*, ONE-EYE?

I-I *DID* IT. BLASTED THE GROUND *BELOW* 'IM...

IT SHOULD *CARRY* HIM OFF...

JUST HOPE I AIMED HIM AT THE *RIVER*... DON'T WANT HIM SPLATTERING ALL OVER THE *SIDEWALK.*

SHE *IS* GOOD... THIS WOULD PROBABLY *CRIPPLE* ANY ORDINARY MAN.

BUT I'M HARDLY *ORDINARY.*

MY BRAIN CAPACITY HAS BEEN INCREASED TO 90%--I'VE GOT *FULL* CONTROL OVER MY BODY.

NOBODY *ELSE* ON EARTH COULD EXECUTE THIS MOVE SO PERFECTLY.

TERMINATOR'S SWORD FLASHES OUT, IMBEDDING ITSELF IN THE STONE WALL OF THE HANDICOTT BUILDING...

16

172

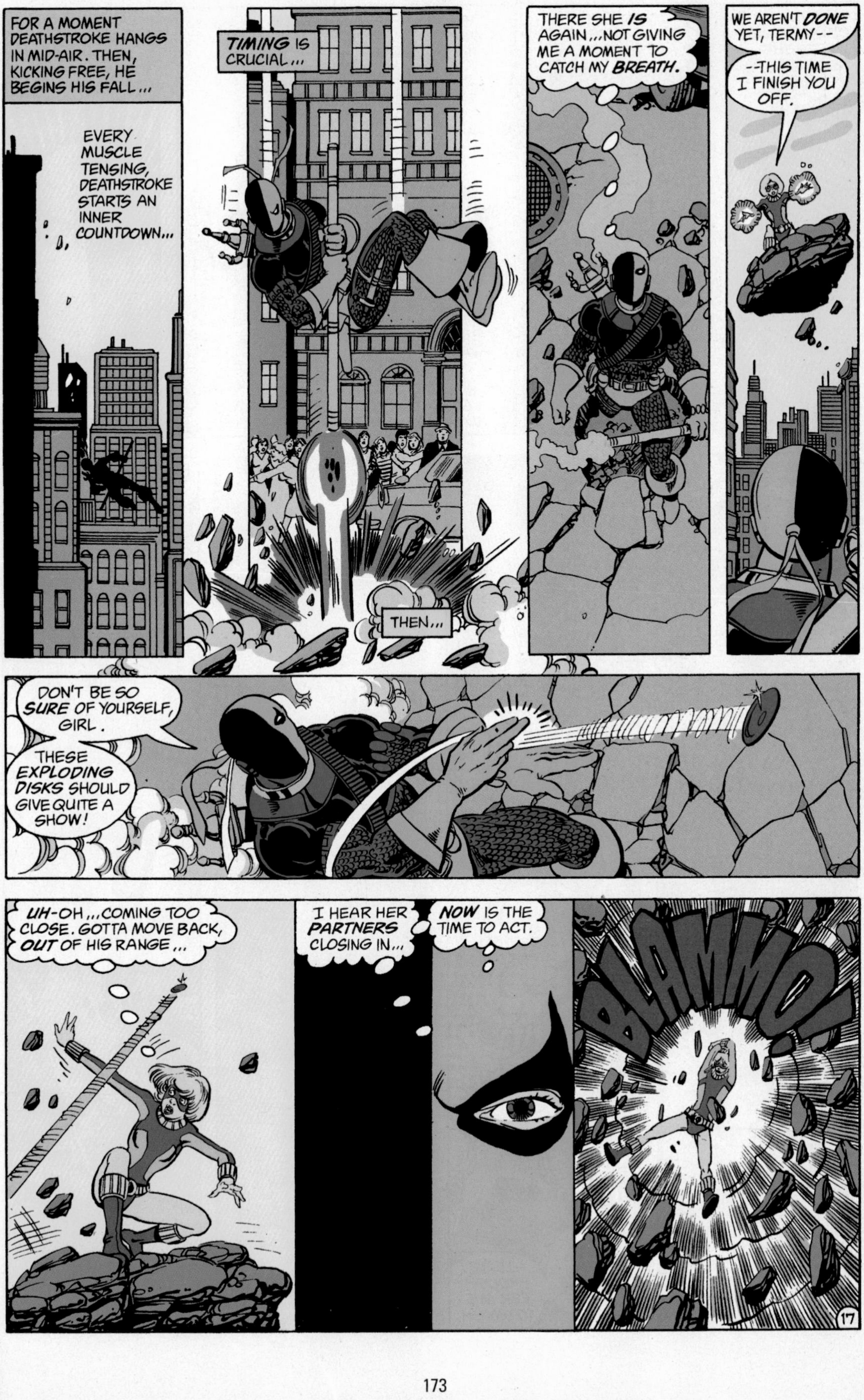
FOR A MOMENT DEATHSTROKE HANGS IN MID-AIR. THEN, KICKING FREE, HE BEGINS HIS FALL...
EVERY MUSCLE TENSING, DEATHSTROKE STARTS AN INNER COUNTDOWN...
TIMING IS CRUCIAL...
THEN...
THERE SHE IS AGAIN...NOT GIVING ME A MOMENT TO CATCH MY BREATH.
WE AREN'T DONE YET, TERMY--
--THIS TIME I FINISH YOU OFF.
DON'T BE SO SURE OF YOURSELF, GIRL.
THESE EXPLODING DISKS SHOULD GIVE QUITE A SHOW!
UH-OH...COMING TOO CLOSE. GOTTA MOVE BACK, OUT OF HIS RANGE...
I HEAR HER PARTNERS CLOSING IN...
NOW IS THE TIME TO ACT.
BLAMMO!
17

THIS IS IT... C'MON, TITANS... WHERE THE HECK **ARE** YOU?

I DIDN'T GET **THAT** MUCH OF A HEAD START.

HOLD IT... FEELING A SUDDEN **UPDRAFT.** I'M SLOWLY BEING **LOWERED.**

I DON'T **SEE** HIM, BUT I BET MY LAST DONUT **KID FLASH** IS DOWN THERE.

YAHOOO! IT WORKED!

WELL, I WAS **WONDERING** IF YOU'D SHOW UP.

WE'RE **HERE,** TERMINATOR.

AND THIS TIME WE'RE PLAYING FOR **KEEPS!**

SKREEEEE!

SHE'S NOT **KIDDING.** ONLY MY SUPER-FAST REFLEXES SAVED ME FROM HER **STARBOLT.**

DON'T TAKE 'IM ALL BY **YOURSELF,** STARRY--

--LEAVE ENOUGH FER **ME** TO SMASH.

KA-BLAM!

HOLD IT. HE'S **MINE.**

HE ALMOST **KILLED** ME. I STILL REMEMBER THE **PAIN.**

I WANT HIM.

BUT WHAT YOU **WANT,** CHANGELING--

18

--IS *NOT* WHAT YOU'RE *GETTING.*

F-WAMM!

THEY'VE BECOME A *REAL TEAM* SINCE WE LAST TANGLED.

CAN'T TAKE THEM ALL ON IN AN *OPEN* CONFRONTATION.

YOU ALL *RIGHT?*

I *THINK* SO. THANKS, FLEET-FEET. YOU SAVED MY *LIFE.*

YOU WOULD'VE DONE THE SAME FOR ME.

IT'S *ALWAYS* THIS WAY--ALWAYS FIGHTING, ALWAYS WORRYING IF SOMEONE YOU CARE FOR WILL DIE OR... CHANGE.

I'VE *HAD* IT. I CAN'T PUT UP WITH THIS PRESSURE ANY LONGER.

SOMETHING *WRONG,* FLASH? YOU'RE *SLOWER* THAN I REMEMBERED.

HARDLY NEEDED MY *INCREASED* REFLEXES TO DOWN YOU.

OKAY, PALS AND GALS-- UNLESS YOU WANT KID FLASH HERE GRINNING OUT OF HIS *THROAT*--

--I SUGGEST YOU *BACK OFF.*

HE'LL *DO* IT.

LET ME *BLAST* HIM.

NO... CAN'T TAKE THE *CHANCE.*

YOU'RE BEING *SMART*... I'M GETTING AWAY-- *EH?*

THAT *S-SOUND?*

GRUMMBLE

19

A FIST OF EARTH? BLAST-- IT'S THAT *TERRA* GIRL.

I GOT *FLASH*...

I CAN STOP THE *OTHER* TITANS, BUT SHE KEEPS *GETTING* ME.

THEN WE CAN *MOVE IN*.

GIVE UP BEFORE I LET THAT HAND *CRUSH* YOU.

YOU'RE *GOOD*, GIRL, BETTER THAN ALL THE OTHERS.

BUT I STILL GOT MY *POWER STAFF*...

NOBODY CAPTURES THE TERMINATOR. *NOBODY!*

SK-B-L-A-M-M!

H-HE'S *GONE?* HE BLEW HIMSELF UP?

NO TROUBLE FIGGERIN' *THIS* GAME'S *MOST VALUABLE PLAYER*.

B-BUT I *LOST HIM*.... HE WAS IN MY *HANDS* AND HE GOT AWAY.

I-- *FAILED*.

NOPE. YOU SAVED MY *LIFE*, TERRA.

WELL, YOU SAVED *MINE*.

AND YOU'VE REALLY *PROVEN* YOURSELF. YOU *ARE* A TITAN.

I--I AM?

YOU *BET*, KID.

HEY, ARE YOU *OKAY?*

Y-YEAH.... I GUESS I'M STILL A LITTLE *STUNNED*.

I GOTTA *DO* SOMETHING.... I-I'LL SEE YOU GUYS *LATER*.

20

SHE REALLY FOUGHT HERSELF THE *GOOD FIGHT*.

I *TOLDJA* SO. IS SHE *OKAY* NOW?

I'D CERTAINLY VOTE SO.

THAT'S IT, THEN. WE TELL HER EVERYTHING-- *TOMORROW*.

BROOKLYN, NEW YORK...

TARA MARKOV HAD BROUGHT GAR LOGAN HERE TO THIS TENEMENT WHERE, SHE SAID, SHE HAD BEEN HELD *CAPTIVE* BY TERRORISTS...

NOW SHE RETURNS, A BIT *FORLORN*.

HOW HER *LIFE* HAS CHANGED...

TERRA.

HUH? *YOU*?

WHY SO SURPRISED, TERRA? YOU *KNEW* WE'D BE TALKING.

YEAH, JUST THOUGHT *I'D* GET HERE FIRST.

HOW DID IT *GO*?

PERFECT. THEY SWALLOWED *EVERYTHING*.

THEY DIDN'T KNOW IT'S ALL BEEN A *SET-UP*.

THEY DIDN'T SUSPECT THE *TERRORISTS* WORKED FOR YOU.

THEY DON'T SUSPECT THAT I'VE BEEN *PLANTED* IN THEIR STUPID GROUP.

21

177

AND THEY CERTAINLY DIDN'T SUSPECT OUR WHOLE *FIGHT* WAS WORKED OUT IN ADVANCE.

TERMINATOR, YOU PULLED OFF A CONVINCING *DEATH.*

I COULDN'T HAVE DONE IT WITHOUT THE *SAFETY TUNNEL* YOU CHANNELED.

I THINK THEY'RE GOING TO TELL ME THEIR *SECRETS* AT OUR NEXT FULL MEETING.

EXCELLENT. THEN THE TEEN TITANS ARE AS GOOD AS *DEAD!*

UPTOWN IN MANHATTAN...

I'M FED UP, CHASE-- YOU *USED* ME.

TO PUT SCARAPELLI BEHIND BARS I *BENT* A FEW LAWS.

MY GOD -- IF YOU HAD A *WARRANT,* WE DIDN'T NEED TO BREAK IN LIKE THAT.

I WANTED SCARAPELLI TO KNOW HE COULDN'T *ESCAPE* ME.

BUT YOU'RE A *DISTRICT ATTORNEY.* YOU'RE SUPPOSED TO *OBEY* THE LAW.

THE LAW IS *USELESS.* ONLY *JUSTICE* COUNTS.

MY GOD. AND I THOUGHT *THE BATMAN* WAS *OBSESSED.*

DON'T CALL ME *AGAIN,* CHASE.

IS IT *TRUE,* ADRIAN? DID YOU BREAK THE *LAW?*

DORIS, *SCARAPELLI* BROKE THE LAW AND HE WAS *RELEASED.*

I HAD TO FORCE HIS *HAND.*

ADRIAN, I'M *WORRIED.*

DON'T BE, HONEY. I'D NEVER DO ANYTHING *WRONG.* OR ANYTHING THAT WOULD *HURT* YOU.

22

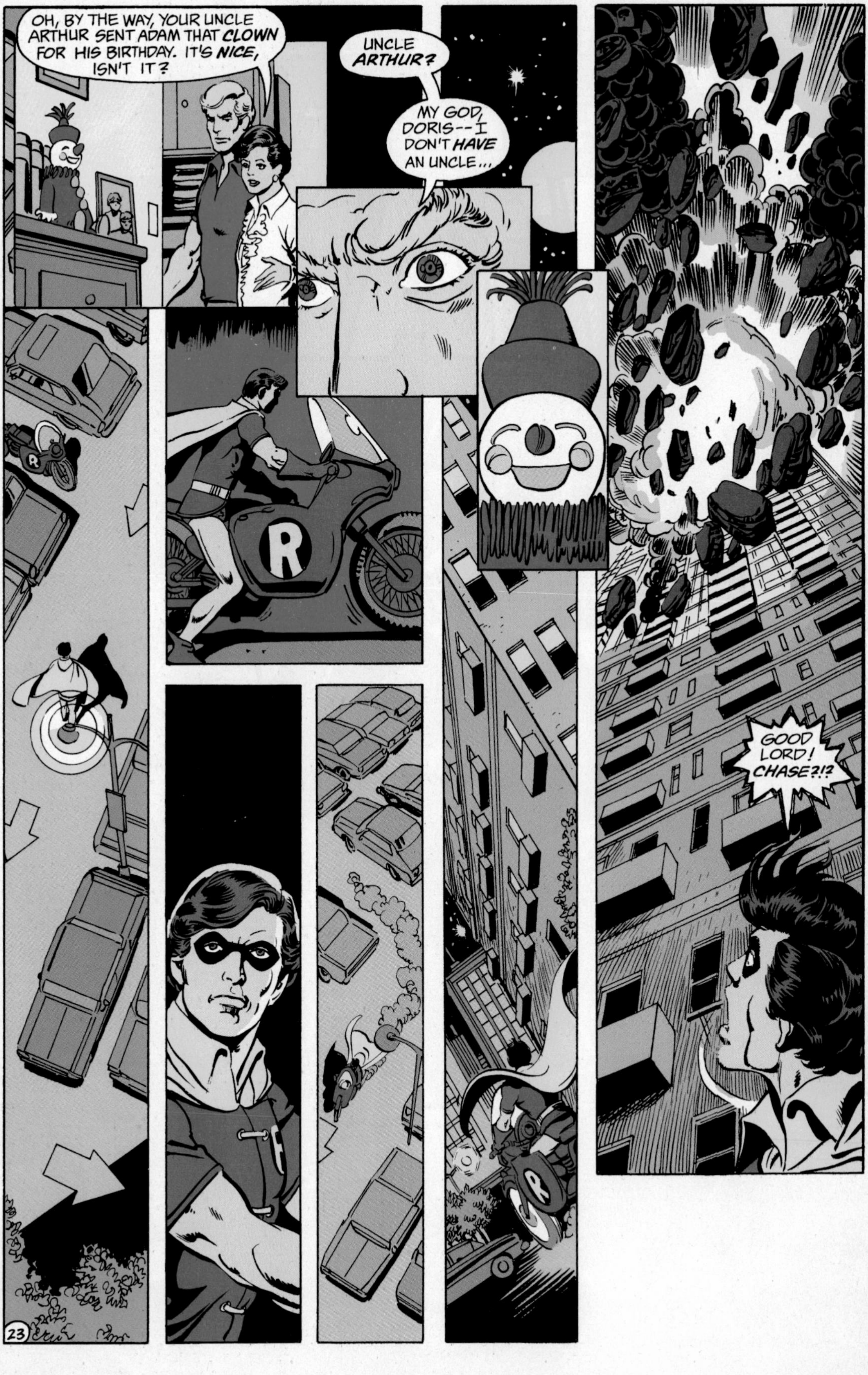
OH, BY THE WAY, YOUR UNCLE ARTHUR SENT ADAM THAT CLOWN FOR HIS BIRTHDAY. IT'S NICE, ISN'T IT?
UNCLE ARTHUR?
MY GOD, DORIS--I DON'T HAVE AN UNCLE...
GOOD LORD! CHASE?!?
23

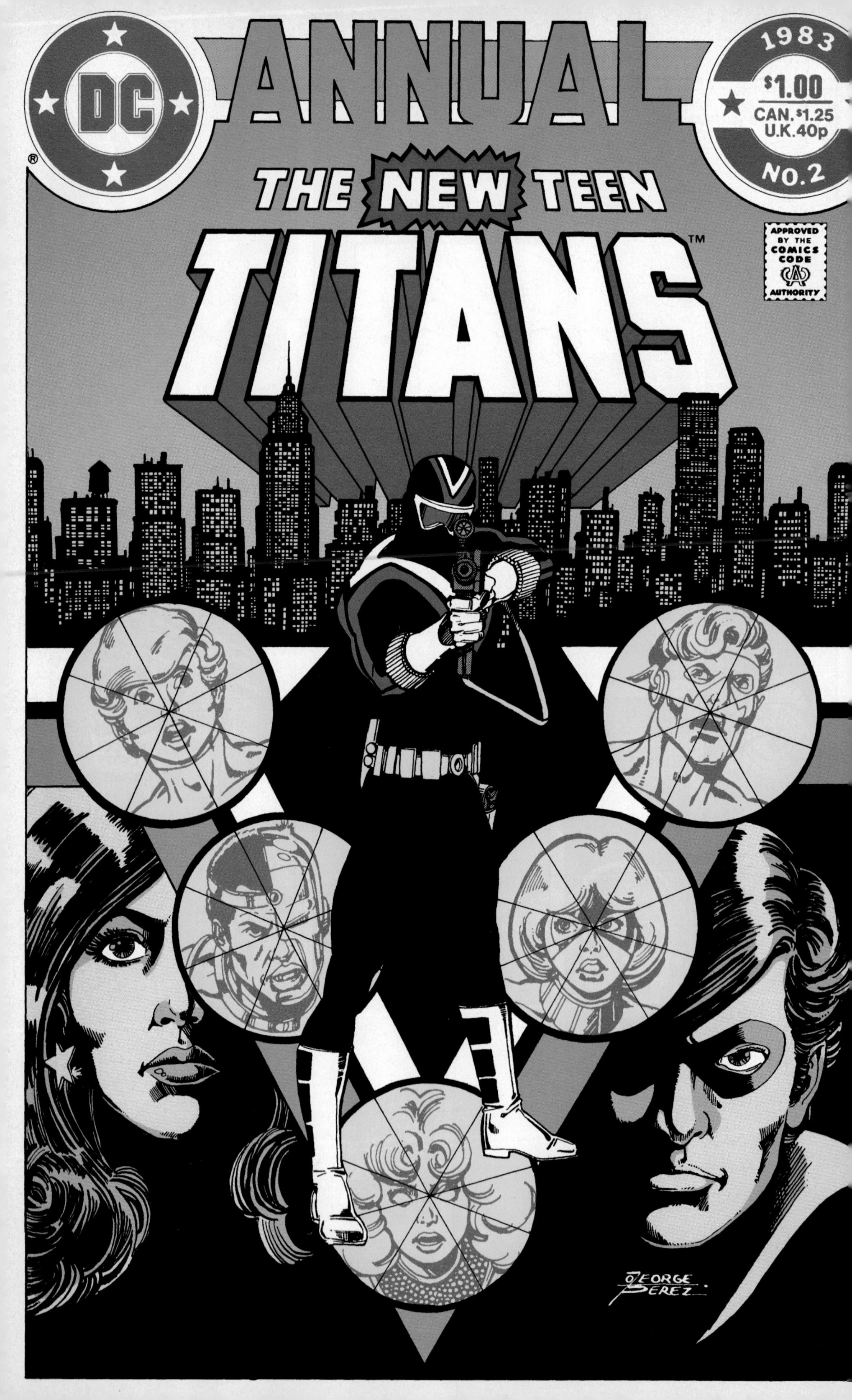

DC
ANNUAL
1983
$1.00
CAN.$1.25
U.K.40p
NO.2
THE NEW TEEN
TITANS™
APPROVED BY THE COMICS CODE AUTHORITY
GEORGE PEREZ

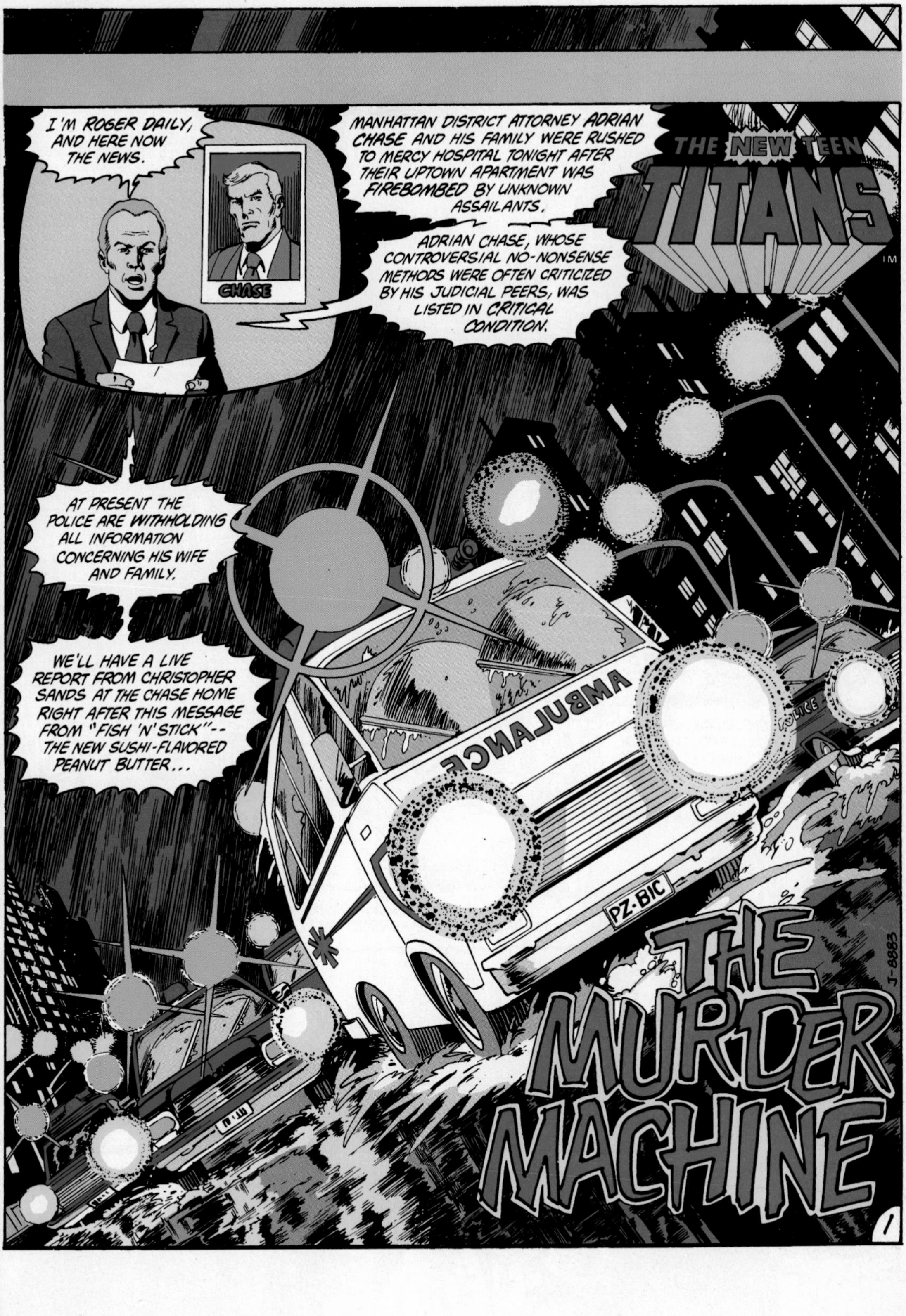
THE NEW TEEN TITANS
I'M ROGER DAILY, AND HERE NOW THE NEWS.
CHASE
MANHATTAN DISTRICT ATTORNEY ADRIAN CHASE AND HIS FAMILY WERE RUSHED TO MERCY HOSPITAL TONIGHT AFTER THEIR UPTOWN APARTMENT WAS FIREBOMBED BY UNKNOWN ASSAILANTS.
ADRIAN CHASE, WHOSE CONTROVERSIAL NO-NONSENSE METHODS WERE OFTEN CRITICIZED BY HIS JUDICIAL PEERS, WAS LISTED IN CRITICAL CONDITION.
AT PRESENT THE POLICE ARE WITHHOLDING ALL INFORMATION CONCERNING HIS WIFE AND FAMILY.
WE'LL HAVE A LIVE REPORT FROM CHRISTOPHER SANDS AT THE CHASE HOME RIGHT AFTER THIS MESSAGE FROM "FISH 'N' STICK"-- THE NEW SUSHI-FLAVORED PEANUT BUTTER...
AMBULANCE
PZ-BIC
POLICE
THE MURDER MACHINE
J-8883
1

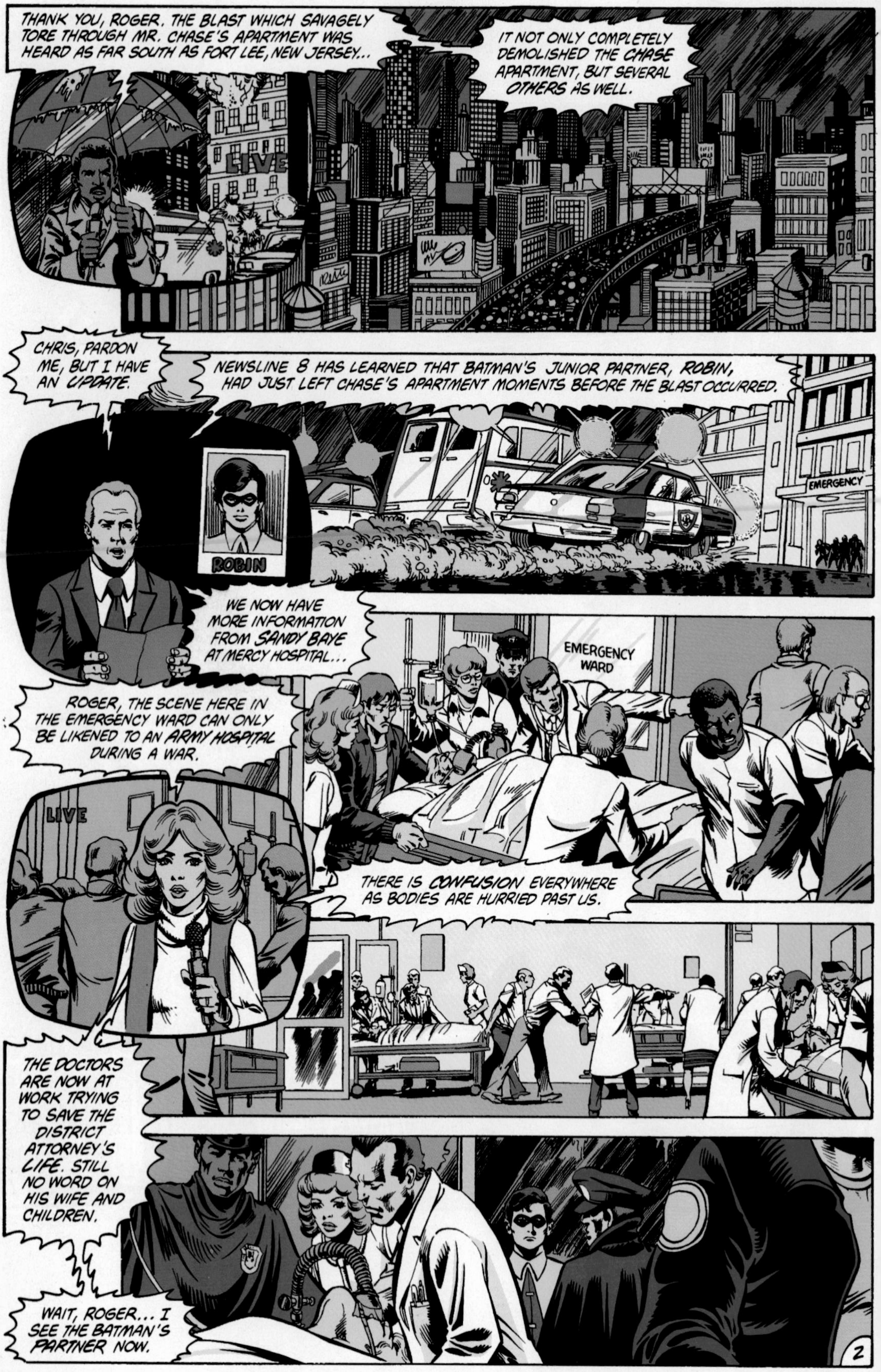
THANK YOU, ROGER. THE BLAST WHICH SAVAGELY TORE THROUGH MR. CHASE'S APARTMENT WAS HEARD AS FAR SOUTH AS FORT LEE, NEW JERSEY...
IT NOT ONLY COMPLETELY DEMOLISHED THE CHASE APARTMENT, BUT SEVERAL OTHERS AS WELL.
LIVE
CHRIS, PARDON ME, BUT I HAVE AN UPDATE.
NEWSLINE 8 HAS LEARNED THAT BATMAN'S JUNIOR PARTNER, ROBIN, HAD JUST LEFT CHASE'S APARTMENT MOMENTS BEFORE THE BLAST OCCURRED.
ROBIN
EMERGENCY
WE NOW HAVE MORE INFORMATION FROM SANDY BAYE AT MERCY HOSPITAL...
EMERGENCY WARD
ROGER, THE SCENE HERE IN THE EMERGENCY WARD CAN ONLY BE LIKENED TO AN ARMY HOSPITAL DURING A WAR.
LIVE
THERE IS CONFUSION EVERYWHERE AS BODIES ARE HURRIED PAST US.
THE DOCTORS ARE NOW AT WORK TRYING TO SAVE THE DISTRICT ATTORNEY'S LIFE. STILL NO WORD ON HIS WIFE AND CHILDREN.
WAIT, ROGER... I SEE THE BATMAN'S PARTNER NOW.
2

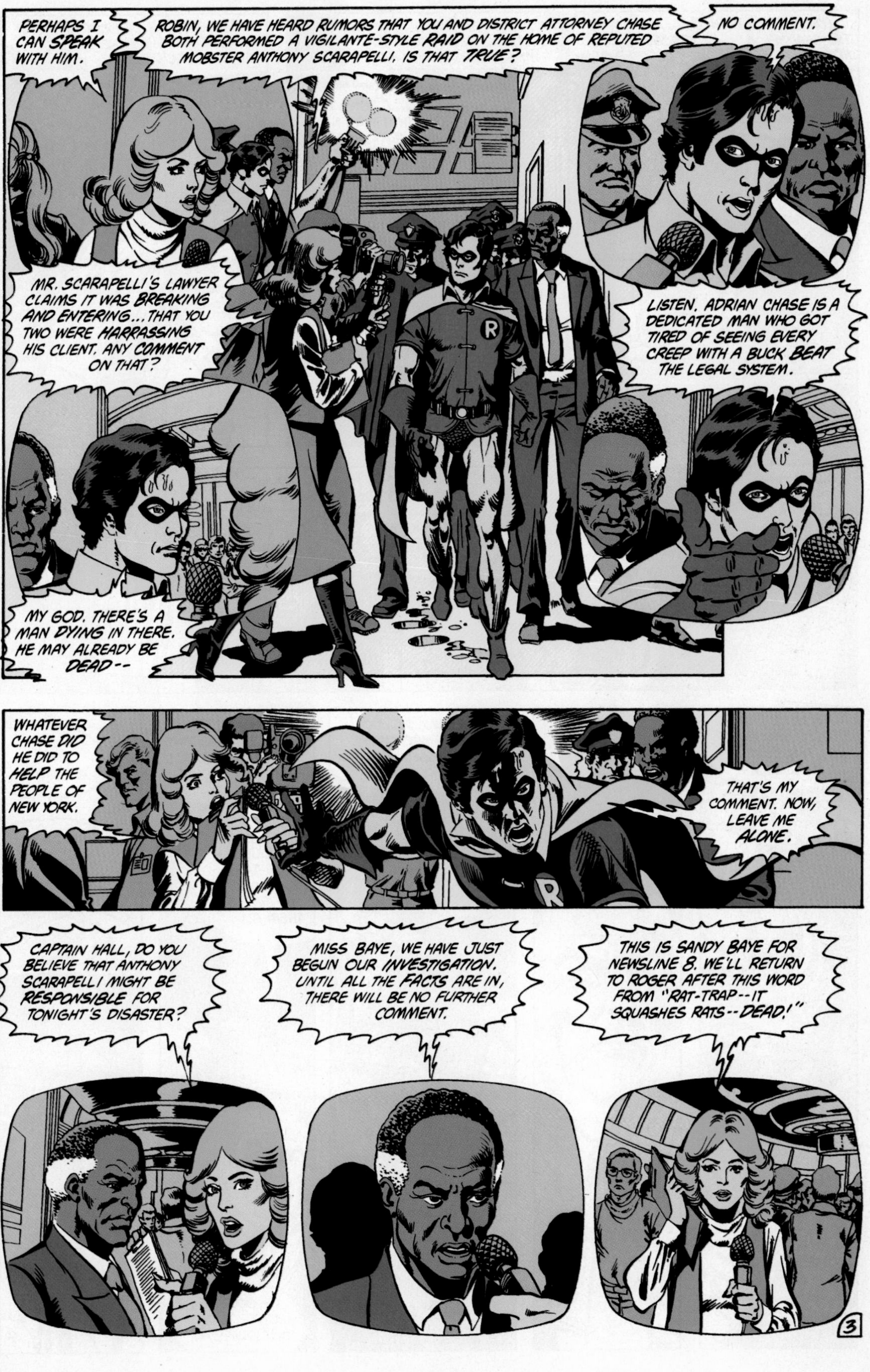
PERHAPS I CAN SPEAK WITH HIM.
ROBIN, WE HAVE HEARD RUMORS THAT YOU AND DISTRICT ATTORNEY CHASE BOTH PERFORMED A VIGILANTE-STYLE RAID ON THE HOME OF REPUTED MOBSTER ANTHONY SCARAPELLI. IS THAT TRUE?
NO COMMENT.
MR. SCARAPELLI'S LAWYER CLAIMS IT WAS BREAKING AND ENTERING... THAT YOU TWO WERE HARRASSING HIS CLIENT. ANY COMMENT ON THAT?
LISTEN. ADRIAN CHASE IS A DEDICATED MAN WHO GOT TIRED OF SEEING EVERY CREEP WITH A BUCK BEAT THE LEGAL SYSTEM.
MY GOD. THERE'S A MAN DYING IN THERE. HE MAY ALREADY BE DEAD--
WHATEVER CHASE DID HE DID TO HELP THE PEOPLE OF NEW YORK.
THAT'S MY COMMENT. NOW, LEAVE ME ALONE.
CAPTAIN HALL, DO YOU BELIEVE THAT ANTHONY SCARAPELLI MIGHT BE RESPONSIBLE FOR TONIGHT'S DISASTER?
MISS BAYE, WE HAVE JUST BEGUN OUR INVESTIGATION. UNTIL ALL THE FACTS ARE IN, THERE WILL BE NO FURTHER COMMENT.
THIS IS SANDY BAYE FOR NEWSLINE 8. WE'LL RETURN TO ROGER AFTER THIS WORD FROM "RAT-TRAP--IT SQUASHES RATS--DEAD!"
3

...LORNA TOLLE WITH THE CHANNEL 6 HOTLINE. INVESTIGATION ON THE ATTACK OF NEW YORK DISTRICT ATTORNEY ADRIAN CHASE CENTERS ON THIS MAN...

A. SCARAPELLI

...ANTHONY SCARAPELLI, A REPUTED MEMBER OF THE NEW YORK MAFIA.

ALTHOUGH MR. SCARAPELLI HAS NOT BEEN CHARGED, MY SOURCES IN CITY HALL SAY AN INDICTMENT IS FORTHCOMING.

TONY, TONY, THAT WAS NOT VERY GOOD WHAT YOU DID.

RUBBING OUT A DISTRICT ATTORNEY WITHOUT ADVISING THE FAMILY IS TROUBLE.

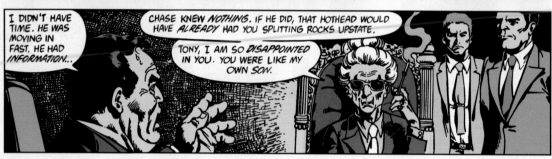

I DIDN'T HAVE TIME. HE WAS MOVING IN FAST. HE HAD INFORMATION...

CHASE KNEW NOTHING. IF HE DID, THAT HOTHEAD WOULD HAVE ALREADY HAD YOU SPLITTING ROCKS UPSTATE.

TONY, I AM SO DISAPPOINTED IN YOU. YOU WERE LIKE MY OWN SON.

IT APPEARS I MUST BECOME INVOLVED WITH THIS DIRTY BUSINESS.

DONNA OMICIDIO, DO YOU REMEMBER WHAT WE DISCUSSED EARLIER? HIS RECORDS?

I DID NOT FORGET, DON GEORDAN. TONY, YOU WILL BRING ALL YOUR FILES TO ME, TONIGHT.

GODMOTHER, I CAN'T... IT WOULD-- UH TAKE TOO LONG TO GET THEM ALL.

OF COURSE, TONY...I AM NOT UNFAIR.

YOU HAVE UNTIL TOMORROW.

MORNING.

4

184

THIS JUST IN.

CHASE

1952 – 1983

UPDATE

DORIS CHASE, WIFE OF ADRIAN CHASE, AND HER TWO CHILDREN WERE DECLARED *DEAD*...

IT'S STRANGE, CAPTAIN HALL, BUT WHEN ADRIAN SHOWED ME HIS *SEARCH WARRANT*, I REALIZED HE WAS USING ME TO *COERCE* SCARAPELLI. HE OBVIOUSLY DIDN'T HAVE ENOUGH INFOR-MATION TO GET A *CONVICTION*.

WHY DID YOU GO ALONG WITH CHASE?

I GUESS I *BELIEVED* IN CHASE ...THOUGHT HE WANTED TO *HELP*.

MY PROBLEM IS I TEND TO *FOLLOW* MORE THAN I LEAD.

WHAT ARE YOU GOING TO DO ABOUT *SCARAPELLI?*

NOTHING... *YET*. WE HAVEN'T ANY *EVIDENCE* LINKING HIM WITH THE FIREBOMBING.

OH COME ON, DON'T GIVE ME THAT *GARBAGE*.

THIS IS *LOUSY*, HALL--DAMN *LOUSY*.

EXCUSE ME, ARE YOU ONE OF THE *TITANS?*

ENTERING THE HOSPITAL NOW ARE *THE NEW TEEN TITANS*. YES, I EVEN *RECOGNIZE* ONE OR TWO. I BELIEVE THAT'S *ROBOTMAN* COMING IN FIRST.

NO. I'M *SNOW WHITE*, AND THESE ARE MY *SEVEN DWARFS*. GET OUTTA MY *WAY*.

GAWD! THERE WERE MORE *REPORTERS* DOWN THERE THAN FLIES AROUND *LOGAN*.

WHAT HAPPENED, ROBIN? WE HEARD THE *REPORT*.

ARE ADRIAN AND DORIS *DEAD?*

HE *IGNORED* ME AGAIN...WHAT IS *WRONG*, DICK--? WHY DO YOU DO THIS TO ME?

GUYS, IT'S UP TO *US* TO GET SCARAPELLI.

I WANT HIM TO *PAY*.

5

185

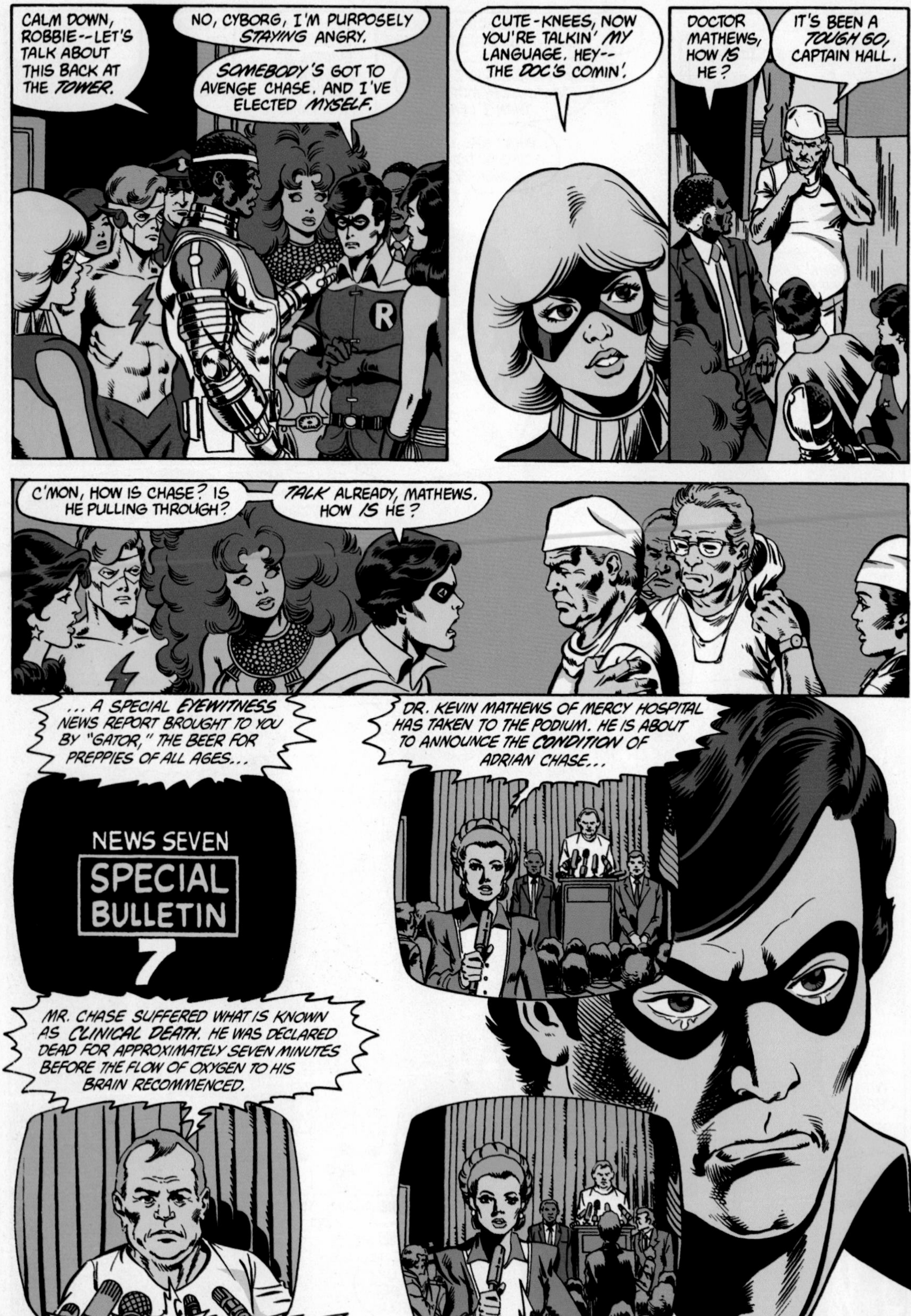
CALM DOWN, ROBBIE--LET'S TALK ABOUT THIS BACK AT THE TOWER.
NO, CYBORG, I'M PURPOSELY STAYING ANGRY.
SOMEBODY'S GOT TO AVENGE CHASE. AND I'VE ELECTED MYSELF.
CUTE-KNEES, NOW YOU'RE TALKIN' MY LANGUAGE. HEY-- THE DOC'S COMIN'.
DOCTOR MATHEWS, HOW IS HE?
IT'S BEEN A TOUGH GO, CAPTAIN HALL.
C'MON, HOW IS CHASE? IS HE PULLING THROUGH?
TALK ALREADY, MATHEWS. HOW IS HE?
... A SPECIAL EYEWITNESS NEWS REPORT BROUGHT TO YOU BY "GATOR," THE BEER FOR PREPPIES OF ALL AGES...
NEWS SEVEN
SPECIAL BULLETIN
7
DR. KEVIN MATHEWS OF MERCY HOSPITAL HAS TAKEN TO THE PODIUM. HE IS ABOUT TO ANNOUNCE THE CONDITION OF ADRIAN CHASE...
MR. CHASE SUFFERED WHAT IS KNOWN AS CLINICAL DEATH. HE WAS DECLARED DEAD FOR APPROXIMATELY SEVEN MINUTES BEFORE THE FLOW OF OXYGEN TO HIS BRAIN RECOMMENCED.
X-RAYS HAVE FURTHER REVEALED A PIECE OF SHRAPNEL LODGED JUST BELOW HIS HEART, TOO CLOSE TO OPERATE.
THIS IS ALLISON COOKE FOR EYEWITNESS NEWS. WE'LL RETURN AS MORE INFORMATION IS PASSED TO US.
6

THEY CAN'T *DO* THIS TO ME. OMICIDIO GETS MY FILES, I'M A *DEAD MAN.*

AWRIGHT. IT MEANS ME AGAINST THE GOD-MOTHER. BUT OMICIDIO ISN'T GOING TO TAKE THIS *LYING DOWN.*

SHE'S A *DANGEROUS WITCH.* I'M GONNA NEED *PROTECTION.*

WE HAVE ALWAYS SERVED YOU *FAITHFULLY,* MR. SCARAPELLI.

YEAH. I KNOW, GARROTE -- BUT FOR THIS I NEED SOME-THING *SPECIAL.*

I NEED -- *THE MONITOR!*

ELSEWHERE...

SIR...

...THE *FILES* YOU REQUESTED...

THANK YOU, LYLA...

MR. SCARAPELLI, YOU ARE ASKING FOR...

A *DOZEN* SPECIAL GUARDS... AND I NEED THEM *FAST.*

I'M SORRY. ACCORDING TO MY COMPUTER READ-OUT, I CAN LOCATE ONLY *HALF* THAT NUMBER.

ARE YOU STILL INTERESTED IN MY *REFERRAL SERVICE?*

OF COURSE, MONITOR -- GET ME AS MANY AS YOU *CAN.*

EXCELLENT. AS SOON AS THEY COMPLETE THEIR *CURRENT* ASSIGNMENTS, I'LL PUT THEM IN TOUCH WITH YOU...

...FOR MY *USUAL* COMMISSION.

7

ROGER DAILY FOR NEWS ELEVEN. THE PRELIMINARY HEARINGS FOR REPUTED MOBSTER ANTHONY SCARAPELLI BEGAN TODAY WITH THE CALLING OF BATMAN'S JUNIOR PARTNER, ROBIN, TO THE WITNESS STAND.

UNDER CROSS-EXAMINATION THE YOUTHFUL CRIME-FIGHTER APPEARED UNCERTAIN AND CONFUSED.

HE ADMITTED TO JOINING FORMER DISTRICT ATTORNEY CHASE ON A VIGILANTE-STYLE RAID ON SCARAPELLI'S HAMPTONS' ESTATE...

...AND BECAME ABUSIVE WHEN QUESTIONED ON HIS CONDONING OF VIGILANTE-STYLE JUSTICE.

MR. SCARAPELLI'S LAWYER, CARLO GIONETTI, HAS RECEIVED A COURT ORDER PREVENTING ROBIN FROM HARASSING HIS CLIENT IN THE FUTURE.

IN THE MEANTIME, ADRIAN CHASE HAS LEFT THE COUNTRY TO RECUPERATE.

THERE IS NO INFORMATION AS TO WHERE MR. CHASE HAS GONE, AND NOW A WORD FROM "TWEET"! THE BIRD-FLAVORED CAT FOOD.

CAFE ITALIA, SOMETIME LATER...

BENITO, FETTUCINE ALFREDO AND YOUR FINEST WINE.

NO, MAKE THAT YOUR FINEST CHAMPAGNE. WE CELEBRATE, EH, GARROTE?

YES, SIR.

TONY, WE'LL REALLY CELEBRATE TONIGHT, HUH, HONEY?

GARROTE, Y'FIND OUT WHERE CHASE WENT?

NO, SIR. EITHER NO ONE KNOWS, OR NO ONE'S TALKING.

MAYBE HE DECIDED TO PUT EVERYTHING BEHIND HIM.

MAYBE HE HAS, BUT I HAVEN'T.

GEE, I THOUGHT HE WAS A BOY. BUT HE'S A MAN.

YOU COULD BE HELD IN CONTEMPT FOR THIS, PUNK.

YOU PEOPLE ARE IN CONTEMPT...

...OF THE HUMAN RACE.

YOU HAVE A COURT ORDER BARRING YOU FROM HARASSING MR. SCARAPELLI.

I SUGGEST YOU HONOR IT.

LEMME UNDER-STAND THIS, YOU WANT ME TO OBEY THE LAW?

I'D BE GLAD TO... RIGHT AFTER I LEAVE THIS MESSAGE. I'M WATCHING YOU, SCARAPELLI.

AND SOMEHOW... I'M GOING TO GET YOU.

I DON'T THINK SO, BOY. GINO!

I GOT 'IM, BOSS.

AN' I'M KICKIN' 'IM OUT ON HIS BUTT.

GOOD. I WAS COUNT-ING ON YOU MAKING THE FIRST MOVE.

BECAUSE I INTEND TO MAKE THE *LAST*.

SKRAKK

THAT *DOES* IT, KID.

I'LL HAVE YOU BEHIND BARS BY *DAWN*.

NO. I DON'T WANT ANY MORE *PUBLICITY*. WE'LL *FORGET* THIS, ROBIN--

--BUT *DON'T* SHOW UP NEAR ME *AGAIN*.

SCUM, I'M STICKING *CLOSER* TO YOU THAN PAINT TO A WALL.

AND I'M GOING TO HOUND YOU TILL YOU'RE WARMING THE *ELECTRIC CHAIR*.

ROBIN, PLEASE *STOP*.

WHAT ARE *YOU* DOING HERE.

MAKING SURE YOU DON'T DO SOMETHING YOU'LL LATER *REGRET*.

THIS ISN'T YOUR *BUSINESS*.

YOU'RE WRONG. I *LOVE* YOU, AND I KNOW YOU LOVE ME.

YOU'RE ALSO THE ONE WHO TOLD ME *I* HAD TO LEARN RESTRAINT.

NOW I THINK THE SHOE'S ON THE OTHER *FOOT*.

C'MON HOME.

SCARAPELLI, IT'S JUST *BEGINNING*.

10

WHY DID YOU BRING ME *HERE*?

SO YOU COULDN'T *LEAVE*.

DICK, PLEASE, I CARE FOR YOU TOO MUCH TO SEE YOU *DO* THIS TO YOURSELF.

I'M NOT DOING *ANYTHING*.

OH? THE DICK GRAYSON *I* FIRST MET WAS WARM, CARING... *FUN*.

THAT DOESN'T DESCRIBE YOU *NOW*.

THE *OTHERS* ALL SENSE IT, TOO. YOU'VE SHUT US ALL OUT OF YOUR LIFE.

YOU DON'T TELL US WHAT'S *WRONG*.

FOR X'HAL'S SAKE, DICK--WE ALL *CARE*. WE WANT TO *HELP* YOU.

A FEW *MONTHS* AGO YOU SHOWED YOU *LOVED* ME... I STILL WANT TO LOVE *YOU*.

STARFIRE, I... UHH...

DON'T TALK... PLEASE DON'T *TALK* ANY MORE.

RIGHT IN TARGET.

...BOY WONDER ATTACKS SUSPECTED MOBSTER AND CHERYL LADD TO PORTRAY MOTHER THERESA. MORE NEWS AND SPORTS AT ELEVEN...

THE SCARAPELLI MANSION...

NOK NOK

SIR, MR. SCARAPELLI TOLD ME *NOT* TO OPEN THE DOOR.

SECURITY REASONS, ANNA. I'LL GET IT.

MAMA MIA!

MR. SCARAPELLI!

DEAD? AS DILLINGER!

CHASE IS OUT OF THE COUNTRY. THAT MEANS ONLY THE *BATMAN* KID--WHAT'S-HIS-NAME-- DID THIS.

BUT, SIR, *KILLING'S* NOT HIS STYLE.

MEBBE NOW IT *IS*. I GOT TO *THINK* THINGS OUT.

I DON'T LIKE WHAT'S GOING *DOWN*.

OKAY, LOOK-- I KNOW THIS ISN'T MUCH TO GO ON, BUT IT'S ALL THE *INFO* I'VE GOT.

ROBIN, THIS IS PRIMARILY *CIRCUMSTANTIAL*. IT WON'T HOLD UP IN *COURT*.

CHASE AND I KNOW *SCARAPELLI* WAS BEHIND THIS. *WE* ALL KNOW HE WAS RESPONSIBLE FOR THE *"RUNAWAY"* TROUBLES.

AND FROM WHAT BATMAN'S STREET CONTACTS TELL ME, SCARAPELLI IS IN DUTCH WITH THE MOB.

SO MAYBE WE CAN *PUSH* HIM A BIT AND FORCE 'IM TO THINK WE KNOW MORE THAN WE DO.

12

I DON'T WANT RIDDLES, LADY-- WHO ARE YOU?

ALL WORK, STARFIRE? VERY WELL, THEN.

SIMPLY PUT, DEAR GIRL-- WITH OR WITHOUT MY POISONOUS CLAWS--

--I AM YOUR DEATH!

SKROOOOM

Y-YOU'RE THE ONE WHO ALMOST HIT ME?

THAT WAS A MISTAKE, HONEY--

--AN' SLASHER DON'T MAKE THEM KIND TWICE!

MAN, ONE SECOND SLOWER, AND SHE'D'VE CUT A RUT IN MY BUTT.

YOU GOTTA BE KIDDIN', BOY. THEIR AIN'T NOTHIN' TOO SMALL FOR SLASHER TO HIT!

MY WINGS!

GOTTA MOVE-- THEN CHANGE INTO SOMETHING HER KNIVES CAN'T CARVE UP LIKE SOME THANKSGIVING TURKEY.

C-CAN'T HOLD THE CHANGE... TURNIN' BACK INTO HUMAN FORM.

GOD! MY SHOULDER-- IT'S BLEEDING LIKE BLAZES!

WELL, WELL, HON--TRAPPED LIKE A RAT, EH?

DON'T WORRY NONE, THE TRAP IS ABOUT TO SPRING!

YOU'RE RIGHT ABOUT THAT, SLASHER--

--BUT IT'S NOT THE CHANGELING THAT IT'S CLOSING ON.

27

OH, LORD-- SHE'S BEEN *SHOT!*

S-SOMEONE *KILLED* HER.

B-BUT *WHO--?*

AIN'T GOT A *LEG* TO STAND ON, *EH* BOY?

WELL, DON'T YEW *WORRY* NONE-- IN TWO SECONDS THAT WON'T BE YORE *PROBLEM* NO MORE.

CREEP, ARE *YOU* EVER WRONG!

HEY! TAKE YORE BLASTED *HAND* OFF MAH--

SK-BLAMM!

I DON'T *ENJOY* KILLING WOMEN, WONDER GIRL--

FACT IS, BEFORE THE *ACCIDENT,* I WAS *MARRIED*...HAD TWO *DAUGHTERS*...

ONE WOULD HAVE BEEN *YOUR AGE,* I BELIEVE.

THEN WHY ARE YOU *DOING* THIS, TANKER?

YOU CAN *STOP.*

28

I SUPPOSE I COULD, IF I *WANTED* TO.

BUT EVER SINCE THE ACCIDENT, I'VE COME TO *ENJOY* MY NEW LIFE AS A MERCENARY.

THERE'S A SATISFYING FEELING OF *POWER* IN KNOWING THAT I CAN KILL *ANYONE* I CHOOSE AND NEVER BE *STOPPED*.

IT MAKES UP FOR SO MUCH OF MY *LOSS*.

HE'S *INSANE*, YET HE'S STRONG ENOUGH TO *CARRY OUT* HIS THREAT.

HE'LL *STRANGLE* ME UNLESS I CAN SUMMON ALL MY INNER STRENGTH.

HELP ME, HERA--

-- HELP ME STOP THIS MADMAN!

BA-WHOOM

WHEW, IT'S *OVER*... FUNNY, AWHILE AGO I THOUGHT ABOUT *QUITTING*.

BUT MAYBE PREVENTING LUNATICS LIKE HIM FROM INFLICTING HIS INSANITY ON THE REST OF US IS THE *REASON* I STICK THIS OUT.

SOMEONE'S GOT TO DO THE JOB.

YO! WONDY-- NOT *SHABBY*.

YOU FIGURE OUT WHAT THIS IS ALL *ABOUT?*

NO IDEA, CYBORG. THEY WERE OBVIOUSLY *HIRED* TO KILL US-- BUT I DON'T KNOW *WHY*, OR BY *WHOM*.

MEBBE WE OUGHTA MAKE ONE OF 'EM *TALK*.

HEY, RED-- Y'THINK YOU CAN GET "MR. T" THERE TO *CHIRP?*

WHAM

KID, WHEN WE'RE THROUGH, HE'LL BE SINGING *ARIAS*.

RIGHT, HANDSOME?

29

YEAH, KID-- C'MON RIGHT AHEAD A BIT.

YOU'RE ALMOST IN RANGE.

I *ENVY* YOU, KID-- YOU'LL FEEL WHAT MY LOVELY *FLAMES* CAN DO WHEN THEY *CARESS* YOU.

SCORCHER, PUT DOWN YOUR *FLAME-THROWER*.

HUH? MISTER, I DON'T KNOW WHO *YOU* ARE--

--BUT YOU'RE GONNA *FRY!*

I GAVE YOU A *CHANCE*, SCORCHER.

KRAK

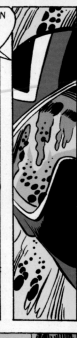

THAT'S MORE THAN *YOU'VE* EVER DONE FOR YOUR *VICTIMS*.

I DON'T BELIEVE THIS-- I'VE FOUGHT AGAINST WARRIORS FROM *TWO DOZEN* WORLDS--

--ON OKAARA I NEVER *MISSED*--

--BUT I CAN'T EVEN GET *CLOSE* TO CHESHIRE.

HONEY, YOU'RE AIMING FAR TOO *WIDE* TO BE EFFECTIVE.

STILL, YOU'RE A *GOOD* FIGHTER, I CAN TELL THAT.

YOU REALLY DESERVE A *BETTER* FATE THAN YOU'LL BE GETTING.

STAND *STILL,* BLAST YOU!

SORRY, HONEY-- NO CAN *DO*--

30

SHE DOESN'T HAVE TO, CHESHIRE--

YOU SEE, WE TITANS STICK TOGETHER.

AND NO MATTER HOW FAST YOU ARE AGAINST STARFIRE--

--YOUR SPEED MEANS NOTHING TO ME.

WELL, HONEY, I DON'T NEED TO MOVE FAST FOR A HUNK LIKE YOU.

MY POISONOUS CLAWS.

TASTE MY CLAWS, SWEETS.

IN SECONDS YOU'LL BE PARALYZED. AND IN MINUTES, WHY YOU'LL BE--DEAD!

IT'S BEEN A REAL PLEASURE, HONEY.

WHAT A SHAME IT HAS TO END SO SOON.

I REALLY COULD HAVE GOTTEN OFF WITH A GUY LIKE YOU.

BLAM

X'HAL-- WALLY! H-HE'S SO HOT...HE'S BURNING UP.

SOMEBODY-- DO SOMETHING BEFORE HE DIES!

RAVEN?!?

C-COLD...SO C-COLD... R-RAVEN...R-RAVEN... FOR GOD'S SAKE... WHERE ARE YOU?

31

HOW DID YOU KNOW?

I AM HERE.

KETTLEBRAIN'S RIGHT--SHE IS A WITCH!

I SENSED HIS PAIN...I WAS AWARE OF HIS NEEDS.

IF HE IS NOT ALREADY DOOMED, MY POWERS MIGHT BE ALL THAT CAN SAVE HIM.

RAVEN, IF TRIGON FREES HIMSELF BECAUSE YOU--

WONDER GIRL, I--I MUST DO THIS.

...THIS JUST IN. A FIRE HAS BROKEN OUT AT THE SCORPIO MERCHANDISING DOCKSIDE WAREHOUSE, FOR AN ON-THE-SCENE REPORT, LET'S SWITCH TO CAL DAVIS...

THOUGH POLICE WILL NOT CONFIRM IT, REPORTS ARE CIRCULATING THAT THE TEEN TITANS WERE SEEN ENTERING THE WAREHOUSE MOMENTS BEFORE THE FIRE BEGAN...

J..JUST SPOKE WITH LOGAN. THE DOC'S TOLD HIM TO REST. HE SENDS HIS LOVE...'SPECIALLY TO GOLDIE.

ROBIN, I CAN'T GO ALONG WITH THIS ANY LONGER.

WE'VE ALWAYS WORKED WITH THE LAW, BUT NOW YOU'RE TURNING US INTO VIGILANTES.

GIVE US ONE PIECE OF FACTUAL EVIDENCE AND WE'LL BE RIGHT ALONGSIDE YOU.

YOU SHOULD BE ANYWAY. ROBIN'S NEVER LED US WRONG.

HE'S NEVER BEEN THIS EMOTIONALLY INVOLVED BEFORE, EITHER.

32

212

IF YOU'RE DONE *CHASTISING* ME, LISTEN TO THIS.

WELL, DON'T STAND THERE GAWKING...YOU DON'T HAVE TO *STARE* AT A TAPE RECORDER.

THAT'S ADRIAN CHASE'S VOICE.

ROBIN, I'M ACTUALLY GETTING HARD EVIDENCE, BUT FRANKLY, BOY, I'M WORRIED.

SCARAPELLI KNOWS I'VE OVERHEARD ONE OF HIS SECRET MEETINGS...

I THINK HE'S GOING TO TRY TO *KILL* ME. JUST HAVE TO HOPE HE FAILS.

HE MADE THIS *BEFORE* THE BOMBING? BLAST, WHY DIDN'T HE ASK FOR HELP?

THAT ISN'T CHASE'S STYLE. KEEP LISTENING.

THE MOB WANTS HIM *OUT*, BUT BEFORE THEY KILL HIM, THEY NEED CERTAIN *INCRIMINATING* RECORDS HE'S KEPT.

BUT SCARAPELLI KNOWS HE'S GOING TO BE *SHARK BAIT*, SO HE'S PLANNING A LITTLE SURPRISE FOR HIS PALS-- --ON WEDNESDAY, AT HIS *DESERT* PROPERTY.

ROBBIE, I ALSO HEAR HE'S HIRED SOME *SPECIAL HITMEN* TO GET YOU GUYS, SO WATCH OUT.

BUT, IF SOMETHING HAPPENS TO ME, GET OUT THERE AND *STOP* HIM.

TAKE CARE, KIDDIE COPS. HOPE TO SEE YOU AGAIN.

WELL?

WHAT CAN I SAY?

LET'S GO!

WEDNESDAY AT DAWN...

A COLD, HOWLING WIND RAISES EXPECTATIONS OF...

...DEATH.

I SEE HIS LIMO.

DO YOU THINK HE'LL BRING THOSE FILES?

MAYBE, MAYBE NOT, BUT THEY'RE NOT IMPORTANT TO ME NOW.

ANTHONY HAS BROUGHT *EMBARRASSMENT* TO THE FAMILY.

HE HAS ALSO *DISOBEYED* US.

PUNISHMENT IS IN ORDER.

33

213

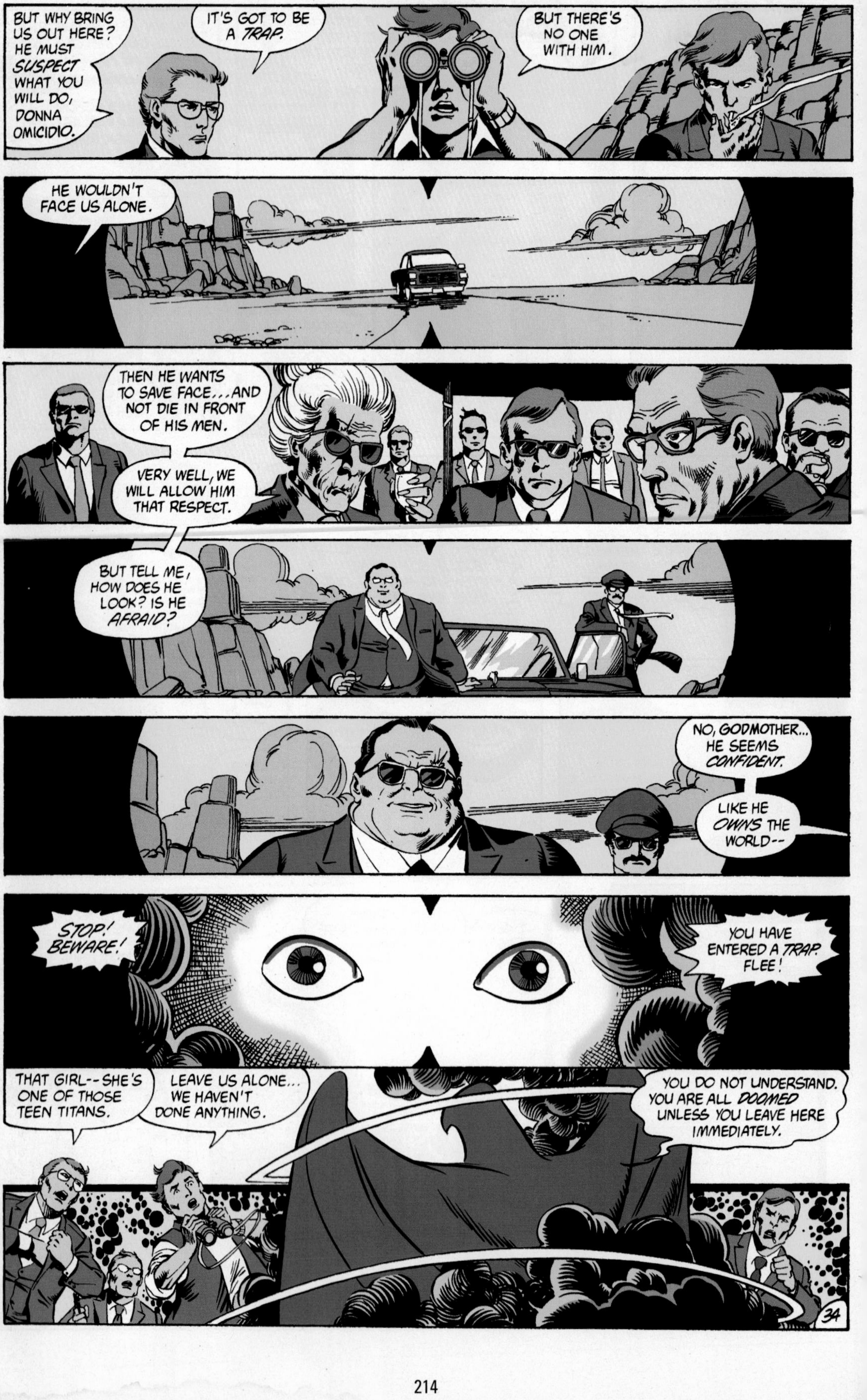
BUT WHY BRING US OUT HERE? HE MUST SUSPECT WHAT YOU WILL DO, DONNA OMICIDIO.
IT'S GOT TO BE A TRAP.
BUT THERE'S NO ONE WITH HIM.
HE WOULDN'T FACE US ALONE.
THEN HE WANTS TO SAVE FACE...AND NOT DIE IN FRONT OF HIS MEN.
VERY WELL, WE WILL ALLOW HIM THAT RESPECT.
BUT TELL ME, HOW DOES HE LOOK? IS HE AFRAID?
NO, GODMOTHER... HE SEEMS CONFIDENT.
LIKE HE OWNS THE WORLD--
STOP! BEWARE!
YOU HAVE ENTERED A TRAP. FLEE!
THAT GIRL--SHE'S ONE OF THOSE TEEN TITANS.
LEAVE US ALONE... WE HAVEN'T DONE ANYTHING.
YOU DO NOT UNDERSTAND. YOU ARE ALL DOOMED UNLESS YOU LEAVE HERE IMMEDIATELY.
34

WHAT DO YOU MEAN? *EXPLAIN* YOURSELF, GIRL.

I DON'T *LIKE* HER. KILL HER!

JOSEPH, JOSEPH...DON'T BE SO *RASH.*

YOU MUST *LISTEN.* ANTHONY SCARAPELLI INTENDS TO *DESTROY* YOU ALL.

THAT DAMN GIRL, SHE'LL *BLOW* EVERYTHING.

THE *MONITOR* SAID THE MEN WOULD BE IN *PLACE.*

GOOD. Y'KNOW SOMETHIN'--?

"OMICIDIO *LAUGHED* AT ME BACK IN THE SIXTIES FOR INSTALLIN' A *BOMB SHELTER* ON THIS LAND.

"NOW I'M HAVING THE *LAST LAUGH!*"

THERE!

35

215

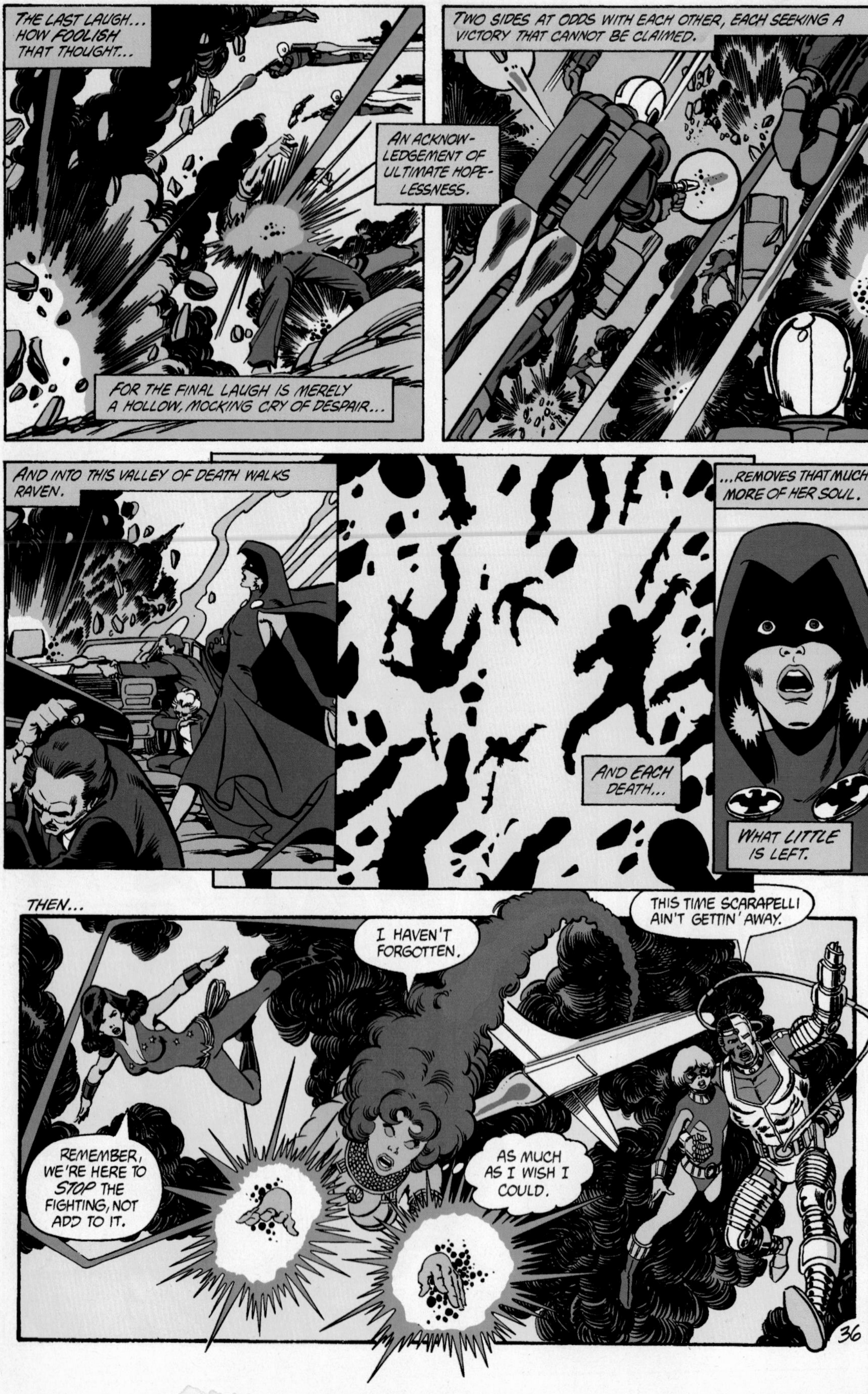

THE LAST LAUGH... HOW FOOLISH THAT THOUGHT...
AN ACKNOWLEDGEMENT OF ULTIMATE HOPELESSNESS.
FOR THE FINAL LAUGH IS MERELY A HOLLOW, MOCKING CRY OF DESPAIR...
TWO SIDES AT ODDS WITH EACH OTHER, EACH SEEKING A VICTORY THAT CANNOT BE CLAIMED.
AND INTO THIS VALLEY OF DEATH WALKS RAVEN.
AND EACH DEATH...
...REMOVES THAT MUCH MORE OF HER SOUL.
WHAT LITTLE IS LEFT.
THEN...
I HAVEN'T FORGOTTEN.
THIS TIME SCARAPELLI AIN'T GETTIN' AWAY.
REMEMBER, WE'RE HERE TO STOP THE FIGHTING, NOT ADD TO IT.
AS MUCH AS I WISH I COULD.
36

C'MON, MOVE IT. I DON'T WANT TO BE ANYWHERE *NEAR* HERE.

SIR, IF I MAY ASK, WHY DID YOU SHOW UP IN THE FIRST PLACE?

YOU *COULD* HAVE REMAINED HOME.

YOU CRAZY? I HADDA MAKE SURE THE GODMOTHER WAS THERE.

ALSO, I DIDN'T EXPECT THOSE *BRATS* TO SHOW.

IT SHOULD'VE BEEN *CLEAN*. NO PROBLEMS.

SUDDENLY REALIZED... WHERE'S DICK?

HE'S NOT HERE.

DON'T LIKE DOIN' THIS... STOMPIN' OUT THE *MOB*.

BUT I GOTTA KEEP *PRETENDIN'* TO BE A TITAN--

--TILL ALL THEIR INFO IS *MINE!*

THEY'RE FALLIN', BUT I KEEP WONDERIN'--

--WHERE'D A HOOD LIKE SCARAPELLI GET SOUPED-UP ASSASSINS LIKE THESE?

DICK SHOULD BE HAPPY... HE'S GOTTEN THE *PROOF* HE WANTS.

NOW MAYBE HE CAN *SETTLE DOWN*... MAYBE WE CAN GET BACK TOGETHER AGAIN.

CAN YOU CALL OFF THIS WASTEFUL KILLING? NO ONE CAN WIN.

I'LL CALL IT OFF, LADY--

--WHEN ANTHONY SCARAPELLI IS *DEAD!*

37

217

THE EASTERN TIP OF LONG ISLAND. ONLY THE VERY *RICH* CAN AFFORD TO LIVE HERE...

BUT, AS ANTHONY SCARAPELLI WILL MOMENTARILY LEARN, NOT EVEN WEALTH CAN BUY YOU...LIFE.

C'MON, I GOT A PRIVATE JET THAT'LL TAKE US TO *HAITI.*

AND WITH THESE RECORDS, *DONNA OMICIDIO* WON'T DARE TOUCH ME.

THEY COULD BLOW THE *LID* OFF THE WHOLE BLASTED MOB.

THAT IS WHAT I'VE BEEN *WAITING* FOR.

WHAT?

WH-WHO ARE YOU?

YOU ARE *GUILTY* OF CRIMES AGAINST YOUR FELLOW MAN.

YOU HAVE PROVEN A LACK OF CONCERN FOR ANY OTHER THAN YOURSELF.

IF YOU WERE *POOR,* IF YOU WERE AN ORDINARY MAN, YOU WOULD HAVE BEEN *IMPRISONED* YEARS AGO...

BUT YOUR WEALTH AND YOUR POLITICAL CONNECTIONS HAVE BOUGHT YOU YOUR FREEDOM TIME AND TIME AGAIN.

YOUR WEALTH CANNOT BUY *ME.*

AND YOUR POLITICAL CONNECTIONS WON'T FREE YOU WHEN THE CONTENTS OF THESE BOOKS ARE REVEALED.

YOU'RE FINISHED.

WHO ARE YOU!?

38

218

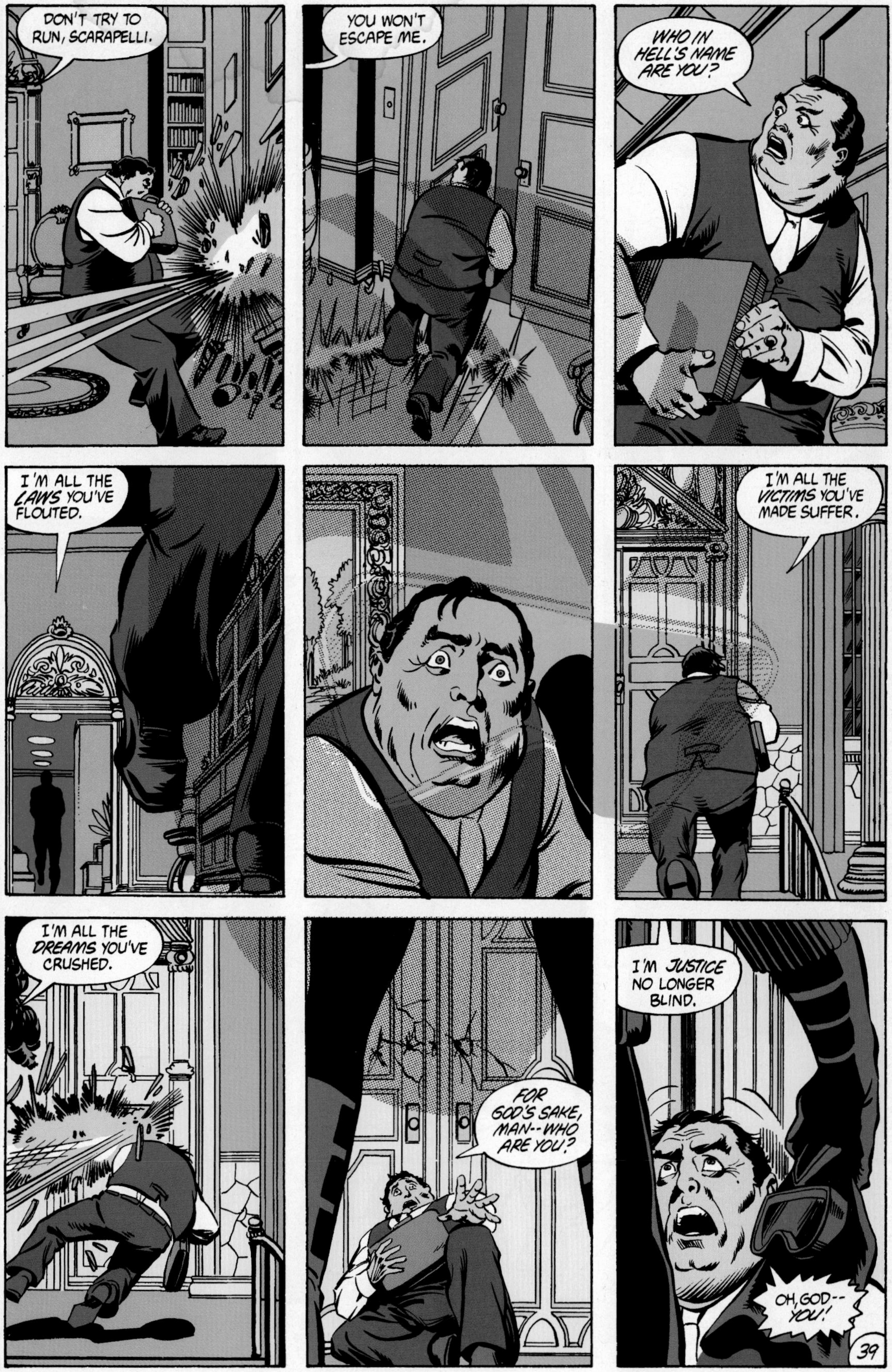
DON'T TRY TO RUN, SCARAPELLI.
YOU WON'T ESCAPE ME.
WHO IN HELL'S NAME ARE YOU?
I'M ALL THE LAWS YOU'VE FLOUTED.
I'M ALL THE VICTIMS YOU'VE MADE SUFFER.
I'M ALL THE DREAMS YOU'VE CRUSHED.
FOR GOD'S SAKE, MAN--WHO ARE YOU?
I'M JUSTICE NO LONGER BLIND.
OH, GOD--YOU!
39

CHASE!?!

ADRIAN CHASE IS DEAD.

NO.

I AM... THE VIGILANTE!

I--I'M SORRY ABOUT YOUR WIFE AND KIDS, I REALLY AM. THEY WEREN'T SUPPOSED TO GET HURT...

BELIEVE ME... PLEASE BELIEVE ME.

DON'T HURT ME... I DON'T WANT TO DIE.

I--I'M SORRY ABOUT YOUR FAMILY...

GET UP. ON YOUR FEET. NOW.

OKAY, OKAY... SURE...WHATEVER YOU WANT. BUT PLEASE...DON'T SHOOT.

HE WON'T.

HOW DID YOU KNOW?

THAT YOU WERE BEHIND THIS? THAT YOU WERE THE ONE WHO STOPPED SCARAPELLI'S ASSASSINS?

I'M A DETECTIVE, CHASE. THAT TAPE YOU SENT HAD TO BE MADE AFTER SCARAPELLI BOMBED YOUR APARTMENT, NOT BEFORE, LIKE YOU WANTED US TO BELIEVE.

HIS PEOPLE HAD NO REASON TO KILL HIM UNTIL THEN.

CHASE IS DEAD...

SO I KNEW YOU WERE STILL IN NEW YORK.

DON'T HAND ME THAT CRUD. I'VE LIVED WITH THAT KIND OF THINKING SINCE I WAS A KID.

40

AND WHAT DO YOU WANT FROM ME?

IF YOU *BELIEVE* IN THE LAW LIKE YOU SAY YOU DO, YOU'LL LET ME TAKE SCARAPELLI TO TRIAL.

BUT IF YOU SHOOT HIM, YOU'LL BE AS BAD AS HE IS.

MAYBE...

AGHHH!

BAM!

CHUD-UD-AH!

...BUT... MAYBE NOT...

LATER...

ROBIN? ROBIN, THIS IS WONDER GIRL... COME IN.

ROBIN!?!

41

221

...WE INTERRUPT "LENNY AND SQUIGGY GO TO THE WHITE HOUSE" FOR THIS SPECIAL NEWS BULLETIN NOW IN PROGRESS.

REPUTED MOBSTER ANTHONY SCARAPELLI WAS FOUND SHOT TO DEATH IN HIS HOME TONIGHT ALONGSIDE THE WOUNDED BODY OF ROBIN, LEADER OF THE NEW TEEN TITANS.

POLICE CAPTAIN HALL SAID SCARAPELLI HAD SHOT ROBIN, BUT THERE WERE NO CLUES AS TO WHO HAD KILLED SCARAPELLI.

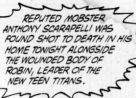

HALL DID SAY, HOWEVER, THAT HE RECEIVED AN ANONYMOUS CALL INFORMING THE POLICE OF THE SHOOTING AND REQUESTING AN AMBULANCE FOR THE WOUNDED TEEN HERO.

WE NOW GO TO CLIVE PHILLIPS AT FLYNN HOSPITAL.

ROBIN, THE POLICE HAVE CLEARED YOU IN SCARAPELLI'S MURDER, BUT THE QUESTION STILL REMAINS--

--DID YOU SEE WHO KILLED HIM?

MR. PHILLIPS, I CAN TRUTHFULLY SAY I WAS ALREADY UNCONSCIOUS BY THE TIME THAT SHOT WAS FIRED.

SO YOUR GUESS IS AS GOOD AS MINE.

AND SO THE MYSTERY STILL REMAINS. WHO KILLED ANTHONY SCARAPELLI? WHO CALLED FOR THE AMBULANCE WHICH SAVED YOUNG ROBIN'S LIFE, AND WHO SENT SCARAPELLI'S PRIVATE DOCUMENTED RECORDS OF MOB ACTIVITY TO POLICE CAPTAIN HALL?

TRADITIONALLY, SUPER-HEROES SUCH AS SUPERMAN, BATMAN, WONDER WOMAN AND THE TEEN TITANS DO NOT WILLINGLY TAKE LIVES, DO WE NOW HAVE A NEW KIND OF HERO IN TOWN? OR DO WE SIMPLY HAVE YET ANOTHER KILLER ON THE LOOSE? ONLY TIME WILL TELL.

NOW, BACK TO OUR REGULARLY SCHEDULED SHOW...

VIGILANTE JUSTICE

NOT THE END!

42

222

READ MORE ADVENTURES OF YOUR FAVORITE HEROES IN THESE COLLECTIONS FROM DC COMICS:

KINGDOM COME

THE GREATEST SUPER HERO EPIC OF TOMORROW!
KINGDOM COME
ELSEWORLDS
Mark WAID Alex ROSS

Mark Waid and **Alex Ross** deliver a grim tale of youth versus experience, tradition versus change and what defines a hero. KINGDOM COME is a riveting story pitting the old guard — Superman, Batman, Wonder Woman and their peers — against a new uncompromising generation.

WINNER OF FIVE EISNER AND HARVEY AWARDS, INCLUDING BEST LIMITED SERIES AND BEST ARTIST

IDENTITY CRISIS

NEW YORK TIMES BEST-SELLING AUTHOR OF THE ZERO GAME
BRAD MELTZER
RAGS MORALES MICHAEL BAIR
IDENTITY CRISIS
Introduction by JOSS WHEDON, creator of BUFFY THE VAMPIRE SLAYER and FIREFLY
"The IDENTITY CRISIS mystery involves the biggest DC heroes. . . and uses all of Mr. Meltzer's skills as a thriller novelist."
— The New York Times

BRAD MELTZER
RAGS MORALES
MICHAEL BAIR

CRISIS ON INFINITE EARTHS

CRISIS
ON INFINITE EARTHS
MARV WOLFMAN
& GEORGE PÉREZ

MARV WOLFMAN
GEORGE PÉREZ

DC: THE NEW FRONTIER VOLUME 1

DC: The New Frontier
VOLUME ONE
BY DARWYN COOKE WITH DAVE STEWART

DARWYN COOKE
DAVE STEWART

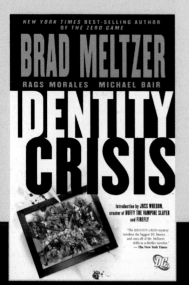